SAVED BY FAITH AND HOSPITALITY

Saved by Faith and Hospitality

Joshua W. Jipp

WILLIAM B. EERDMANS PUBLISHING COMPANY
GRAND RAPIDS, MICHIGAN

Wm. B. Eerdmans Publishing Co.
2140 Oak Industrial Drive N.E., Grand Rapids, Michigan 49505
www.eerdmans.com

ISBN 978-0-8028-7505-1

Library of Congress Cataloging-in-Publication Data

Names: Jipp, Joshua W., author.
Title: Saved by faith and hospitality / Joshua W. Jipp.
Description: Grand Rapids : Eerdmans Publishing Co., 2017. |
    Includes bibliographical references and index
Identifiers: LCCN 2017008739 | ISBN 9780802875051 (pbk. : alk. paper)
Subjects: LCSH: Hospitality—Religious aspects—Christianity. | Hospitality—Biblical teaching.
Classification: LCC BV4647.H67 J57 2017 | DDC 241/.671—dc23
    LC record available at https://lccn.loc.gov/2017008739

Contents

CONTENTS

Foreword

The concept of hospitality has gained significant traction in the last couple of decades. Rescued from tame understandings that primarily associated it with hosting dinner parties and entertaining friends or business associates, it is once again being recognized as important theologically, morally, and socially. Numerous excellent books and articles have recently been written to recover, critique, and apply the practice of hospitality.

Many writers have looked at the biblical and historical tradition with fresh eyes. and they have recovered a remarkable number of ancient texts that address hospitality, finding in them a wonderfully rich resource. Sometimes, however, the concept of hospitality has been retrieved from these sources without much attention to the variety of assumptions and other practices within which ancient hospitality was embedded.

Concerns for persons who are vulnerable, as well as tensions between maintaining community identity and offering welcome to strangers, are apparent in some of the earliest biblical texts. Living between the mystery of hospitality as an encounter with God and the challenges of limited resources has occupied people of faith for millennia. The possibilities of encountering Jesus in the stranger and the risks of welcoming false teachers or ill-intentioned visitors continue to challenge us.

Not all of these tensions fit comfortably into contemporary understandings of hospitality that tend to equate it with tolerance, but neither do they support the current and common fear-mongering about strangers. Most of the blessings and challenges of hospitality, along with some abuses, can be found in Scripture. Without attending to the tensions within the biblical tradition itself, it is hard to make sense of how followers of Jesus can sometimes land in such very different places regarding whether or not to welcome certain groups of people.

In this book, Joshua Jipp engages an extraordinary range of sources in arguing that God's hospitality is the basis of the human practice and that "those who have experienced divine welcome will seek to share God's hospitality with others." "Saved by faith and hospitality" has a particular meaning in the early Christian tradition. Jipp explores the surprising importance of offering welcome—an importance so significant that the practice of hospitality in the ancient church is connected to salvation itself as a "sign that one has embraced the message and person of Jesus."

As a New Testament scholar, Jipp deftly discusses hospitality themes as they appear in the Gospels and other New Testament materials. In addition, he effectively draws on many other disciplines. His fine, accessible writing is combined with exceptional scholarship. He masterfully draws together the wide range of biblical scholarship on hospitality that has been generated in the last twenty years to reinforce the significance of Christ's welcome for the church's identity.

Undergirding his careful scholarship is a deep passion and a profound compassion. This book is far more than an academic study of an interesting topic; Jipp understands what is at stake. Hospitality matters—it matters theologically and it matters socially; and it matters especially for the church. Jipp argues convincingly that God's hospitality creates a community that embodies hospitality in its practices and also in its composition.

Jipp identifies small subtleties in the biblical texts that open up startlingly new insights into hospitality. Making excellent use of recent New Testament scholarship, he thoughtfully discusses the importance of shared meals, generous giving, and mutuality in guest-host roles. He provides a fascinating look at Paul's experience of practicing hospitality with nonbelievers, and he uses the biblical accounts of Paul's efforts to be a "good" guest to break open a discussion of the importance and challenge of real friendship with persons of other faiths. His discussion of Paul's willingness to receive hospitality is both original and important.

Struggles over how we handle difference in the church community are not new. The role of hospitality in addressing ethnic, gender, racial, cultural, and socio-economic differences among Christians is evident even in the New Testament. We can learn from the early Christian struggles and their wisdom, and Jipp brings these opportunities to life. While recognizing the difficulties, he shows how hospitality helps Christians form a communal identity that transcends social distinctions without crushing or eliminating difference.

Jipp does not shy away from hard questions in hospitality. His concern with current immigration issues takes him into the Old Testament materials on how the people of God responded to the alien in their midst. He again demonstrates the wealth of wisdom that can be mined from Scripture for issues today.

For anyone interested in a robust understanding of the biblical texts and background, and in the significance of hospitality for contemporary life, this is a wonderfully succinct, substantive, and engaging treatment. Jipp succeeds in showing that divine and human welcome are at the heart of our Christian faith, and that hospitality is a central practice for all who follow Christ. Along the way, he clearly accomplishes his self-described task of showing "how the texts address us, our problems, our questions, and our needs," and brings to life a fascinating and fruitful conversation between the ancient texts and our current challenges. His work is a gift to the church and a major contribution to the recovery of the practice of hospitality.

CHRISTINE D. POHL

Abbreviations

ABRL	The Anchor Bible Reference Library
BBR	*Bulletin for Biblical Research*
BibInt	Biblical Interpretation Series
BTB	*Biblical Theology Bulletin*
CBQ	*Catholic Biblical Quarterly*
ECCon	Early Christianity in Context
ESEC	Emory Studies in Early Christianity
HTR	*Harvard Theological Review*
JBL	*Journal of Biblical Literature*
JSNT	*Journal for the Study of the New Testament*
JSNTSup	Journal for the Study of the New Testament Supplement Series
JSOT	*Journal for the Study of the Old Testament*
JSOTSup	Journal for the Study of the Old Testament Supplement Series
JSPL	*Journal for the Study of Paul and His Letters*
JTI	*Journal of Theological Interpretation*
JTS	*Journal of Theological Studies*
LNTS	The Library of New Testament Studies
NICNT	New International Commentary on the New Testament
NovT	*Novum Testamentum*
NovTSup	Novum Testamentum Supplement Series
NTM	New Testament Message
NTMon	New Testament Monographs
NTS	*New Testament Studies*
OBT	Overtures to Biblical Theology
PCNT	Paideia Commentaries on the New Testament

Abbreviations

SBLAB	Society of Biblical Literature Academia Biblica
SBLDS	Society of Biblical Literature Dissertation Series
SNTSMS	Society for New Testament Studies Monograph Series
StPatr	Studia Patristica
THC	The Two Horizons Commentary Series
WTJ	*Westminster Theological Journal*
WUNT	Wissenschaftliche Untersuchungen zum Neuen Testament

Preface

The title of this book, *Saved by Faith and Hospitality*, was inspired by the reading of Scripture found in the early Christian book of 1 Clement. The author of this text makes the claim that Abraham, Lot, and Rahab were saved by their faith *and hospitality*. While those of us with Protestant commitments to *sola fide* may perhaps initially bristle at this claim, the author presents a very plausible reading of the Old Testament Scriptures that suggests that hospitality to strangers is at the heart of the Christian faith.

My interest in hospitality to strangers stems from my doctoral studies at Emory and particularly my dissertation, which sought to provide a convincing literary and socio-historical explanation for Luke's account of Paul's time on Malta in Acts 28.[1] At the time I was primarily interested in the relationship between the early Christian movement and Greco-Roman religion and philosophy as seen in the book of Acts. One of the fundamental insights of my study was that hospitality to strangers permeated Luke-Acts from its beginning to its end, and in fact it played a central role in many of the New Testament compositions. I was fortunate enough to have a wonderful dissertation director, Luke Timothy Johnson, who encouraged me to do the typical New Testament historical critical work *and* to examine the importance of hospitality for our particular historical moment. If this work makes one point it is simply that hospitality to strangers—both understood as extending hospitality as host and receiving it as guest—is indeed at the heart of the Christian faith. In this book I try to present coherent and convincing readings of the Scriptures on

---

1. Joshua W. Jipp, *Divine Visitations and Hospitality to Strangers in Luke-Acts: An Interpretation of the Malta Episode in Acts 28:1–10*, NovTSup 153 (Leiden: Brill, 2013).

hospitality *and* to put them in conversation with some of the more pressing issues facing the church in North America. Of course, I do not expect every reader to agree fully with how I move from the biblical text to contemporary challenges facing the church. I do, however, hope that my readers will feel the challenge and call that the Scriptures present to the contemporary church.

I count it as a great blessing that I have been able to teach regularly a seminar on hospitality to strangers at Trinity Evangelical Divinity School (TEDS). It is a joy to have students who can match my enthusiasm and push my own thinking and acting. I have been blessed to have students who have researched and presented papers that explored the relationship between hospitality and incarceration, the Black Lives Matter movement, the condition of intersex, adoption, mental illness, and more. I would like to extend my thanks to all of the students at TEDS who have participated in my course "Hospitality to Strangers in the New Testament." I have learned much from you about the practical, social, and ecclesial implications of what the Scriptures teach about hospitality. In particular, thanks to Stephanie Lamour, Steven Durgin, Matthew Henderson, Dustin Hacker, Will Horne, Matt Cyr, Nic Cageo, Zach Caddy, Tyler Chernesky, R.A. Atanus, Stacy Simon, Gregory Campeau, Adam Darbonne, Daniel Waldschmidt, Sally Jackson, Kevin Holmen, Seongeun Ban, and Andrew Brantley. Many thanks to my wonderful graduate assistants Matthew Robertson and Katie Whiteside for their valuable contributions to this project.

I would like especially to thank the many friends and colleagues who read portions of the book and offered helpful criticism, feedback, and encouragement. Thanks to Timothy Baldwin, Christopher Skinner, Amber Jipp, Eric Tully, Drew Strait, Matthew Bates, Peter Cha, Michael Bird, Darren Carlson, David Luy, Justin Jeffcoat Schedtler, and David Pao. Thanks to Taylor Worley for the tip on the Coen brothers' film *A Serious Man*. Special thanks to Alec Lucas for the many conversations about this book and for the encouragement to write it. My editor Michael Thomson has been a joy to work with, and I hope we can collaborate again in the future. Thanks for your help.

My wife Amber truly loves to support and encourage my teaching and writing. I couldn't even begin to be able to indicate how her faith, love for others, and encouragements and exhortations have shaped the ideas now found in this book. As always, all my love, Little One.

I dedicate this book to my two sons, Josiah and Lukas. Every morning that I have the chance to drop them off at kindergarten and preschool, I tell them: "Remember, love God and love people." My prayer for them is that they will both experience God's loving hospitality in their own lives and then extend it *and* receive it from others.

Saved by Faith and Hospitality

The opening scene of the Coen brothers' film *A Serious Man*, set in pre–World War II in Eastern Europe, begins with a Jewish man returning to his humble home late at night after his visit to the village. The man tells his wife that he has had a fortunate encounter with Reb Groshkover, who offered him help when his cart tipped over on his way back home. And, by the way, he has invited Reb Groshkover to come to their home for soup, for it is a cold winter night. The wife is seriously shocked and then displeased and finally mutters, "God has cursed us." She claims that Reb Groshkover has been dead now for some years, and so her husband must have encountered a dybbuk (that is, a ghost) who wishes to visit them with some harm. The husband finds this ludicrous at first, and an argument ensues between the wife and husband as to the identity of the stranger. A knock at the door interrupts the argument, however, and the couple must decide what they will do. "Who is it?" the wife asks. "I invited him here for some soup, to warm himself," says the husband. The struggle is real as the husband and wife are caught between feeling a sense of obligation to welcome the cold, hungry stranger *and* fear that the stranger might not be who he says he is and will harm or contaminate them in some way. Will they open the door and offer the man some hot soup, warmth, and rest, or will they ignore the knocking and keep the door shut?

I imagine all of us have experienced the same kind of tension. We sense that we should probably open our doors, at least at times, to strangers. We may even remember experiences when hosts have taken a risk to show hospitality to us, to make us feel safe and welcome. We may remember that the Scriptures even command hospitality to strangers as a necessary virtue for Christians. But we are nervous that the stranger might do us harm. What if the stranger is morally corrupt, or violent, or takes advantage of my hospitality? What if by opening up my doors to this person I expose myself or my loved ones to physical harm? What if the guest doesn't leave? Do I have enough resources to share with those outside of my family and friendship network?

In this book I make a simple argument: the God of the Christian Scriptures is a God of hospitality, a God who extends hospitality to his people and who requires that his people embody hospitality to others. Stated simply, God's hospitality to us is the basis of our hospitality to one another. God's relationship to his people is fundamentally an act of hospitality to strangers, as God makes space for "the other," for his people, by inviting humanity into relationship with him. This experience of God's hospitality is at the very heart of the church's identity. We are God's guests and friends. And it is because of God's extension of hospitality and friendship to us that the church can offer hospitality to one another *and* to those seemingly outside the reach of our faith communities. Just as God extends welcome and hospitality toward his people, so also God's people extend hospitality to one another, and as we imitate God, we offer hospitality—particularly to "the other," the one who is not like us, the one outside. This does not mean that there are not challenges, limitations, and boundaries to our showing hospitality. There most certainly are. But it does mean that hospitality to strangers is an inextricable component of the identity of the church and its vocation.[1]

Hospitality is the act or process whereby the identity of the stranger is transformed into that of guest. While hospitality often uses the basic necessities of life such as the protection of one's home and the offer of food, drink, conversation, and clothing, the primary impulse of hospitality is to create a safe and welcoming place where a stranger can be converted into a friend. The practice of hospitality to strangers very frequently hopes to create relationships and friendships between those who were previously either alienated, at enmity, or simply unknown to one another. Thus, the language of "friendship" or "fictive" kinship is closely related to hospitality to strangers. One can think of friendship or non-biological familial connections *as the result* or outcome of

---

1. Many of the best New Testament ethics books seem to me to underestimate and at times almost entirely ignore the significance of hospitality to strangers for Christian ethics. Two of the most helpful NT ethics works which could be well supplemented through attention to hospitality to strangers are Richard B. Hays, *The Moral Vision of the New Testament: A Contemporary Introduction to New Testament Ethics* (San Francisco: HarperCollins, 1997) and Richard A. Burridge, *Imitating Jesus: An Inclusive Approach to New Testament Ethics* (Grand Rapids: Eerdmans, 2007).

hospitality to strangers. Thus, in this book I will generally reserve the language of hospitality for the process of making space for *strangers* and the language of friendship or fictive kinship to describe the result of hospitality to strangers.

In this book I demonstrate that hospitality to strangers is an inextricable component of the Christian faith. To some extent, the claim that hospitality to strangers is at the heart of Christianity needs little justification. After all, from the very first pages of the Bible we encounter the hospitable Abraham (Gen 18:1–8), apostles exhorting their churches to show hospitality to strangers (see, for example, Rom 12:13; Heb 13:2–3; 1 Tim 3:2; Titus 1:8; 1 Pet 4:9), and the church frequently portrayed as hospitably receiving itinerant missionaries and sending them on their way (see, for instance, Rom 16:23; Col 4:10). But the importance of the church's practice of hospitality to strangers depends upon the broader way in which the early church understood itself to be recipients of *God's hospitality* and thereby agents of hospitality to one another. Israel in the Old Testament and the church in the New Testament understood its identity as founded upon God's hospitality, a divine welcome that joined Israel and the church to God. In a sense, then, we learn something about who God is from the human practice of hospitality to strangers, given that the practice is predicated upon our understanding of who God is—the one who extends hospitality to the stranger. We will see, then, that hospitality to strangers is at the core of the church's identity and mission; it is part and parcel of what we celebrate when we partake in the Eucharist; it is foundational for how members of the church relate to one another; and it provides direction for the church's mission in and to the world. Thus, the biblical texts speak of the necessity of hospitality to strangers in ways that might surprise us. Let's take a brief and simply suggestive look at the way in which some New Testament and early Christian texts speak of hospitality to strangers as related to salvation.

Salvation and Hospitality

If I were to ask, "By what means was the biblical hero Abraham justified?" I imagine many of you would give the good Pauline answer, "Abraham was justified by faith, of course!"[2] But we may be more surprised to see that at least some early Christians thought Abraham was justified by his faith *and hospitality to strangers*. We'll turn to the New Testament in a moment, but

---

2. Gen 15:6; Rom 4:1–8; Gal 3:6–9.

let's take a look first at how one early Christian understood how Abraham was justified. Many of us might not be familiar with this text, but I want you to notice the importance he places on God's people demonstrating hospitality to strangers. Sometime toward the end of the first century CE (95–97), a letter now known as 1 Clement was penned from the church in Rome to the church in Corinth (1). The goal of the letter was to instruct the Corinthians to put away factionalism, schisms, and jealousy, which were damaging the church (1.1; 39.1).[3] The author sets forth a series of biblical models for the church to emulate, with a thematic focus on how following these scriptural models will enable the church to eradicate jealousy and dissension and procure peace (see esp. 4.1–6.4). Three of these biblical heroes are Abraham, Lot, and Rahab—all of whom are said to have been saved as a result of their hospitality (10.1–12.8).

> And again he says: "God led Abraham forth and said to him, 'Look up to heaven and count the stars, if you are able to count them; so shall your seed be!' And Abraham believed God, and it was reckoned to him as righteousness.'" *Because of his faith and hospitality [dia pistin kai philoxenian]* a son was given to him in his old age, and for the sake of obedience, he offered him as a sacrifice to God on one of the mountains that he showed him. (10.6–7)
>
> *Because of his hospitality and godliness [dia philoxenian kai eusebian],* Lot was saved from Sodom, when the entire region was judged by fire and brimstone. In this way the Master clearly demonstrated that he does not forsake those who hope in him, but destines to punishment and torment those who turn aside. (11.1)
>
> *Because of her faith and hospitality [dia pistin kai philoxenian] Rahab the harlot was saved.* For when the spies were sent to Jericho by Joshua the son of Nun, the king of the land realized that they had come to spy out his country, and so he sent out men to capture them, intending to put them to death as soon as they were caught. The hospitable Rahab, however, took them in and hid them in an upstairs room under some flax-stalks. (12.1–3)

We may be surprised that the author seems to be giving a rather important and remarkable role to hospitality with respect to salvation, but it is clear that

3. See Clayton N. Jefford, *Reading the Apostolic Fathers: An Introduction* (Peabody, MA: Hendrickson, 1996), 101–6.

he is not simply making off-handed assertions to rhetorically manipulate the Corinthians to pursue peace, order, and hospitality (though, of course, he does want that!). Rather, the author of 1 Clement is offering a serious reading of the biblical texts, an interpretation that sees hospitality to strangers (along with faith for Abraham, godliness for Lot, and the scarlet robe signifying the bloody death of the Lord for Rahab) as the causal basis for the salvation of Abraham, Lot, and Rahab.[4]

The author has good reason to discern in the biblical text a connection between the hospitality of these three figures and their salvation. God's promise to Abraham that he would be the father of many nations (Gen 15:1–6; 17:1–14) is confirmed in Genesis 18 *after he has demonstrated his faith and piety through offering hospitality to the three men* (18:1–15). In other words, Abraham's faith, exemplified in his welcome of the three men within his tent, results in God's confirmation to give Abraham and Sarah a child in their old age. With respect to the claim in 1 Clement that Lot was saved by godliness and hospitality, we can see that whereas Sodom and Gomorrah are destroyed because of their flagrant inhospitality and abuse of strangers, Lot's hospitality to the divine visitors (Gen 19:1–3) is the basis for God's rescuing of Lot and his family. Lot's hospitality is probably the sole reason 2 Peter refers to him as "righteous Lot" (2 Pet 2:7).[5] And Rahab's hospitality to the spies is taken as a sign of her faith in the God of Israel (Josh 2:8–13) and results in her being shown "kindness and mercy" when Israel enters into the land (Josh 2:14). So the author of Hebrews says that Rahab's faith was manifested in her "welcoming the spies in peace" (Heb 11:31).

But 1 Clement isn't the only early Christian text that connects hospitality to salvation. James argues that judgment will be severe for those "who do not show mercy, for mercy triumphs over judgment" (Jas 2:13b [my trans.]). Faith without acts of mercy—exemplified in the provisions of food and clothes to the needy (2:15)—is dead and powerless to save (2:17–19). The kind of faith that saves, however, is seen in Abraham and Rahab, who demonstrate saving faith through the merciful acts of hospitality to strangers.[6] James declares that Abraham was justified *by his works*, and the plural

---

4. That the author of 1 Clement is engaging in a reading of the biblical texts does not seem to me to be emphasized as clearly as it should in H. Chadwick, "Justification by Faith and Hospitality," StPatr 4 (1961): 281–85.

5. T. Desmond Alexander, "Lot's Hospitality: A Clue to His Righteousness," *JBL* 104, no. 2 (June 1985): 289–91.

6. In other words, though faith alone is constitutive of salvation and the Christian's appropriation of saving grace, *both faith and acts of mercy* are ultimately necessary for salvation.

works, in addition to speaking of his willingness to sacrifice his son Isaac (Gen 22), almost certainly refers to his hospitality to strangers (see Gen 18:1–18).[7] James also argues that Rahab's saving faith was demonstrated through hospitality: "in the same way, wasn't Rahab the prostitute also justified by works when she welcomed the messengers and sent them out by a different way?" (2:25 [my trans.]).

In his parable of the sheep and the goats (Matt 25:31–46), Jesus famously declares that those who will inherit the kingdom of God are those who perform merciful acts of hospitality: "for I was hungry and you gave me food, I was thirsty and you gave me something to drink, I was a stranger and you welcomed me, I was naked and you gave me clothing, I was sick and you took care of me, I was in prison and you visited me" (25:35–36). Alternatively, those who will depart "into the everlasting fire prepared for the devil and his angels" (25:41b [my trans.]) are those who fail to show the merciful acts of hospitality. Both groups are surprised to learn that Jesus had fully identified with the impoverished, the stranger, the sick, the naked, and the imprisoned such that the merciful acts of hospitality to "the least of these brothers of mine" (25:40, 45) were performed to Jesus himself (25:37–39, 44–45). Regardless of whether "the least of these" refers to any human in need, or Christian missionaries, or any Christian at all, the fact remains that the sheep's inheritance of eternal life is dependent upon the merciful acts of hospitality.

Both the Gospel of Luke and the Acts of the Apostles, as we will see in more detail, also connect salvation with hospitality. In Luke Jesus is frequently depicted as a guest or a traveler, and those who experience salvation and the blessings of the kingdom are those who welcome Jesus into their home and demonstrate loving hospitality to him and his disciples (see, for example, 5:27–32; 7:36–50; 10:1–16; 19:1–10). Alternatively, those who reject Jesus and the kingdom manifest this rejection through inhospitality toward Jesus (7:36–39; 9:51–56; 11:37–41; 14:1–6; 19:41–44). None of this is to deny the importance of responding to Jesus with faith (see, for instance, 5:20; 7:9; 7:50), but it is to say that hospitality to Jesus appears to function in the

7. That James has in mind Abraham's hospitality is likely for the following reasons: a) the depiction of "merciful acts" as providing the hospitable provisions of food, warmth, and clothing (James 2:13–16), b) the popular depiction of Abraham as a paragon of hospitality (for example, Gen 18:1–8), and c) the second example of Rahab who "in the same way" demonstrated her faith through hospitality (2:25–26). See further R. B. Ward, "The Works of Abraham: James 2:14–26," *HTR* 6 (1968): 283–90; Luke Timothy Johnson, *Brother of Jesus, Friend of God: Studies in the Letter of James* (Grand Rapids: Eerdmans, 2004), 178–79.

Gospel as a sign that one has embraced the message and person of Jesus. In the Acts of the Apostles' description of Paul and Silas's missionary journey, Lydia (16:11–15), the Philippian jailer (16:25–34), Jason (17:5–8), and Titius Justus (18:7–8) all manifest their receptivity to the gospel through welcoming and hosting Paul and Silas in their homes.

The early Christian texts, then, of 1 Clement, James, Matthew, and Luke-Acts, testify that hospitality to strangers was not an optional practice for the church, but is something that is deeply related to salvation. These texts would not justify some form of "works-righteousness," as though we could accumulate merit with God by loving the stranger; but their deep connection to salvation does suggest that hospitality is a tangible testimony to our wholehearted embrace of Jesus's person and message. The Scriptures indicate that hospitality to strangers is one of the primary ways in which followers of Jesus fulfill the command to "love your neighbor as yourself." Human hospitality is necessary precisely because we, as God's people, are constituted by God's extension of hospitality to us. Reinhard Hütter states this dynamic nicely: "[T]he Triune God is both truth and host in one. In his self-giving in Christ, God offers abundant, costly, and holy hospitality to a humanity hopelessly entangled in practices and habits of sin. God's own distinct and radical hospitality culminates in opening Israel and thus in welcoming Gentiles into God's house."[8] What we will see throughout our foray into the biblical texts is that God's hospitality in the loving gift of Christ to a broken and lost humanity creates a people constituted by hospitality to one another, to strangers, and to the world.

Church, Society, and Hospitality to Strangers

The church today in North America is faced with an incredible test. How can it open its door to the outsider? Our culture betrays its deep need for meaningful relationships that can flow from hospitality. Loneliness, cultural/social divisions, mass incarceration, homelessness, the treatment of undocumented migrant workers, racism in manifold forms but especially towards black men, fear and rejection of the religious other, and the need for the provision of services for the mentally ill are just a few of the major chal-

---

8. Reinhard Hütter, "Hospitality and Truth: The Disclosure of Practices in Worship and Doctrine," in *Practicing Theology: Beliefs and Practices in Christian Life*, ed. Miroslav Volf and Dorothy C. Bass (Grand Rapids: Eerdmans, 2002), 206–27, here, 214.

lenges our society faces today. While I am not qualified or trained to engage in detailed analysis of these challenges, I believe the Bible offers insight to the church for a variety of social challenges such as immigration, incarceration, and racism. I see this *primarily* as a matter of the church intentionally making space for immigrants and refugees, for continuing the early church's legacy of visiting prisoners, and rejecting all forms of xenophobic rhetoric about the religious other. Henri Nouwen describes the church's vocation in this way: "Our society seems to be increasingly full of fearful, defensive, aggressive people anxiously clinging to their property and inclined to look at their surrounding world with suspicion, always expecting an enemy to suddenly appear, intrude and do harm. But still—that is our vocation: to convert . . . the enemy into a guest and to create the free and fearless space where brotherhood and sisterhood can be formed and fully experienced."[9]

One of the primary calls upon the church is to create this "free and fearless space" where "our hostilities can be converted into hospitality."[10] The church may fulfill its vocation by actively engaging in building friendship with adherents of other religions in their own neighborhoods and/or workplaces, by educating themselves about where refugees are resettled and pursuing intentional relationships with them, and in looking for ways to intentionally reintegrate and welcome the formerly incarcerated into one's church and society. What Christine Pohl said in 1999 still rings true almost twenty years later: "Even among Christians, many of the current discussions about poverty and welfare, inclusion and diversity, scarcity and distribution, are conducted without the benefit of any coherent theological framework. Often, the result is that our stands on complex social and public policy concerns are little affected by our deepest Christian values and commitments. Hospitality as a framework provides a bridge which connects our theology with daily life and concerns."[11]

While I do not offer specific suggestions for public policy, I do suggest that when churches begin to evaluate the alignment between the Bible's mandate to care for the other with how contemporary North American society and public policy often treat undocumented workers, the incarcerated, and the religious other (to give just three examples) this should create stances of solidarity with these marginalized communities that will inevitably result

9. Henri J. M. Nouwen, *Reaching Out: The Three Movements of the Spiritual Life* (New York: Doubleday, 1975), 65–66.

10. Nouwen, *Reaching Out*, 65.

11. Christine D. Pohl, *Making Room: Recovering Hospitality as a Christian Tradition* (Grand Rapids: Eerdmans, 1999), 7–8.

in prophetic challenges against unjust social structures. While this book is primarily a biblical examination of hospitality to strangers and not a sociological analysis, I do attempt to make some *suggestions* about how hospitality might stimulate our imaginations to think more boldly and creatively about contemporary issues inside and outside of the church.

The Scriptures emphatically reject xenophobia. The people of God are meant to show another way. Yet increasingly, some quarters in the North American church make a virtue out of excluding outsiders, be they moral outsiders or merely non-American, or even non-white, outsiders. Pockets of evangelical Christianity in North America are guilty of supporting the most radically xenophobic, intolerant public policies and public servants. While I do not offer concrete public policy prescriptions, I do attempt to show how Christians must reject *anything* that dehumanizes, stigmatizes, and perpetuates violence against the marginalized and vulnerable. Few Christians today understand that hospitality to strangers and to the marginalized is a constituent component of their faith. This book forcibly argues that hospitality to strangers is not an optional practice for Christians. The biblical texts consistently speak of the identity and vocation of Christians as those who have experienced God's hospitality whereby all of us are welcomed into God's family.

Method and Outline of the Book

Finally, let me say a brief word about my method or approach in this book.[12] I read the biblical texts primarily as an exegete and not as a trained sociologist, ethicist, or theologian—though I have benefited and continue to benefit greatly from those who have articulated the importance of hospitality to strangers for the practical life of the Christian and the church.[13] But given that the subject matter of these texts is God as revealed to humanity in the Scriptures, Jesus, and the Spirit-gifted church, I believe that my task is ines-

---

12. For a fuller articulation of my method, see Joshua W. Jipp, "The Beginnings of a Theology of Luke-Acts: Divine Activity and Human Response," *JTI* 8, no. 1 (Spring 2014): 23–44, esp., 24–28. Similarly, see Luke Timothy Johnson, "Imagining the World Scripture Imagines," *Modern Theology* 14 (1998): 165–80.

13. In addition to Henri Nouwen's *Reaching Out*, I think here especially of the following: Pohl, *Making Room*; Amy G. Oden, *God's Welcome: Hospitality for a Gospel-Hungry World* (Cleveland: The Pilgrim Press, 2008); Jean Vanier, *Community and Growth*, 2nd ed. (New York: Paulist Press, 1989).

capably self-involving. As opposed to most "biblical-theology" approaches that are solely descriptive, I try to convey the way in which the Scriptures press us to understand our own lives, wills, and practices in light of the God who extends hospitality to his people and demands we show hospitality to one another. In other words, while I avoid preaching or prescriptive calls for "application," my scriptural exegesis tries to show how the biblical texts call us to belief, obedience, confession, repentance, and to understand the entirety of our existence in light of the hospitality of God. Thus, while the middle sections of each chapter are largely exegetical in nature, I draw upon a variety of disciplines such as missiology, sociology, church history, social psychology, political/economic theory, and systematic theology as a means of bringing the biblical texts to bear upon real human lives and communities. Of course, my expertise is limited and I am an outsider to those disciplines, but I hope the supplementing of my exegetical work with cross-disciplinary reflections will stimulate the reader to think about the demands the biblical texts make upon the contemporary reader.

I think readers will be better equipped to understand my argument if they understand my own personal investment in this book. When I was working on my dissertation, I remember that my wife Amber prayed that God would use my research even in some small way for the church. Little did I know that my research for my dissertation would take me so deeply into the practice of hospitality to strangers (both in the Bible and in the ancient world more broadly).[14] I was simply stunned at how deeply love for the stranger was woven into so many biblical texts and was truly fundamental for understanding the Gospel of Luke. This coincided with my opportunity to co-teach a course on "Introduction to the Bible" at the women's state prison in Atlanta.[15] At the same time, my wife and I had been leading a small group of about 15–20 young adults at our church in Atlanta. We met together to read the Scriptures, pray, share meals, and serve together at local ministries. At this same time, my wife and I had built a meaningful but challenging friendship with refugees through World Relief, had developed real friendships with students involved in the Muslim Student Association at Emory University, and were participating in a local ministry to the urban homeless in Atlanta. I should probably also mention that it was at

14. See my *Divine Visitations and Hospitality to Strangers in Luke-Acts.*

15. For which I am thankful to my co-teacher Marian Broida, as well as to the director of the program, Jennifer M. McBride, who powerfully embodied the virtues of hospitality, solidarity, and friendship in her relationship with the women inmates at Metro State Prison. Jenny's powerful book of lived theology, *Radical Discipleship: A Liturgical Politics of the Gospel* (Minneapolis: Fortress Press, 2017), was written after the completion of this book.

this time that I began to learn and read from the likes of Christine Pohl, Henri Nouwen, and Jean Vanier. The biblical teachings on hospitality and "the other" gradually became a significant lens and conversation partner for how I viewed my own identity, my relationships and friendships both in and outside the church, and *how* I conducted myself in ministries focused on acts of mercy.

I'm sure my readers will have no difficulty in discerning that I am white, educated, midwestern, heterosexual, and male. I am an evangelical who teaches New Testament at an evangelical seminary in the wealthy suburbs of Chicago. I live in a relatively safe neighborhood on the northwest side of Chicago with my wife and two young children. Unlike some of the contemporary heroes in this book, I am not an expert practitioner of the practice I describe in this book. I don't mention any of this as an apology, but I recognize the limitations and social-cultural situatedness of my own suggestions and calls for the church's engagement to practice hospitality to strangers. I speak out of my own limited experiences and observations. My hope is not so much that my practical contemporary exhortations will be taken as prescriptive but that, rather, they will stimulate you into thinking and reflecting upon what it might look like to hear and follow the biblical vision of hospitality to strangers in your own particular, local, and ecclesial context. I have no doubt my encouragements to the church to embody a more hospitable manner of life are already being lived out and enacted in powerful ways in many local assemblies, many of which are ethnic minority congregations and leaders that often do not receive the same amount of attention in the broader North American Christian places of power.[16] My knowledge of "the church" is primarily of Protestant churches in North America. And I would invite you, if you are so inclined, to share those stories with me and with others.[17] When I make observations about or suggestions for the church, my own limitations are probably in obvious view, but I offer what are, I hope, suggestions that are faithful for any church that would follow the vision of hospitality to strangers found in our Christian Scriptures. Again, my hope is that reading this book and encountering the Bible's teaching on hospitality will enable you to think freshly, creatively, and boldly about how love for the stranger is taking form in churches all over the world and by the Spirit can take form in new ways in our local church contexts.

16. I recommend here Soong-Chan Rah, *The Next Evangelicalism: Freeing the Church from Western Cultural Captivity* (Downers Grove, IL: InterVarsity Press, 2009); Sandra Van Opstal, *The Next Worship: Glorifying God in a Diverse World* (Downers Grove, IL: InterVarsity Press, 2015).

17. You can reach me at jjipp@tiu.edu.

In the first part of *Saved by Faith and Hospitality* I show how Luke-Acts, Paul, and the Gospel of John portray Jesus serving as God's host who bestows God's welcome to all people, including sinners, outcasts, and foreigners. Each New Testament writer shows us Jesus mediating God's hospitality, literally extending the table in sharing meals with various outsiders. Jesus's salvation, healing, forgiveness, and peace are revealed to Israel, to the church, and to the world in these simple, prophetic encounters. To those who follow Jesus, these New Testament writers offer a new kind of community of friendship with each other, marked by the inclusion of others, rejection of hierarchy, joy, and sharing goods and money. This experience of God's hospitality creates communities of human hospitality and friendship. The church in the New Testament is marked by these inclusive friendships. Christ is the divine host. He extends hospitality to outsiders through table-fellowship, and he insures that the church remember and celebrate his divine hospitality in the form of the Eucharist. In the Gospel of Luke outsiders become insiders and friends. Paul describes Christ as the one who welcomes the strong and weak in faith, the wealthy and the poor, and the Jew and the Gentile. John shows how Christ offers hospitality in daily life through wine, water, bread, and foot-washing. John describes the community of disciples as a circle of God's friends. It is the friends of God who embody the presence of God in their practical love for one another.

In the second part, I unpack how God's hospitality elicits human hospitality and enables the church to overcome three challenges or barriers to extending hospitality to others. In chapter four I look at one of the missionary strategies of Paul, namely, his embrace of the role of the good and ideal guest, and suggest that we, too, are encouraged to enter into the role of guest with non-Christians as a means of engaging in meaningful friendships and beneficial other-regarding relationships with the religious other for their own sakes as well as with the hope that they will encounter the life-giving presence of Jesus. In chapter five I show how the story of Israel in the Old Testament imparts to God's people today an immigrant identity that enables God's people to overcome a posture of xenophobia, or fear of the immigrant. Israel's experience of divine hospitality is the reason they are called to be merciful to the stranger and immigrant in their midst. Finally, in chapter six I examine the ways in which economic structures can facilitate greed and consumerism and suggest that recovering the church's call to almsgiving, or simply stated, "merciful acts," provides a way toward combatting greed as an inhibitor of hospitality.

Study Questions

1. Describe an experience that made you feel pulled between "opening your doors" to a stranger or "keeping your doors closed." Why did you experience this tension? What did you do and why?

2. What comes to your mind when you hear the word "hospitality" used in contemporary speech? In what ways do your thoughts cohere (or not) with the author's definition of hospitality?

3. The author of 1 Clement sees a causal connection between hospitality and salvation with respect to Abraham, Lot, and Rahab. Is this a convincing interpretation or reading of these Old Testament passages? Why or why not?

PART ONE

Divine Hospitality

CHAPTER 1

Food, Stigma, and the Identity
of the Church in Luke-Acts

Whom you eat with can say a lot about who you are or at least about who you think you are. Think about the meals you've shared with another person or group in the past few weeks or so. Who comes to mind? For most of us, the companions at our meals will be friends, family, and co-workers—people who are generally *already* part of our normal societal surroundings. It is unlikely that our table companions will include anyone of a different socio-economic bracket or another religion, someone struggling with a severe addiction, someone chronically homeless, or someone with a physical disability or with a serious mental illness. I am not trying to make you feel guilty. My meals generally also revolve around family, friends, and colleagues or students at my seminary. Handing a homeless person some money for food is much easier and, of course, much less intimate than sharing a meal together. Sharing meals, eating with someone at the same table, and receiving guests into one's home (and entering into others' homes as a guest) function as opportunities to increase our friendship and intimacy with others.

Luke's Gospel and his second volume, the Acts of the Apostles, are filled with the language and elements of hospitality—food, meals, houses, and traveling—in order to express something significant about Jesus's identity, namely, how God's hospitality is extended to his lost, broken, needy, and often stigmatized people. This divine hospitality comes to us in the person of Jesus, the divine host who extends God's hospitality to sinners, outcasts, and strangers and thereby draws them—and us—into friendship with God. God's embrace of humanity into friendship with him is the ultimate form of welcoming the stranger. But divine hospitality does not end with our experience of God's welcome; it also elicits human hospitality. In other words, our friendship with God is the foundation of and cause for our friendship with one another. Jesus grants divine hospitality to the "other" without distinction, and this is exemplified in his welcome to sinners and the religious, men and women, rich and poor, and Jews and Gentiles. Jesus shows no apprehension or fear of associating with the stigmatized in society. And, further, he is markedly unimpressed by appeals to ethnicity, status, formal religious observance, and gender as means of social worth or worth before God. Thus, divine welcome does not correspond to some type of merit or preexisting social worth, for Jesus's extension of divine hospitality appears as indiscriminate—which is precisely the feature of Jesus's ministry that annoys so many of the religious leaders of his time.

God's hospitality toward us and our friendship with God create the foundation for friendship within the church. In other words, divine hospitality is enacted in our friendship and hospitality toward others who have been welcomed into God's family. Humans are created for friendship with God and for friendship with one another, but both sets of relationships have been fractured by disordered desires for wealth, status, and power, by the creation of boundaries and divisions that separate and prevent peaceful and authentic communication and result in judgments upon one another, and ultimately by sin and hubris that mar our relationship with God. The Gospel of Luke introduces us to a Savior who both restores our broken friendship with God *and* thereby heals our broken relationships with one another.

This divine hospitality is often enacted through Jesus's sharing of meals, meals that are anticipations of the final feast with the Messiah. These meals are marked by joy, generosity, inclusivity, the rejection of status and hierarchy, and most importantly—the experiential and saving presence of the Messiah among his people. Jesus's final meal with his disciples ritualizes his hospitality practices and insures that the presence of the risen Messiah will continue to meet, heal, and transform those who share in the meals of the church. The church's hospitality meals indicate that the primary marker of the identity of the church is that it is the recipient of God's hospitality. And if Jesus's extension of hospitality is the basis of our friendship with God, then the fact that he is markedly unconcerned with purity or contamination by the intimate act of sharing meals with sinners and society's stigmatized should have consequences for how we, too, think about the vocation of the church. In other words, the church is called to participate in Jesus's hospitality among sinners and outcasts by embracing a stigmatized identity that follows from sharing life together with *all of God's people*. The church must recover its role as the context for embodying God's hospitality by considering what it might look like to embrace a stigmatized identity through acts such as visiting and caring for the incarcerated community in North America.[1]

The Year of the Lord's Welcome

Clearly, Jesus's identity and teaching are foundational for the church's understanding of its identity and vocation. Before we begin to examine what Jesus says about his mission, we need to take note of one important aspect of divine hospitality, namely, *the depiction of God as the divine host who nourishes his people.*[2] In Israel's Scriptures God is often portrayed as the host of Israel as he provides manna and quail in the wilderness (Exod 16:4, 15; Num 11:1–9; Deut 8:3, 16; Pss 78:24–38 and 105:40; Neh 9:15), spreads a table of peace and divine nourishment for the Psalmist (Ps 23), and, as the owner of the land, grants Israel the gift of benefiting from that land as his guests (Lev 25:23). But God also promises his people that one day he will act to inaugurate his kingdom, will save his people, and will make known his presence in full *by means of a banquet feast between God and his people.* God's climactic act of salvation for his people will come, then, in the form of God sharing his presence with his people through shared hospitality.

Multiple Old Testament texts look forward to this day. For instance, Isaiah 25:6–9 says,

> On this mountain the Lord of hosts will make for all peoples a feast of rich food, a feast of well-aged wines, of rich food filled with marrow, of well-aged wines strained clear. And he will destroy on this mountain the shroud that is cast over all peoples, the sheet that is spread over all nations; he will swallow up death forever. Then the Lord God will wipe away the tears from all faces, and the disgrace of his people he will take away from all the earth, for the Lord has spoken. It will be said on that day, Lo, this is our God; we have waited for him, so that he might save us. This is the Lord for whom we have waited; let us be glad and rejoice in his salvation.

---

1. While we might reflect on many marginalized, stigmatized communities, I have chosen the incarcerated community in North America as a result of my own particular experiences and my belief that this constitutes one of the more vulnerable and oppressed communities in my North American context.

2. See here especially Geoffrey Wainwright, *Eucharist and Eschatology* (Oxford: Oxford University Press, 1981), ch. 2.

Isaiah is obviously looking forward to something more than a tasty meal. The full and complete shared presence between God and his people, an experience of divine presence such that we cry out, "This is our God! We have waited for him," is symbolized through God providing and sharing with us this banquet feast.[3] The prophet Isaiah anticipates God's fulfillment of the promises made to David and invites the hungry and thirsty:

> Ho, everyone who thirsts, come to the waters; and you that have no money, come, buy and eat! Come, buy wine and milk without money and without price. Why do you spend your money for that which is not bread, and your labor for that which does not satisfy? Listen carefully to me, and eat what is good, and delight yourselves in rich food. (Isa 55:1–2)

The prophet Ezekiel says that when God sends his Davidic Messiah to shepherd his people, one of his tasks will be to provide food and nourishment for them (Ezek 34:23–24). In other words, Israel looks forward to a time when God and God's Messiah come to share divine welcome, salvation, and peaceful relationship with Israel *by means of shared hospitality and table fellowship between God and his people.*[4]

This is the context for understanding Jesus's meals and table-fellowship, as Jesus's meals extend God's hospitality and offer a foretaste of the eschatological banquet to all kinds of people in the Gospel of Luke. Let's begin with Jesus's well-known Nazareth sermon in Luke 4:16–30.[5] When Jesus enters into the synagogue in his hometown of Nazareth, he turns to Isaiah and reads:

> The Spirit of the Lord is upon me. He has anointed me to proclaim good news to the poor. He has sent me to preach release for the captives and sight for the blind, and to give release to the oppressed, *to proclaim the year of the Lord's welcome.* (4:18–19; emphasis added [my trans.])

---

3. See further Isa 49:9–10; 62:8–9; 65:13–18; Amos 9:13–15.

4. This hope for a coming banquet feast between the Messiah and his people continues in Second Temple Jewish literature. See, for example, 1 En. 25:4–6; 62:13–16; 2 Bar. 29:1–30:4. Further, see Brant Pitre, *Jesus and the Last Supper* (Grand Rapids: Eerdmans, 2015), 452–58. Also helpful is Craig L. Blomberg, *Contagious Holiness: Jesus' Meal with Sinners*, vol. 19, *New Studies in Biblical Theology* (Downers Grove, IL: InterVarsity Press, 2005), 32–96.

5. Much has been written on the programmatic nature of Luke 4:16–30. See, for example, Christopher J. Schreck, "The Nazareth Pericope: Luke 4:16–30 in Recent Study," in *L'évangile de Luc—The Gospel of Luke*, ed. Frans Neirynck, 2nd ed. (Leuven: Leuven University Press, 1989), 399–471.

First, Jesus's ministry enacts the *Lord God's* hospitality. Jesus declares that "the Spirit of *the Lord* is upon me" (4:18a) and that his ministry is "to proclaim the year of the *Lord's* welcome" (4:19). The phrase "Spirit of the Lord" refers to *God's* Spirit, and the second phrase (in 4:19) is a quotation of Isaiah 61:2a, so no doubt the primary referent of "Lord" is the God of Israel. Jesus's ministry, then, is both empowered by God's Spirit and a manifestation of God's welcome.[6] In other words, "the year of the Lord's welcome" is established and enacted throughout Luke's Gospel in the ministry of the Lord Jesus.[7] The point is simple but important: Jesus is more than a prophet or important religious leader; his ministry is an embodiment of God's hospitality toward the stranger and the oppressed.

Second, most English translations of the Bible render the italicized portion of Jesus's speech as "to proclaim the year of the Lord's favor" instead of "welcome." While this is a perfectly acceptable translation of the Greek word *dektos*, given that Luke uses the same word in 4:24 to refer to a prophet's *lack of welcome* in his hometown, Luke's frequent use of the *dech-* root for hospitality (for instance, in 9:5, 48, 53; 10:8–10; see also Acts 10:35), and the fact that the recipients of the Lord's welcome are stereotypical outsiders in need of welcome, it makes good sense to understand 4:19 as Jesus's programmatic proclamation that he has come to enact divine welcome and hospitality to the stranger and the outcast. The programmatic function of Jesus's Nazareth sermon invites the reader to pay attention to the way in which the entirety of Jesus's ministry *and particularly his meals with strangers* enact divine hospitality to the poor, the captives, the blind, and the oppressed.

Third, the phrase "to give release to the oppressed," quoted by Jesus in Luke 4:18b, comes from Isaiah 58:6, and it is worth quoting the prophetic oracle in more detail: "Isn't this the fast I choose: to break the chains of wickedness, to loose the ropes of the yoke, to give release to the oppressed, and to tear off every yoke? Is it not to share your bread with the hungry, to bring the poor and homeless into your house, to clothe the naked when you see him and not to ignore your own flesh and blood?" (Isa 58:6–7). Both Isaiah 61:1–2 and 58:6–7, which are the texts quoted by Jesus in Luke 4:18–19, share the words "release" and "welcome" and indicate that Jesus's ministry will provide the social justice, release, forgiveness of debts, and hospitality

---

6. On this passage, see C. Kavin Rowe, *Early Narrative Christology: The Lord in the Gospel of Luke* (Berlin: Walter de Gruyter GmbH & Co. KG, 2006), 78–82.

7. Rowe, *Early Narrative Christology*, 81.

that Israel's prophets had demanded of Israel.[8] The entire ministry of Jesus is appropriately captured in the phrase "divine hospitality to the stranger and sinner."[9]

Jesus—Divine Host to Strangers and Sinners

If Jesus's mission is to enact the Lord's hospitality as set forth in Isaiah, then it is no surprise that Luke portrays Jesus as an actual host who dispenses the Lord's welcome by sharing meals with strangers, sinners, and outsiders. In fact, one of the primary ways in which Jesus enacts the year of divine welcome is by sharing his saving presence with *all kinds of people* at meals. It is precisely through Jesus's eating meals with outsiders that he creates the hospitable space where outsiders experience the saving presence of God and are thereby transformed from strangers to friends of God. For example, Jesus interprets the "great feast" (5:29) that is hosted by Levi the tax collector as signifying Jesus's healing of Levi's ruptured relationships (5:31–32). Jesus's meal with Simon the Pharisee, ironically, provides the hospitable space for the so-called "sinful woman" to encounter the saving presence of Jesus, a presence that enables her to experience divine forgiveness, peace, and incorporation into the people and kingdom of God (7:36–50).[10] Zacchaeus's quest to see Jesus is more than fulfilled when Jesus demands hospitality from the tax collector: "I must receive hospitality in your house today" (19:5). After their shared hospitality, Jesus makes a similar declaration: "Salvation has come to this house today" (19:9). The shared hospitality between Jesus and Zacchaeus has provided the context for Jesus to share his presence with the outcast and incorporate him into God's family as a "son of Abraham" (19:9).

In the ancient world it was common practice to share meals with one's family, friends, and clients. As a result, many statements offer wise advice or moral philosophical instruction to give counsel as to the kinds of people with whom one should and *should not* share meals. The Jewish sage Sirach offers counsel that may seem quite sensible: "Do not invite *everyone* into

---

8. See further Richard B. Hays, *Echoes of Scripture in the Gospels* (Waco, TX: Baylor University Press, 2016), 225–29.

9. Similarly, see Brendan Byrne, *The Hospitality of God: A Reading of Luke's Gospel* (Collegeville, MN: The Liturgical Press, 2000), 48–50.

10. For much more detail, see my *Divine Visitations and Hospitality to Strangers in Luke-Acts: An Interpretation of the Malta Episode in Acts 28:1–10*, NovTSup 153 (Leiden: Brill, 2013), 171–82.

your home, for many are the tricks of the crafty. . . . Receive strangers into your home and they will stir up trouble for you, and will make you a stranger to your own family" (Sir 11:29, 34).[11] Instead of strangers and indiscriminate table-fellowship companions, it is better to "let the righteous be your dinner companions" (Sir 9:16). One of the major marks of Jesus's table-practices is his indiscriminate and non-calculating offer of hospitality to all people, and this might easily seem to conflict with Jewish heroes who separated themselves from impure people and their food.[12] Instead, Jesus eats with tax collectors (Luke 5:27–32; 19:1–10; see also 3:10–14; 7:29, 34; 18:9–14), a sinful woman (7:36–50), two women (10:38–42), the poor and ritually unclean (9:11–17), his disciples (22:15–20), and even with the Pharisees (7:39; 11:37–54; 14:1–6). It is no surprise, then, that Israel's religious leaders are said to have taken offense and complain about the guests to whom Jesus extends hospitality (5:30–32; 15:1–2; 19:6–7). Jesus is tangibly extending God's friendship to those who, in the eyes of others, are not righteous, have a low status, and are viewed as unworthy of friendship with God.[13]

Many of you will remember Jesus' parable of the lost son (15:11–32) and likely even the stories of the lost sheep and the lost coin (15:3–10), but how many remember *why* Jesus told these stories? Jesus tells these stories as a response to the Pharisees and scribes who were angrily complaining about his extension of hospitality to the wrong people: "And all the tax collectors and sinners were coming near to listen to him. And the Pharisees and scribes were grumbling, saying, 'This one extends hospitality [*prosdechetai*] to sinners and he eats with them!' (15:1–2 [my trans.]). It should not escape the reader that the charge brought against Jesus (extending hospitality to sinners and tax-collectors) is exactly what Jesus himself had described as the very purpose of his mission ("to proclaim the year of the Lord's welcome," 4:19). Jesus' three parables, then, are commentary upon the meaning of his extension of welcome through shared meals with the sinners and tax collectors.

When Jesus shares table-fellowship with sinners, this is an enactment of the divine Shepherd's recovery of the lost sheep of Israel (15:3–7; see also Ezek 34:11–12). His table-fellowship with outcasts is the embodiment of di-

---

11. See Robert J. Karris, *Eating Your Way through Luke's Gospel* (Collegeville, MN: Liturgical Press, 2006), 26–30.

12. See, for example, Dan 1:10–12; 1 Macc 1:43, 62–63; 2 Macc 6:4–7; Jdt 12:1–2, 19; Tob 1:5, 10–12; Jos. Asen. 7:1.

13. On the use of labels to identify these Lukan characters, see Joel B. Green, *Conversion in Luke-Acts: Divine Action, Human Cognition, and the People of God* (Grand Rapids: Baker, 2015), 106–13.

vine celebration (15:10) over sinners who, like a lost coin, were "lost" but are now "found" (15:8–9). Jesus's extension of hospitality to sinners is the expression of the father's welcome of "my son who was dead and is alive again, who was lost and now is found" (15:24; see also 15:32). The father's response to the recovery of his lost son is significant for, like Jesus's meals with sinners and outcasts, his response is one of joyous and celebratory feasting (15:27; see also v. 30). The elder son epitomizes the stance of the Pharisees who reject a divine hospitality that would welcome sinners. Both the elder son and the Pharisees "do not want to enter in" (15:28) and participate in the feast. The father's words to his elder son are significant, for they declare he must acknowledge the necessity of rejoicing over recovery of the lost: "we must celebrate and rejoice. . ." (15:32a). And while the father's words to the elder son provide a warning, Jesus's teaching affirms the elder son's place in the family as well: "Son, you are always with me and everything I have is yours" (15:31 [my trans.]). In other words, Jesus compassionately extends God's hospitality to any of the religious leaders who might relate with the elder son and be in need of a reorientation in their understanding of their relationship with their merciful Father *and* fellow neighbors who are being welcomed into God's family (see 15:1-2). Thus, in these three parables Jesus links his hospitality to sinners with divine joy ("heaven," 15:7; "before God's angels," 15:10; the Father rejoices, 15:24-32).[14] The joy that occurs when sinners are restored to friendship with God through Jesus's extension of hospitality corresponds to the joy that is shared between Jesus and sinners over these shared meals (see 19:6).

Feasting with the Messiah

In order to fully appreciate Jesus's meals with strangers, we must examine the three most important meals in Luke, each of which functions as a conclusion to the major divisions of Jesus's ministry.[15] At the conclusion of his Galilean ministry, Jesus is shown as the divine host when he feeds the five thousand near Bethsaida (9:10-17). Robert Karris rightly recognizes that Jesus is por-

14. John Koenig, *New Testament Hospitality: Partnership with Strangers as Promise and Mission* (Eugene, OR: Wipf and Stock, 2001), 115; David P. Moessner, *Lord of the Banquet: The Literary and Theological Significance of the Lukan Travel Narrative* (Minneapolis: Fortress Press, 1989), 159.

15. Arthur A. Just, *The Ongoing Feast: Table Fellowship and Eschatology at Emmaus* (Collegeville, MN: The Liturgical Press, 1993), 156–57.

trayed as divine host to the hungry: "This miracle is a glowing example of Jesus's inclusive table, to which he invites sinners and the unclean."[16] He "welcomes" the crowd (9:11), makes all of them "recline" (9:14–15), commands his disciples to "distribute" the food (9:16), and "they all ate and were satisfied" (9:17). That this takes place within the context of Jesus's proclamation of the kingdom of God (9:11), healing of the sick (9:11), and revelation of Jesus's identity as the suffering and crucified Messiah (9:18–22) indicates that God's benevolent salvation for his people is made known through these meals with the Messiah.[17] The literary placement of Peter's confession of Jesus as the Messiah (9:18–20) and Jesus's teaching about his impending death (9:21–27) indicate that these meals anticipate feasting upon and with Jesus in the kingdom of God. Luke's wording to describe Jesus's feeding of the five thousand is important: "And then he took the five loaves and the two fish, and he looked up to heaven and he blessed and broke them. And he was distributing the food to the disciples in order to set before the crowd" (9:16 [my trans.]).

Jesus's proclamation of the kingdom of God, his gesture of looking up to heaven, and his prayer of blessing indicate that this is the manifestation of God's presence and hospitable benevolence to the crowd. But the language also points forward to Jesus's climactic final meal with his disciples where he explicitly identifies the bread with his broken body and the drink with his shed blood (22:15–20). In this celebration of the Passover Jesus again plays the role of the host who gives his sacrificial presence to the disciples through his food and his drink.[18] Jesus has "the apostles recline with him" (22:14b). As the servant-host, Jesus "gives to them" his body for their food: "this [bread] is my body given on your behalf" (22:19). The phrasing "he took bread, gave thanks, broke it, and gave it to them" (22:19a) recalls Jesus's feeding of the multitude (9:16) and anticipates his Emmaus meal (24:30)—occasions where Jesus's role as host and his "giving bread" effect his revelatory presence. As host he serves them the drink of "the new covenant in my blood poured out

---

16. Karris, *Eating Your Way Through Luke's Gospel*, 52.

17. The literary frame (9:7–9 and 9:18–36) of the feeding of the five thousand (9:12–17) is concerned with elucidating the nature of Jesus's Messiahship. See Frederick W. Danker, *Jesus and the New Age according to St. Luke: A Commentary on the Third Gospel* (St. Louis: Clayton Publishing House, 1972), 111–19, and 250. Also, Eugene LaVerdiere, *Dining the Kingdom of God: The Origins of the Eucharist according to Luke* (Chicago: Liturgy Training Publications, 1994), 69–70.

18. On Jesus as *both* servant *and* host, see Dennis E. Smith, *From Symposium to Eucharist: The Banquet in the Early Christian World* (Minneapolis: Fortress Press, 2003), 265–67.

for you" (22:20b). The purpose of a covenant, like the extension of hospitality, is to create family and friendship relations, and therefore participation in this meal marks one as belonging to the Lord's family.[19] By giving his "body" and "blood" as food and drink, and by commanding them to "do this in my remembrance" (22:19b), Jesus ensures that the future meals of the apostles will be the locus of his perpetual presence.[20]

With Jesus's death imminent and his covenant meal instituted, Luke shows how the presence of Jesus is continued through the apostles. Jesus confers upon them the kingdom that he has been enacting through his hospitality practices: "so I confer upon you [the kingdom] just as my Father has conferred the kingdom upon me" (22:29 [my trans.]). Within the Septuagint, the particular language of "conferral" is almost always used to refer to the creation or ratification of a covenant,[21] and given that Jesus has just instituted a new covenant, we are invited to see Jesus as "covenanting" his kingdom to the disciples.[22] The kingdom of God has been present in Jesus's extension of divine welcome to sinners and outcasts, and Jesus declares that it will continue within the ministry of the apostles through table fellowship.[23] Thus the purpose of the conferral of his kingdom to the apostles is "in order that you may eat and drink at my table in my kingdom and you will sit on thrones judging the twelve tribes of Israel" (22:30). In other words, the apostles make their rule over God's people known through stewarding "the Lord's table" (22:14–27). Jesus's kingdom has been made manifest through shared hospitality, and now the apostles are commissioned to continue his ministry through the stewardship of food.

This is what happens in Luke's final meal scene, where hospitality and breaking the bread (24:29–35) function as the revelatory context for the

19. See Scott W. Hahn, *Kinship by Covenant: A Canonical Approach to the Fulfillment of God's Saving Promises*, ABRL (New Haven: Yale University Press, 2009).

20. Like the Israelites who "remembered" when they ate the Passover (Exod 12:14 LXX), so the church's meals will be the locus for the experience of the Lord's presence. So J. P. Heil, *The Meal Scenes in Luke Acts: An Audience-Oriented Approach* (Atlanta: SBL Publications, 1999), 175–76; Smith, *From Symposium to Eucharist*, 263.

21. See, for example, Gen 9:17; 15:18; 21:27, 32; 26:28; Exod 24:8.

22. See Hahn, *Kinship by Covenant*, 227–28.

23. Hahn, *Kinship by Covenant*, 230–4. Peter K. Nelson, "Luke 22:29–30 and the Time Frame for Ruling and Dining," *Tyndale Bulletin* 44, no. 2 (November 1993): 355–57, claims that if Luke intended 22:28–30 to correlate with Acts, then one would expect more specific correspondences. His examination of the correspondences, however, is superficial. Most notable is his failure to connect the apostles' sitting on "twelve thrones" (22:30b) with the reconstitution of the Twelve (Acts 1:15–26).

disciples' recognition of Jesus. In Luke 24:13–35, two disciples encounter the risen but disguised Jesus on the Emmaus road. Let's pick up the story where it appears that Jesus will leave the disciples and journey further on the way (24:28b). Despite the disciples' sadness over recent events in Jerusalem (24:17), they respond admirably to the journeying stranger in their offer of hospitality: "They compelled him strongly, saying 'Stay with us, for already it is evening and the day has reclined'" (24:29a). Jesus accepts their offer of hospitality and his role as their guest as "he entered in to stay with them" (24:29b). Our expectations are heightened since we have already seen how meals often function within Luke's Gospel as occasions for deeper disclosure of Jesus's identity (for example, 7:36–50; 9:11–17; 14:1–24; 22:14–38).[24] Thus, it is no great surprise that when Jesus "reclined at the table with them" (24:30a) to share the meal, Jesus the guest assumes the role of the host: "upon taking the bread he gave a blessing and after breaking it he distributed it to them" (24:30b [my trans.]).[25] The precise language evokes Luke's stories of Jesus as host who feeds and nourishes his people *by disclosing himself* to the people (esp. Luke 9:10–17 and 22:15–20). For example, in Luke 9:16 Jesus "takes" bread, "blesses" and "breaks" the bread, and "gives" it to the disciples to feed the crowd. Likewise, at the Last Supper, Jesus assumes the role of host and "takes bread, gives thanks, breaks it and gives it to them [that is, the disciples]" (22:19a). The connections between Luke 9:16, 22:19–20, and 24:30 indicate that the Emmaus meal symbolizes the active, experiential, ongoing presence of the risen Jesus who enacts God's hospitality and welcome to his people.[26] It is the presence of Jesus the divine host, therefore, that finally initiates the disciples' recognition of the stranger's identity, moving them from a state of blindness (see 24:16) to one of insight and recognition: "and their eyes were opened and they recognized him" (24:31a [my trans.]). Shared hospitality between Jesus and the two disciples functions as the catalyst for moving the disciples from blindness to sight, or from non-recognition to recognition. When the two disciples return to the others, Luke highlights that they narrate to them "the things which happened on the way and how he was made known to them in the breaking of the bread" (24:35 [my trans.]).[27]

---

24. See, for example, Just, *The Ongoing Feast*, 128–95.

25. Luke frequently portrays "Jesus the guest" assuming the role of host during meal scenarios (for instance, 5:27–32; 10:38–42; 14:1–24).

26. Rightly, Robert C. Tannehill, *The Narrative Unity of Luke-Acts*, vol. 1 (Minneapolis: Fortress Press, 1986), 290; Karris, *Eating Your Way through Luke's Gospel*, 48–50.

27. The phrase "the breaking of the bread" is a metonymy for the entire meal (compare

Friendship, Food, and the Risen Messiah in Acts

Luke's sequel to his Gospel, the book of Acts, shows how the experiential presence of the risen Lord continues to be found through the breaking of bread, the administration of food, and the imitation of Jesus's hospitality. The community implements Jesus's ethics through the non-reciprocal sharing of hospitality and food within a diverse kinship group composed of diverse social classes (rich, poor, and widows), ethnicities (Hellenists and Hebrews), and genders.

The "Summary Statements" of Acts 2:42–47 and 4:32–35 fulfill this expectation by portraying the community as the place where the Lord is present and "remembered" (Luke 22:19) through food and hospitality. First, the statements' description of the community breaking bread (2:42, 46) and sharing possessions (2:44–45; 4:32–35) fulfills Jesus's promises that the twelve apostles would share in his rule through the distribution of his food, drink, and possessions (Luke 22:30; see also 12:42–46). Second, the repeated phrase "breaking the bread" (2:42b), which is expanded to "they broke bread from house to house and ate their food with a joyful and sincere heart" (2:46), recalls Jesus's acts of breaking bread (Luke 9:16; 22:19; 24:30, 35).[28] Jesus's "breaking of bread" expresses his hospitality for the people (Luke 9:12–17) and signifies his sacrificial and revelatory presence with his people (Luke 22:19–20; 24:29–35). The "breaking of bread," then, is instituted as the means for manifesting the Lord's presence with his people.[29] That the risen Lord is present with his people is indicated by their "rejoicing" (Acts 2:46) and "praising God" (2:47) in their meals—language also used to indicate the response to the divine visit.

Third, these statements are the implementation of Jesus's teachings on hospitality set forth in Luke. Given the note that three thousand converted (Acts 2:41) and the fact that the rich sold property for the needy (2:44–45; 4:34–35; 4:36–5:11), the community includes both rich and poor. Thus, the practice of eating together "daily" (2:46a) depends upon the rich sharing their possessions with "whoever had need" (2:45). This daily provision of

---

Acts 2:46). See B. P. Robinson, "The Place of the Emmaus Story in Luke-Acts," *NTS* 30, no. 4 (October 1984): 484.

28. Hahn, *Kinship by Covenant*, 233–34; Douglas A. Hume, *The Early Christian Community: A Narrative Analysis of Acts 2:41–47 and 4:32–35*, WUNT 2.298 (Tübingen: Mohr-Siebeck, 2011), 106–8.

29. Alan J. Thompson, *One Lord, One People: The Unity of the Church in Acts in Its Literary Setting*, LNTS 359 (London: T&T Clark, 2008), 63–70.

food for the poor would "significantly ameliorate the financial burdens of the impoverished in the community, since food is the primary expense of a poor person."[30] The provision of food for the poor mirrors Jesus's activities as host of the hungry (Luke 9:12–17) and provider of hospitality to *all people* (15:1–2). The non-reciprocal sharing of food is the antithesis of the disposition of those characters who refuse to share possessions and show hospitality to the poor (Luke 16:19–31; 18:18–30) and even the disciples who used the Last Supper as an opportunity to pursue status (Luke 22:25–26).[31] By bestowing food upon the needy, the wealthy follow Jesus's command to engage in indiscriminate sharing of wealth and hospitality (for example, Luke 6:27–38; 14:12–24; 22:24–27).[32] The wealthy Barnabas's selling his field for the sake of the poor is a clear rejection of the system of benefaction, which Jesus also rejected (Luke 22:24–27).[33] Thus, the community admirably implements Jesus's inclusive hospitality ethics (Luke 10:25–37; 14:12–14). Ananias and Sapphira's withholding money, alternatively, threatens the unity of the community, demonstrates their rejection of Jesus's teaching on possessions and hospitality, and proves they are not true kin.[34]

Finally, the language of "fellowship" (2:42), "all things in common" (2:44; see also 4:32b), and "one heart and soul" (4:32) borrows from the language of philosophical friendship. Luke's use of friendship language to depict the community reinforces the notion that this is a new family that has implemented Jesus's hospitality ethics.[35] The practice of table-fellowship and hospitality creates fictive familial relations, and the philosophical friendship implies social equality.[36] Friendship is something that takes place between those of equal status; if not, then the friendship is a patron-client relationship. But Luke expands the scope of friendship to include *all* people, rich

30. Christopher M. Hays, *Luke's Wealth Ethics: A Study in Their Coherence and Character*, WUNT 2.275 (Tübingen: Mohr-Siebeck, 2010), 193. Also, see Reta Halteman Finger, *Of Widows and Meals: Communal Meals in the Book of Acts* (Grand Rapids: Eerdmans, 2007), 230.

31. Hume, *The Early Christian Community*, 108–9.

32. Alan C. Mitchell, "The Social Function of Friendship in Acts 2:44–47 and 4:32–37," *JBL* 111, no. 2 (Summer 1992): 255–72, here 266–67.

33. Luke Timothy Johnson, *The Literary Function of Possessions in Luke-Acts*, SBLDS 39 (Missoula, MT: Scholars Press, 1977), 201–4; Mitchell, "The Social Function of Friendship in Acts 2:44–47 and 4:32–37," 269.

34. See Finger, *Of Widows and Meals*, 133–34.

35. See Finger, *Of Widows and Meals*, 128–36.

36. Plutarch often refers to "the friend-making nature of the dining table" (*Table Talk* 612 D-E). On friendship and equality, see Aristotle, *NE* 8.5.5; 8.6.7–8.8.7; 8.11.5; 8.13.1; Plutarch, *Table Talk* 708; Plato, *Laws* 6.757A.

and poor, Hellenist and Hebrew, man and woman. It is not wealth or status that provides the basis for the community sharing "one heart and soul" but rather faith in the presence of the Lord in the community (2:44). Hume states it well: "By sharing meals together, the believers are enacting a practice of friendship that forms a kind of family, a fictive kinship group that meets their needs for nourishment, social interaction, and joy."[37]

The joy and friendship of the community is threatened, sadly, when "grumbling from the Hellenists against the Hebrews" occurs, "for their widows were being overlooked in the daily meal" (6:1b). It appears as though the widows are being excluded from the community's "daily" (2:46, 47) meal (see Acts 2:42–47).[38] The Hellenists' grumbling recalls Jesus's opponents who grumble about Jesus's friendship with sinners and social outcasts (so Luke 5:29–30; 15:1–2; 19:7).[39] Thus, it is significant that those who are overlooked are Hellenist widows.[40] Within Luke-Acts, widows represent the vulnerable (Luke 7:11–17) and poor in need of justice (Luke 18:1–8; 20:46–47), and this is why Jesus is compassionate to widows and commends their piety (Luke 7:11–17; 21:1–4). Based on Torah, the widows are classified with "the stranger" to whom God promises protection (Deut 10:17–18). Thus, the Hellenists' grumbling is justified, for the community is failing to implement Jesus's hospitality practices in their exclusion of the poor widows. That the challenge to the community's unity centers upon food, "the serving of the daily meal" (Acts 6:1)—the place where the Lord is present with his people (see 2:42–47)—signifies a major challenge to the implementation of Jesus's hospitality ethics.

Luke narrates the successful resolution of this threat through the commission of the Seven Hellenists "to serve at tables" (6:2b). Their charge "to wait on tables" is an extension of Jesus's ministry that was conferred upon the Twelve (Luke 22:24–30).[41] Likewise, the charge of the Twelve to find seven men "full of the Spirit and wisdom whom we will place in charge over

---

37. Hume, *The Early Christian Community*, 110.

38. See further David W. Pao, "Waiters or Preachers: Acts 6:1–7 and the Lukan Table Fellowship Motif," *JBL* 130, no. 1 (Spring 2011): 127–44, here 135–37. Finger, *Of Widows and Meals*, 251–64, suggests that the Hellenist widows are being excluded from the noble task of preparing, organizing, and serving the daily meal.

39. Pao, "Waiters or Preachers," 137–38.

40. On widows, see F. Scott Spencer, "Neglected Widows in Acts 6:1–7," *CBQ* 56 (1994): 715–33; Todd Penner, *In Praise of Christian Origins: Stephen and the Hellenists in Lukan Apologetic Historiography*, ESEC (New York: T&T Clark, 2004), 265–66; Finger, *Of Widows and Meals*.

41. Pao, "Waiters or Preachers," 141–42.

this need" (Acts 6:3b) alludes to the parables in which Jesus promises to reward the faithful by "placing them over" his food and possessions (Luke 12:44).[42] Given Jesus's summary of his ministry "as one who serves [at the table]" (22:27) and his commission to the Twelve to rule through eating and drinking "at my table" (22:30a), Luke has portrayed the Seven as Jesus's faithful successors. The result of the Seven's leadership over the table is successful: "the word of God grew and the number of the disciples in Jerusalem increased greatly" (Acts 6:7 [my trans.]).

Recall that throughout Luke's Gospel one of the primary ways Luke articulates God's salvation of needy, lost, and broken sinners is through Jesus the host who dispenses God's hospitality and welcomes them into friendship with God. These meals nourish and satisfy both the physically and spiritually hungry. Also, Luke expects that Jesus's meals with sinners will call forth a response from his disciples to imitate and share in dispensing the Lord's welcome to others. In other words, those who have experienced divine welcome will seek to share God's hospitality with others. Finally, Jesus's final meals at the Last Supper (22:15-20) and on the Emmaus Road (24:13-35) ritualize Jesus's hospitality practices and suggest that the church will imitate what Jesus has taught and embodied among them with his hospitality ethics. These meals suggest that the church will continue to experience Jesus's presence during these meals as it looks forward to the messianic banquet in God's kingdom.

Embracing Stigma, Subverting Stereotype

God's extension of hospitality does not correspond to some kind of criteria that would respond to the social worth of the individual or group. One of the primary agendas of Luke's two-volume work is to demonstrate, in fulfillment of Isaiah's prophetic vision, that "all flesh will see the salvation of God" (Luke 3:6; see also Luke 2:10-11; 2:30-32; Acts 28:28).[43] One of the ways Luke fulfills this agenda is seen in his frequent raising of a social or cultural stereotype only in order to subvert it. In other words, Luke rejects popular notions of stigmas and stereotypes in order to show how God's saving embrace is truly

42. For further parallels between the Seven Hellenists (including Stephen) and Jesus, see Johnson, *The Literary Function of Possessions*, 50–52, and 212–13. Smith (*From Symposium to Eucharist*, 264) rightly notes the correlation between Luke 12:35–48 and Acts 6:1–6.

43. No one has articulated this theme as clearly and cogently as David W. Pao, *Acts and the Isaianic New Exodus* (Grand Rapids: Baker Academic Press, 2000).

coming to *all people*, and this functions as a serious indictment or warning for those who would place any restrictions upon *who* can experience divine hospitality.

For example, in Acts 28:1-10 Luke's pairing of "barbarian" (*barbaros*) with "humane kindness" (*philanthrōpia*) is intentionally jarring as Paul and the shipwrecked prisoners land on Malta. Barbarians, stereotypically, do not show hospitable kindness to shipwrecked strangers. But Luke deliberately rejects this stereotype by juxtaposing "barbarian" and "love for humanity." For example, Luke's description of hospitable and philanthropic barbarians in Acts 28:1-10 challenges one to put together two impossible (or at least incredibly unlikely based on cultural conventions) descriptions for the same people—"barbarian" and "extraordinarily hospitable"—and in so doing works to subvert and deconstruct the validity of engaging in ethnic stereotyping as a valid means of making sense of the cultural worth and value of *other* ethnicities.[44] This resembles how Luke employs other ethnic and cultural stereotypes, namely, playing on the stereotype in order to deconstruct it. For example, as John Dominic Crossan has noted in the so-called Parable of the Good Samaritan: "The literal point of the story challenges the hearer to put together two impossible and contradictory words for the same person: 'Samaritan' (10:33) and 'neighbor' (10:36). . . . The story demands that the hearer respond by saying the contradictory, the impossible, the unspeakable."[45] As the hearer struggles to make sense of the *seemingly* contradictory terms, Luke effectively renders the stereotype entirely deficient to make sense of human characters. Luke may be doing something similar with his descriptions of Roman centurions. Within Luke-Acts, centurions recognize and submit to Jesus's authority (Luke 7:2-10), confess Jesus's innocence (Luke 23:46-47), are pious and give alms (Acts 10:1-6), and show great kindness toward Paul (*philanthrōpōs*, Acts 27:3; see also 21:37-40). Luke's centurions behave contrary to the majority socio-cultural expectations of the readers in that these Roman military leaders are not brutish and violent, and do not conscript local citizens. Rather, Luke's positive depiction of Roman centurions invites the reader to see that they possess virtue and potential for conversion to the Christ-movement.[46]

---

44. I have written on this in much more detail in Joshua W. Jipp, "Hospitable Barbarians: Luke's Ethnic Reasoning in Acts 28:1-10," *JTS* (2017): forthcoming.

45. John Dominic Crossan, *In Parables: The Challenge of the Historical Jesus* (New York: Harper and Row, 1975), 64.

46. Laurie Brink, *Soldiers in Luke-Acts: Engaging, Contradicting, and Transcending the Stereotypes*, WUNT 2.362 (Tübingen: Mohr-Siebeck, 2014), 166.

Interpreters often underestimate the significance of the fact that in Luke's description of the first Gentile convert, the Ethiopian eunuch is both black and a sexual outcast (according to many cultural scripts for eunuchs).[47] Castrated men or people with "crushed testicles" were prohibited by Torah from full participation in the Jerusalem temple (see, for example, Lev 21:16–23; Deut 23:1). In fact, the prophet Isaiah uses eunuchs as a trope for the kinds of outcasts who will be fully included within God's people when God returns.[48] Eunuchs were not the ideal kind of men lauded in Greco-Roman culture, for they lacked virility and were often considered soft, feminine, and sexually deviant.[49] The eunuch is not, then, a manly man who conforms to good gender stereotypes about strength, power, and masculinity.[50] And yet we should note that Luke's description of the "Ethiopian" (Acts 8:27) "eunuch" (8:27, 34, 38, 39) neither activates stereotypes of Ethiopians as symbols of vice or sexual passion nor tropes of eunuchs as salacious, hybrid/ambiguous monstrosities.[51] Rather, the eunuch is a "model of virtue": he is silent and humble as he reads and listens to the interpretation of Isaiah, and then receives baptism, and rejoices.[52] Philip rightly perceives, then, that nothing "prevents" the eunuch from baptism and full inclusion into the people of God.[53]

47. Perhaps interpreters are more comfortable with the virility and sensibilities of a Roman military man than they are with a dark-skinned sexual outcast. On the racialized interpretation of this passage and the frequent refrain that the man's ethnicity does not matter for most white interpreters, see Clarice J. Martin, "A Chamberlain's Journey and the Challenge of Interpretation for Liberation," *Semeia* 47 (1989): 105–35.

48. An important work that takes this statement (among others) about eunuchs seriously in its theological articulation of sex and gender is Megan K. DeFranza, *Sex Difference in Christian Theology: Male, Female, and Intersex in the Image of God* (Grand Rapids: Eerdmans, 2015), esp. chs. 3 and 6.

49. Peter Brown, *The Body and Society: Men, Women, and Sexual Renunciation in Early Christianity* (New York: Columbia University Press, 1988), 10–11.

50. See also Brittany E. Wilson, *Unmanly Men: Refigurations of Masculinity in Luke-Acts* (Oxford: Oxford University Press, 2015), 113–49.

51. There are, of course, a variety of descriptors for ancient Ethiopians. See *Race and Ethnicity in the Classical World: An Anthology of Primary Sources in Translation*, ed. and trans. Rebecca F. Kennedy, C. Sydnor Roy, and Max L. Goldman (Indianapolis: Hackett Publishing, 2013), 179–201. On the eunuch as a representative example of the outcast, see David W. Pao, *Acts and the Isaianic New Exodus*, WUNT 2.130 (Tübingen: Mohr-Siebeck, 2000), 140–42.

52. See here Gay L. Bryon, *Symbolic Blackness and Ethnic Difference in Early Christian Literature* (London: Routledge, 2002), 108–15.

53. This is nicely stated by Matthew L. Skinner, *Intrusive God, Disruptive Gospel: Encountering the Divine in the Book of Acts* (Grand Rapids: Brazos Press, 2015), 63–64.

The transgression of boundaries, the subversion of stigma and stereotype, and disregard for the belief that "others" pollute or contaminate is institutionalized as part of the church's identity in the Peter-Cornelius encounter in Acts 10.[54] Every reader of Acts knows that God has determined that the Gentiles will experience God's salvation and will be included in God's family, but given the social restrictions between Jews and Gentiles eating together and entering each other's spaces, you may wonder *how* one church can be composed of pagans and Jews together. And the entire passage is oriented around the transgression or breaking of the boundaries that would prevent communion between Jewish believer and Gentile believer. In the first episode, "the angel of God enters in" to the space of Cornelius, a non-Jew (10:3). Peter's heavenly vision commands Peter not to discriminate in his eating practices, and more specifically not to view the clean animals as polluted by their proximity to unclean animals (10:9–16). These surprising divine interventions lead to Peter inviting Cornelius's men into his (technically Simon's) dwelling (10:1–8, 17–23) and then, even more surprisingly, to receive hospitality in Cornelius's home (10:23b–33). The scene is almost comical as Peter is consistently confused by the multiple acts of divine intervention that lead him finally to declare: "In truth, I perceive that God does not show partiality, but in every nation the one who fears him and does righteousness is *welcome* before him" (10:34–35). The language of "welcome" is reminiscent of Jesus's self-described mission to "proclaim the year of the Lord's welcome" (Luke 4:19). Peter speaks of God's welcome of the Gentiles even better than he knows, for the Spirit interrupts Peter's speech by descending upon the non-circumcised believers and enabling them to speak in tongues about the great deeds of God (10:44–46). The story of Peter and Cornelius ends with another hospitality scene, as Peter receives the invitation to stay at Cornelius's home for three days (10:48b). Once again, divine hospitality elicits human hospitality, for God's welcome of Cornelius and the Gentiles results in the creation of one family-friendship group composed of Jews and non-Jews.

---

54. I have written on this in much more detail in Jipp, *Divine Visitations and Hospitality to Strangers in Luke-Acts*, 204–17. I have also benefited from Beverly Roberts Gaventa, *From Darkness to Light: Aspects of Conversion in the New Testament*, OBT (Philadelphia: Fortress, 1986), 107–25; Walter T. Wilson, "Urban Legends: Acts 10:1–11:18 and the Strategies of Greco-Roman Foundation Narratives," *JBL* 120, no. 1 (Spring 2001): 77–99.

The Church Today as the Context for God's Hospitality

If we take seriously the vision of hospitality in Luke-Acts and see it as the charter of the church that sets forth both its identity and vocation, then I suggest the following characteristics must mark our thinking and practices.

1. The Church's Identity as Recipients of God's Hospitality

The fundamental problem in Luke-Acts is alienation from God and alienation from others. Humans were created to be friends with God and friends with one another. Thus, another way to describe the problem of our alienation from God is with the term *sin*, for sin results in both alienation from God and alienation from one another. We are—all of us—those described by Jesus as the poor, the captive, the blind, and oppressed—desperately in need of encountering the saving benefits of "the year of the Lord's welcome" (Luke 4:18–19). As recipients of divine welcome, all of us are positioned as guests and strangers before the Lord. But the good news of the gospel in Luke-Acts is that God's hospitality has transformed us into God's friends and family. Samuel Wells states it like this: "For Jesus, our real problem as human beings is our alienation from God and one another. That is what changes in Jesus. Jesus is the solidarity between us and God that makes those links tangible and visible and permanent and unbreakable."[55] Jesus's extension of divine hospitality is characterized by peace (Luke 7:48–50), healing of alienation from God and others (Luke 5:27–32), deep joy (Luke 19:7–9), and forgiveness (Luke 7:36–50; 22:15–20). Jesus describes God's hospitality as life, namely, as a resurrection from death to life (Luke 15:24, 32). Those who have been welcomed into God's family continue to experience fellowship with the risen Jesus as host of their community and their meals (Luke 24:28–35; Acts 2:41–47).

Luke-Acts witnesses to the fact that, despite a variety of admittedly important factors that make up our identity—gender, ethnicity, age, vocation, status—humans have two options, two competing alternatives, for how we construe our fundamental identity. One alternative is that we see our identity as determined by ourselves, by our own religiosity, education, ethnicity, and vocation. We see our lives as primarily identified by our vir-

---

55. Samuel Wells, *A Nazareth Manifesto: Being With God* (Malden, MA: Wiley Blackwell, 2015), 78–79.

tuous history of obedience and faithfulness to God, our amount of service to God, our many good deeds for others, our religious zeal and all the lives we've transformed through our ministry, or perhaps by our *lack* of these things. Or, alternatively, you see yourself in every facet of your life as one whose identity, the very core of who you are, has been determined by God's gracious and undeserved saving and reconciling welcome of all of us into his family. Jean Vanier, the founder of L'Arche, has repeatedly emphasized that all of God's children are poor, weak, handicapped, and impoverished and in need of one another. But in his words, "[S]ome people recognize their poverty; others do not."[56] God's hospitality, the saving welcome that reconciles us to God and heals us, is the *singular answer* to our fractured relationship with God and with others.[57] And this gift does not correspond to any prior social worth.

Just like Zacchaeus with his need to *see Jesus and who he is* or the "sinful woman" who showed extravagant, loving devotion to Jesus, all of us, too, are desperate, needy, and dependent upon Jesus's welcome to answer and satisfy our deepest longings. Just like the half-dead man in the ditch, "We are the needy ones. We long for relationship, we long for forgiveness, we long for reconciliation, we long for eternal life."[58] Some of us might find it natural to think: "Once I was a little bit like Zacchaeus. Once upon a time I was entirely dependent upon the reconciling welcome of Jesus. But *now* I've lived many years in pursuit of holiness and good things. I've preached many sermons, served in many places, written many helpful things about the gospel." And if we're honest with ourselves, some of us probably don't think we're all that much like the stigmatized social outcasts that pepper the pages of Luke-Acts. Or alternatively, we think of ourselves as defined by our addictions, our marital failings, our economic conditions, our past sins and indiscretions, and/or our mental illnesses. The witness of Luke-Acts, however, demands a transformation of our imaginations, a complete transformation of how we think of ourselves and others, and one that we need to appropriate consistently: *all* of us are desperately needy and dependent in every way upon the welcoming and reconciling presence of Jesus.

56. Jean Vanier, *An Ark for the Poor: The Story of L'Arche* (Toronto: Novalis, 1995), 14.

57. This is not to deny, however, that Luke (and the other NT authors) also use other metaphors to describe God's salvation of humanity in Christ. My argument fits neatly with Joel B. Green's argument that Luke uses a journey metaphor to describe salvation in his Gospel. See Green, *Conversion in Luke-Acts*.

58. Wells, *A Nazareth Manifesto*, 93.

2. *Jesus-Like Meals as Remembrance of Divine and Human Hospitality*

The witness of Luke-Acts calls for a recovery of the practice of sharing meals with one another as opportunities to "remember" and celebrate the presence of Jesus who, as the risen Lord, continues to extend divine welcome indiscriminately to those who come to him. Jesus's meals, and the meals in the early church as well, were the means whereby the sinner, the outcast, and even the enemy encountered God's hospitality and were transformed into friends who were fully included as God's people. As such, we have seen that these meals were marked by joy, inclusivity, the satisfaction of hunger, and the presence of the risen Jesus. This calls for the church to recommit itself to intentional times of eating together with the expectation that, in obedience to both the example and command of Jesus, the risen Jesus is powerfully present in our communities, and that these meals will continue to provide the hospitable context whereby *all people* may encounter God's hospitality. The church's hospitality meals testify that *the defining marker of the church is that they are recipients of God's hospitality* and nothing else. If the sacrament of the Last Supper ritualized and brought to memory all of Jesus's eating and drinking with sinners and outcasts, then the church needs to recover a greater role for meals of fellowship in remembrance of Jesus. Craig Blomberg states this well when he notes that the right response to seeing Jesus's hospitality meals with sinners "is to elevate the significance and 'sacramentalize' the role of other fellowship meals, *when Christians celebrate them intentionally for the sake of creating greater intimacy with fellow human beings before reconciling them to each other and to God*" (italics his).[59]

If we believe that the risen Jesus continues to share his saving presence through Jesus-like meals, then I suggest that we as the church should engage in some intentional reflection and take some creative risk to continue the witness of Jesus's table-fellowship. This may simply take the form of looking for opportunities to institute times of shared meals or potlucks as part of the church's communal life where Jesus's own table practices are remembered and embodied. Soong-Chan Rah's reflections on the communal power of eating together is worth quoting in full:

> Without a shared table fellowship, a major gap develops in the church community, particularly a multicultural community. The power of table

---

59. Craig L. Blomberg, *Contagious Holiness: Jesus' Meal with Sinners*, vol. 19, *New Studies in Biblical Theology* (Downers Grove, IL: InterVarsity Press, 2005), 179.

fellowship is the power of hospitality. An invitation to the table is an invitation to fellowship. Hospitality and community are central to our understanding of the Communion table, to which we are invited. I am called to participate with others in Jesus' hospitality. I am part of a larger community—one body, one loaf, one cup—in the Communion meal. . . . As Christ invites us to share in the messianic banquet table represented by the Communion table, we acknowledge and delight in his hospitality.[60]

In the following chapters we will continue to explore some of the possibilities that meals and food play in the church's mission, but here I suggest that we begin to ask some critical questions: Where have we seen Jesus-like hospitality meals celebrated in our church gatherings, in small group fellowships, or in particular niche ministries? Sometimes it can be helpful to have this as a lens to view and reinvigorate what we may already be doing. When our church or community eats these meals together how do we expect them to be the space where the risen Jesus is present? Do we use them as opportunities to invite others to experience the hospitality of God, especially those whom our broader society may neglect or reject? Whom can we invite? And how might the meals be marked by inclusivity of *all people*, joyous celebration, and the rejection of status distinctions?

3. *The Church's Embrace of Stigma*

The saving experience whereby we become friends with God transforms us into agents of hospitality who extend hospitality and friendship to others. Since, as we have seen, this divine welcome does not conform to *any* social worth on the part of the individual, concerns with purity and pollution are radically minimized as the church is called to break the boundaries of social convention to include society's most stigmatized. And this is clearly rooted in Jesus's inclusive and indiscriminate extension of hospitality, for which he was remembered and criticized as "a friend of tax-collectors and sinners" (Luke 7:34b).[61] The recipients of divine hospitality in Luke-Acts are some of society's most stigmatized and marginalized people: sinners, tax collectors,

---

60. Soong-Chan Rah, *Many Colors: Cultural Intelligence for a Changing Church* (Chicago: Moody Publishers, 2010), 168–69.

61. Greg Carey, *Sinners: Jesus and His Earliest Followers* (Waco, TX: Baylor University Press, 2009), 17–36.

the poor and hungry, a sinful woman, Samaritans, the physically disabled, non-Jews, eunuchs, and barbarians. Jesus in Luke and the apostles in Acts consistently cross religious and cultural boundaries in order to welcome and bless the stigmatized and rejected among society. In other words, God's hospitality is no respecter of ethnicity or culture, religious tradition, socio-economic status, or gender/sexual identity. Greg Carey has stated this well: "Jesus' followers remembered him for identifying himself among sinners, sharing table with them, and appealing to them as heroes in some of his teachings. They recalled how people confronted Jesus with their social impurity, and how Jesus . . . crossed the boundaries that divided the pure from the impure."[62] In his mission to extend God's hospitality to others, Jesus showed no sense of fear of the stranger, worry about a sinner's polluting presence, or desire to conform to societal norms. And yet all too frequently, the (often implicit) attempts of the church to conform itself to the pattern seen in Jesus's ministry are stunted or overwhelmed by its uncritical acceptance of certain societal stereotypes of individuals labeled as dangerous, risky, worthless, or pollutants.[63] The church's mission can similarly be stunted when we refuse to become allies of those who bear the brunt of the societal stereotypes and when, whether out of apathy or a failure to listen to the experiences of others, we do nothing about structural racism, the perpetuation of dehumanizing gender or sexual stereotypes, and violence against people of color. The church shares in Jesus's table-fellowship among sinners when we *together* are known as fellow friends and allies of tax collectors and sinners, the mentally ill, transgendered persons, current and former prisoners, and all who suffer.[64] This can come about only through the church's recognition that it collectively is the recipient of divine welcome. Human welcome and friendship, as Wells notes, will "come [only] from a recognition of your own desperate plight, and then from gratitude, from joy, from an overflowing delight that you have been met by Christ."[65]

---

62. Carey, *Sinners*, 169.

63. I have benefited greatly from the work on stigma theory by Erving Goffman, *Stigma: Note on the Management of Spoiled Identity* (London: Simon and Schuster, 1963); Richard Beck, *Unclean: Meditations on Purity, Hospitality, and Mortality* (Eugene, OR: Cascade, 2011); and Louise J. Lawrence, *Sense and Stigma in the Gospels: Depictions of Sensory-Disabled Characters* (Oxford: Oxford University Press, 2013).

64. See here especially Jürgen Moltmann, "Open Friendship: Aristotelian and Christian Concepts of Friendship," in *The Changing Face of Friendship*, ed. Leroy S. Rouner (Notre Dame, IN: University of Notre Dame Press, 1994), 29–42.

65. Wells, *A Nazareth Manifesto*, 96.

Note that the early church recognized and advocated specific limitations and boundaries to its hospitality. For example, a traveling missionary should be welcomed, but if the missionary stays too long this demonstrates that she or he is a false prophet and should be excluded for taking advantage of the church and "making traffic of Christ" (Did. 12:1–5). A community cannot survive and it will have no stable identity unless it operates with some clear boundaries that define the identity and meaning of the church and provide physical and psychological safety.[66] But the primary call, the first impulse should be one where hospitality and embrace are prior to exclusion or rejection.[67] Again, Jean Vanier says it well: "Jesus' work is to destroy the barriers, prejudices and fear that separate people from 'normal' people, so as to unite them in a single body. It is the complete reversal of a hierarchical society in which the powerful, the influential and the privileged are elevated, and the weak and poor are put down."[68]

If the church today imagines itself, as indeed it must, as continuing the same story and the same mission found in Luke-Acts, then many of our churches need to reject their obsession with the so-called normal, with safety and exclusive boundaries that are privileged over the consistent witness that the church *is a stigmatized community*.[69] I am not arguing that there should be no boundaries or limitations to our hospitality (see, for example, 1 Cor. 5:1–8; 6:12–20; 2 John 7–11). Engaging in hospitality with strangers obviously requires much wisdom and discernment. But intentionally placing limitations on our hospitality is a secondary matter that comes *after* we have adequately heard Jesus's call and followed his example as a friend of sinners and outcasts. Christine Pohl, again, states this well: "We will need to differentiate and sometimes even exclude but our first priority must always be one of welcome, embrace, hospitality. When we begin with a strong presumption

66. I strongly recommend here Christine D. Pohl, *Making Room: Recovering Hospitality as a Christian Tradition* (Grand Rapids: Eerdmans, 1999), 135–49. Also helpful is Steven Bouma-Prediger and Brian J. Walsh, *Beyond Homelessness: Christian Faith in a Culture of Displacement* (Grand Rapids: Eerdmans, 2008), 52: "Without boundaries there can be no sense of 'place' as home, as a site of hospitality, security, and intimacy with local knowledge. Without boundaries there is no locality and thus no sense of membership in a particular community, family, or neighborhood with an identity distinct from other communities, families, and neighborhoods. In short, identity itself is impossible without boundaries."

67. Pohl, *Making Room*, 149.

68. Vanier, *The Story of L'Arche*, 52.

69. Stigma is a means of excluding or discrediting someone that is deemed by the majority culture as socially deviant and is usually identified with bodily deformities, moral or behavioral differences, and difference in ethnicity, culture, and religion. See Goffman, *Stigma*, 4.

in favor of welcoming the stranger, we will be better equipped to handle the more ambiguous situations."[70] We are, and I include myself here, often too quick to take culturally constructed categories for others as the bases for our lack of interactions with those we deem to be unsafe, uncomfortable, contagious, and/or egregiously sinful. But the consistent witness of Luke-Acts is that those stigmatized and negatively stereotyped by the broader society are precisely those who make up the recipients of divine hospitality. The church is called, then, as Heather Vacek has eloquently argued:

> [T]o be a stigmatized people: to resist social norms contrary to Christian belief and practice, to eat with outcasts and tax collectors, with sinners, and with those who fail, and to remember that Christian identity is defined by baptism into the body of Christ, not by adherence (or lack of adherence) to social norms. . . . Being damned by association should be an expected part of Christian witness, but it is a reality difficult to embrace in a society, like modern America, where a safer, more sanitized Christian belief and practice are deemed normative.[71]

Vacek has it exactly right. If the church is simply composed of those the broader culture has deemed "normal" or "safe," then in what way can we plausibly imagine that we are continuing the legacy set forth in Luke-Acts? Or does God's hospitality come only to the socially acceptable? Of course, the broader standards of society and those it values do not determine membership in God's family. The witness of Luke-Acts and its testimony to the hospitality of God demand, therefore, that we reflect upon who are the vulnerable, marginalized, and/or stigmatized in our communities *and* how to intentionally and *fully* incorporate everyone into our churches. Full inclusion into the people of God will entail deconstructing the ways in which the broader society often uses stereotypes to label some people as dangerous, less valuable, or pollutants. In some instances, of course, this will *not* mean minimizing peoples' experiences with, for example, mental illness, physical challenges, incarceration, or substance addictions. And it also does not mean that repentance for wrongs done is ignored, but Jesus seemed quite content to extend hospitality to sinners, trusting that this created the space for sinners and outcasts to encounter his life-giving, healing, and deliver-

---

70. Pohl, *Making Room*, 149.

71. Heather H. Vacek, *Madness: American Protestant Responses to Mental Illness* (Waco, TX: Baylor University Press, 2015), 168–69.

ing presence with the expectation that repentance would follow (see, for example, Luke 19:5–9). In other words, repentance, restitution for wrongs committed, and moral transformation follow upon and after one's experience of divine hospitality.

But hospitality to one another will require unconditional welcome, mutual solidarity with one another, and a fierce rejection of society's standards of worth as a means for structuring our relationships with each other. Taking seriously the vision of God's hospitality in the ministry of Jesus in Luke-Acts for today will mean that many churches must hold loosely (if not outright reject) their concerns for social status and respectability within the broader society. If we embrace and welcome those that our society categorizes as defective and worthless, then this will almost certainly come only through embracing social stigma as *intrinsic* to the identity of the church, namely, as a community of outcasts welcomed into God's family. Cultural normativity becomes, then, something to be rejected, and "religious stigmatization [is] evidence of faithful practice."[72] As Christine Pohl has said: "In contrast to a more tame hospitality that welcomes persons already well situated in a community, hospitality that welcomes 'the least' and recognizes their equal value can be an act of resistance and defiance, a challenge to the values and expectations of the larger community."[73]

What I am calling for is easier said than done, as social stigma is incredibly powerful and difficult to overcome as a tool for labeling who is deviant, risky, and without full worth. One way that churches might work toward practicing the vision of divine hospitality seen in Luke-Acts is by intentionally hosting support groups, and partnering with and standing in mutual solidarity with marginalized and vulnerable communities, such as those who have alcohol addiction (through such support groups as Alcoholics Anonymous, Women for Sobriety, Celebrate Recovery) or those who face the challenge of mental illnesses (through joining the National Alliance on Mental Illness). The importance of listening to the stories of those who have experienced stigma and rejection can deeply unsettle our stereotypes and fears of the "socially deviant."[74] We might also reflect on whether our ministries or interactions with vulnerable peoples reinforce the perceptions that they are deviant, powerless, and forever in a guest-like status. Do our

72. Vacek, *Madness*, 167.

73. Pohl, *Making Room*, 62.

74. See, for example, the important theological and *personal* reflections on mental illness by Kathryn Greene-McCreight, *Darkness Is My Only Companion: A Christian Response to Mental Illness*, rev. ed. (Grand Rapids: Brazos Press, 2015).

food pantries or services to the homeless offer any meaningful opportunities for the homeless to serve or develop friendships with those outside of their usual social network, or do our ministries humiliate and reinforce their own feeling of subjugation and vulnerability?[75]

Numerous communities in North America are marginalized and stigmatized today, but I would like to highlight one of the more vulnerable of these, namely, the 2.3 million persons who are incarcerated. I confess that I was almost entirely oblivious to this community and the injustices perpetrated against them until my own experience teaching at Metro State Prison in Atlanta, Georgia, opened my eyes to the reality of mass incarceration in our country and the effects of recidivism on our urban communities. Along with my co-teacher I was able to participate in a program through Emory University that offered a certificate in theology to those who completed the required coursework at the women's state prison. Here I witnessed the power and dignity of simply building friendships and relationships with those stigmatized by the broader society as violent, poor, social deviants. I also saw, however, the pain, suffering, exploitation, and injustices these women had experienced—as a result of careless judges, incompetent or apathetic state-appointed defense attorneys, exploitative and abusive relationships with men (fathers, husbands, boyfriends, pimps, etc.). I don't mean to paint my experience in such black-and-white terms that the inmates appear to be innocent or free from criminal activity, nor do I mean to suggest that everyone involved in the criminal justice system has impure and unjust motives, but I do suggest that the structural system dehumanizes *those who are already the most vulnerable in our society and brands them with labels and stereotypes from which they can almost never escape.* My hope is that my very limited analysis and suggestions will stimulate our imaginations to think about the motivations and possibilities for our churches to extend divine hospitality to the most stigmatized and vulnerable communities in our own contexts (on both structural and individual levels).

The early church often went to great length to show hospitality to prisoners.[76] The early Christian apologist Aristides said this of early Christian hospitality: "And if they hear that some are condemned or imprisoned on

75. Pohl, *Making Room*, 61–84, offers sage warning and counsel regarding the danger of failing to honor and dignify the recipient of hospitality.

76. See here especially, Helen Rhee, *Loving the Poor, Saving the Rich: Wealth, Poverty, and Early Christian Formation* (Grand Rapids: Baker Academic Press, 2012), 125–27; Rowan A. Greer, *Broken Lights and Mended Lives: Theology and Common Life in the Early Church* (University Park: The Pennsylvania State University Press, 1986), 119–28.

account of the name of their Lord, they contribute for those condemned and send to them what they need, and if it is possible, they redeem them" (*Apology* 15.7). Hospitality to prisoners often took the form of providing material assistance, food and clothing, and medical care for the incarcerated.[77] Ignatius of Antioch, for example, who was being led to his martyrdom, spoke of being visited, fed, and refreshed by the churches in Asia Minor in his journey as one imprisoned (Eph. 1:2–3; 2:1; Magn. 1:2; 15:1; Trall. 1:1–2; 12:1; 13:1). Lucian of Samosata, who was no friend or admirer of the early Christians, testifies to the Christian response to the imprisonment of Peregrinus (one of their teachers). When Peregrinus was thrown in prison, Lucian (with some obvious sarcasm) notes that:

> [T]he Christians, regarding the incident as a calamity, left nothing undone in their efforts to rescue him. Then, as this was impossible, every other form of attention was shown to him. . . . And from the very break of day, aged widows and orphaned children could be seen waiting near the prison, while some of their officials even slept inside with him having bribed the guards. Then elaborate meals were brought in and sacred books of theirs were read to him. Indeed, people even came from the cities of Asia Minor, sent by the Christians at their own expense, to help and defend their hero. They take incredible speed to help whenever such a public action is taken and in no time they lavish all their resources.[78]

Hospitality to their own, who had been imprisoned, as we see above, often took the form of seeking to ransom the incarcerated—with money or even with their own lives by selling themselves into slavery (see also 1 Clem. 55:2).

Why did the early Christians visit prisoners, care for their needs, and attempt to secure their release from prison? They did so simply because of the scriptural teaching on hospitality to strangers. For example, after reminding his audience, "do not forget to show hospitality to strangers, for in this way some have unknowingly entertained angels," the author of Hebrews provides the imprisoned as an example of whom they are to remember (Heb 13:2–3).[79] We have seen that Jesus describes his mission in Luke 4:18 as centered upon proclaiming "release for the imprisoned" and "release for

---

77. See also 1 Clem. 59:4; Cyprian, *Epistles* 4.1; 76.1–6; Tertullian, *Mart.* 1.

78. Lucian, *The Passing of Peregrinus* 12–13.

79. William L. Lane, "Unexpected Light on Hebrews 13:1–6 from a Second Century Source," *Perspectives in Religious Studies* 9, no. 3 (Fall 1982): 267–74.

the oppressed." The release of prisoners, then, is part and parcel of Jesus's proclaimed "year of the Lord's welcome" (Luke 4:19). In Jesus's parable of the sheep and the goats, the glorious Son of Man receives the sheep into the kingdom because—among other acts of hospitality and albeit unknowingly—"I was in prison and you came to me" (Matt 25:36 [my trans.]). We should not underestimate the force of Jesus's words—those who will inherit the kingdom and enter into life are those who care for and visit prisoners. Furthermore, for a variety of reasons, not least the fact that Christ had taken sin and its guilt upon himself and thereby executed it (see, for instance, Rom 8:3–4; 2 Cor 5:21), the scriptural texts are decidedly critical of retributive justice and vengeance, namely, inflicting punishment upon law-breakers for its own sake.[80] The Scriptures, rather, are decidedly oriented toward restorative justice, namely, a process of forgiveness, restitution/reparation, and healing for those who have inflicted some kind of harm.[81]

If churches today wish to continue the early Christian legacy of building friendships with and extending hospitality to prisoners, then churches should educate themselves about the destructive and horrific effects that incarceration has on individuals, families, and our society.[82] Many important works have critically examined the current prison-industrial complex and its social effects on society, so my sketch here is simply suggestive and anecdotal.[83] It's important, first, to recognize that the percentage of people incarcerated in the US is unprecedented and the rate has been steadily increasing.[84] For example, in 1998 more people were incarcerated in the state of California than in "France, Great Britain, Germany, Japan, Singapore, and the Netherlands combined." Between 1975 and 2005, the US incarceration rate more than quadrupled.[85] And if one includes those in jail, the num-

---

80. On retributive justice and its relationship to contemporary forms of punishment, see William Placher, "Visiting Prisoners," *The Blackwell Companion to Postmodern Theology*, ed. Graham Ward (Oxford: Blackwell Publishing, 2007), 181–85.

81. On this, see the important work of Christopher D. Marshall, *Beyond Retribution: A New Testament Vision for Justice, Crime, and Punishment* (Grand Rapids: Eerdmans, 2001).

82. I have benefited here greatly from the work of Trinity Evangelical Divinity School student Matthew Henderson and his illuminating research.

83. See here especially Michelle Alexander, *The New Jim Crow: Mass Incarceration in the Age of Colorblindness* (New York: The New Press, 2012); also Elizabeth Hinton, *From the War on Poverty to the War on Crime: The Making of Mass Incarceration in America* (Cambridge, MA: Harvard University Press, 2016); Löic Wacquant, *Prisons of Poverty* (Minneapolis: University of Minnesota Press, 2009).

84. Eric Schlosser, "The Prison Industrial Complex," *Atlantic Monthly*, December 1998, 52.

85. Steven Raphael and Michael Stoll, "Introduction," *Do Prisons Make Us Safer? The*

ber increases to six hundred per one hundred thousand.[86] This incredible increase in our nation's incarceration population is *not* the result of better policing tactics, and higher rates of incarceration *have not* corresponded in any way to a reduction in violent crimes.[87]

Rather, as Michelle Alexander, Elizabeth Hinton, and others have shown, the current state of mass incarceration is closely related to the retributive "tough on crime" and "war on drug" policies that began during Lyndon B. Johnson's presidency and were seen in New York during Governor Nelson Rockefeller's leadership in the early 1970s.[88] Politicians adopted a "get tough on crime" mentality which has had a national impact that created longer, harsher, and more punitive prison terms for many non-violent, urban, and minority drug offenders.[89] The harsher severity of sentences for drug charges has meant that a repeat offense will inevitably result in an increasingly strict sentencing.[90] Further, it is now well known that the targets of the war on crime have been largely black and brown minorities in urban communities.[91] While it is estimated that whites participate in criminal drug-related activity at higher rates than blacks, blacks are convicted on drug charges far more frequently and often as a result of discriminatory policing tactics.[92] Though blacks and Latinos account for fewer than 30 percent of the

---

Benefits and Cost of the Prison Boom, ed. Steven Raphael and Michael Stoll (New York: Russell Sage Foundation, 2009), 3.

86. Placher, "Visiting Prisoners," 178–79.

87. This point is readily apparent to any viewer of HBO's portrait of urban Baltimore in the television show *The Wire*. See here Jonathan Tran and Myles Werntz, eds., *Corners in the City of God: Theology, Philosophy, and the Wire* (Eugene, OR: Cascade, 2013). But see also Shawn Bushway and Raymond Paternoster, "The Impact of Prison on Crime," in Raphael and Stoll, *Do Prisons Make Us Safer?*, 143–45.

88. Schlosser, "The Prison Industrial Complex," 56. But see now also Elizabeth Hinton's *From the War on Poverty to the War on Crime*. Hinton argues that the roots of mass incarceration begin with Lyndon B. Johnson's "War on Crime" through "law enforcement agencies, criminal justice institutions, and jails as the primary public programs in many low-income communities across the United States" (4).

89. See here David Weiman and Christopher Weiss, "The Origins of Mass Incarceration in New York State: The Rockefeller Drug Laws and the Local War on Drugs," in Raphael and Stoll, *Do Prisons Make Us Safer?*, 86.

90. Weiman and Weiss, "The Origins of Mass Incarceration in New York State," 86.

91. See throughout, Hinton, *From the War on Poverty to the War on Crime*; Nicole Gonzalez Van Cleve, *Crook County: Racism and Injustice in America's Largest Criminal Court* (Stanford, CA: Stanford University Press, 2016).

92. Mark Lewis Taylor, *The Executed God: The Way of the Cross in Lockdown America*, 2nd ed. (Minneapolis: Fortress Press, 2015), 177; Alexander, *The New Jim Crow*, 189.

population in the United States, they account for two thirds of our prison population.[93]

While many have profited financially from the increased number of incarcerated persons, most recognize that our current prison system rarely rehabilitates the prisoner and/or restores him/her to society, and also that the dehumanizing practices of the institution often turn non-violent offenders into more violent persons. Many prisons are remarkably overcrowded and beyond population capacity. Inmates are often subjected to all kinds of power plays that result in violence and sexual abuse. Violence, including sexual violence and exploitation, is often a given in most prisons.[94] Those who are unable to defend themselves from sexual violence may become flamboyantly effeminate as they trade becoming sexually passive partners in exchange for protection.

When our churches' consciousness is awakened to the brutal injustice and continued racism of our current penal system, churches must rise up to seek more just alternatives for crime and punishment in our society, speak out against racist and exploitative legislations, and actively seek ways to re-integrate prisoners into society.[95] Churches can also partner with organizations like Prison Fellowship that hold Bible studies, lead educational seminars, and build friendships through regular visits and written letters. One should not underestimate the importance of simple but consistent face-to-face visits with those who are incarcerated (or correspondence through phone conversations and writing letters) as a form of Christian hospitality.[96] Our prison system successfully transforms its population into stigmatized, marginalized strangers. Churches should actively and imaginatively look for ways to develop long-lasting committed relationships with those in prison that last *through and beyond* their sentences and for opportunities to become allies who fight against the structural injustice of our policing tactics and criminal courts. In this way, they could then turn those who have been incarcerated into friends by incorporating them into the life of the church family.

---

93. Hinton, *From the War on Poverty to the War on Crime*, 310.

94. For a particularly harrowing and painful description, see James Samuel Logan, *Good Punishment? Christian Moral Practice and US Imprisonment* (Grand Rapids: Eerdmans, 2008); Placher, "Visiting Prisoners," 179–80.

95. While not directed to the church specifically, this is the call also given by Gonzalez van Cleve, *Crook County*, 189–90.

96. See Dick Allison, "Spiritual Friendship: Portrait of a Prison Ministry," in *Prison: Christian Reflection*, ed. Robert B. Kruschwitz (Waco, TX: Baylor University Press, 2012), 62–66.

Incorporation into the church community, and intentionally making space for them to act as host and bring their gifts to the church, could counter the strong recidivism rates.

Likewise, churches can partner with ministries like the Hospitality House, a ministry in Texas that focuses on helping families and friends visit their incarcerated friends and family. The Hospitality House provides clothing to those visiting their loved ones that is in compliance with prison visitation dress codes, thereby preventing the frequent and sad experience of being denied access to visit their family member or friend.[97] The Hospitality House also offers food and lodging for those who have traveled great distances, and even provides large common areas for church members to welcome the visitors through conversation, eating together, and entertainment.[98] The significance of these kinds of ministries is articulated clearly by one inmate who said: "[Visits are] a reminder that we do matter; that we are not alone, we are not forgotten, and we have a chance to refocus our minds and goals. We live in a place full of drama, pressures, stress, no privacy . . . where it is so easy to feel forgotten, alone, hopeless, and to fall into despair."[99]

Study Questions

1. Why is it necessary to experience God's hospitality to us as the basis for our sharing hospitality with and receiving it from others?

2. If it is true that one of the primary ways Luke articulates God's salvation is through Jesus the host who dispenses God's hospitality and welcomes people into friendship with God, then why is this depiction of God's salvation so rarely taught and proclaimed? What would be the tangible benefits of recovering this metaphor to describe salvation?

3. Who are those in your community who are marked by stigma and stereotypes? What are the effects for these individuals or communities for bearing these burdens?

97. Mary Alice Wise, "The Hospitality House: Portrait of a Prison Ministry," in *Prison*, ed. Robert B. Kruschwitz, 80.
98. Wise, "The Hospitality House," 80.
99. Wise, "The Hospitality House," 81.

4. Have you experienced or celebrated Jesus-like meals as occasions for remembering Jesus's hospitality to his people? If not, in what ways might you and your community recover this practice of Jesus?

5. To what extent do you agree or disagree with the author's claim that the church should be a community that *embraces* stigma? What would this look like in your own context?

CHAPTER 2

Ecclesial Hospitality amidst Difference and Division in Paul

If we attempt to embody the vision of hospitality that we see in Luke-Acts, this will inevitably involve making friendships with those who are very different from us. And this raises an important question: is it possible to have real difference and diversity in our churches without this leading to division? We all know that the church has been afflicted by all kinds of rivalries, schisms, and divisions. Peter Leithart states the problem well: "Churches are set up on conscious opposition to churches from other traditions. Pastors preach *against* other churches as much as from the text of Scripture. Theologians . . . magnify slight divergences in formulation and shape entire theological systems to reinforce the fact that *we* are not *them*."[1] On a broader cultural level, Robert Bellah has observed that despite "all the lip service given to respect for cultural differences, Americans seem to lack the resources to think about the relationship between groups that are culturally, socially, or economically quite different."[2] The question arises: is unity amidst inevitable diversity even possible? Can churches embrace the Bible's vision of the unity (not uniformity) of God's people as those marked as recipients of God's hospitality without simultaneously forcing ethnic, cultural, and/or religious minorities to assimilate into majority culture definitions of Christianity?[3] I will discuss in a later chapter whether it is possible to welcome

1. Peter J. Leithart, *Delivered from the Elements of the World: Atonement, Justification, Mission* (Downers Grove, IL: InterVarsity Press, 2016), 274–75.

2. Robert N. Bellah et al., *Habits of the Heart: Individualism and Commitment in American Life*, rev. ed. (Berkeley, CA: University of California Press, 2008), 206.

3. Curtiss Paul DeYoung et al., *United by Faith: The Multiracial Congregation as an Answer to the Problem of Race* (New York: Oxford University Press, 2003), 128.

outsiders or people with different religious traditions, but here I am asking whether we can actually show hospitality *to fellow Christians* with whom we have ethnic, cultural, sociological, or political differences.

We might rightly respond to this question by appealing to certain biblical texts that promote unity among God's people amidst ethnic, status, and gender diversity. The creation account in Genesis 1–2 indicates that God creates the man and the woman different from each other for the purpose of mutuality and interdependence. Isaiah envisions a coming day when Jews and pagans together will worship the God of Israel, precisely *as* Jews *and* non-Jews (Isa 11:10–16; 66:17–24). Paul, of course, says that in Christ the old distinctions of male/female, slave/free, and Jew/Greek are somehow rendered inconsequential (Gal 3:28; 1 Cor 12:13; Col 3:9–11). In fact, Paul even mentions that those in Christ should be content with, and should not try to transform their own social identities (1 Cor 7:19–24). In 1 Corinthians 12:1–13 Paul argues that the church's diverse gifts and ministries stem from one God who himself is characterized by relational diversity as God, Lord, and Spirit. The book of Revelation indicates that the people who worship the Lamb will come together from "every nation, tribe, people, and language" (Rev 7:9 [my trans.]). Curtiss Paul DeYoung has argued that Jesus's practice of inclusive table-fellowship and his vision of the temple as a house of prayer for all people foreshadow culturally diverse multiethnic congregations.[4] We could go on, as many other passages and theological doctrines support the Bible's vision of the unity of God's people even amidst difference. But the point is that the Bible—or at least significant portions of the Bible—offers a vision of human identity that acknowledges heterogeneous and significant social differences. And this is a good thing, for despite the fact that all humans obviously share some kind of common human existence, we are clearly irreducibly different in many ways from each other: gender, race and ethnicity, culture, political views, theological commitments, wealth, profession, and social status. I don't need to belabor the point, as many ways in which we are quite simply not the same can be empirically verified. And again, difference is not a bad thing in itself.[5] My own understanding of my identity is the result of a continued process of distinguishing myself from others. I know who I am, in other words, precisely by knowing who and what I am not.[6]

---

4. DeYoung et al., *United by Faith*, 9–20.

5. Of course, I am not denying that the Scriptures declare some kinds of heterogeneity to be sinful (take, for example, Paul's vice lists, idolatry, sacrifices to idols, etc.; see, for instance, Rom 1:18–32).

6. Paul Ricoeur, *Oneself as Another* (Chicago: The University of Chicago Press, 1992).

The problem arises, however, when I move from recognizing difference to making the judgment that the other is *necessarily* inferior and thereby engage in exclusion or inhospitality to the other.[7]

So to return to our question: is it possible to recognize and embrace difference and diversity within the church without it leading to division, separation, and inhospitality to the other? The United States is becoming more diverse, and yet most of our local churches are growing in ethnic and socio-cultural sameness.[8] Social psychology explains more precisely what most of us already know, namely, that people generally prefer to be with people who are like themselves.[9] Christena Cleveland has argued "our need for affirmation creates a greater desire to surround ourselves with those who subscribe to our culturally distinct ways of life and an aversion to those whose mere difference threatens our unstable identities."[10] Our cultural and ethnic homogeneity, then, often leads us to categorize the other as not simply different but as inferior or, even worse, as a polluting agent whose very presence may contaminate our church or us.[11] This obviously has disastrous ramifications for the unity of the body of Christ and especially for ethnic, cultural, and/or theological minorities, for again as Cleveland has argued:

> When we idolize our cultural group identity, giving it higher priority than our common group identity, minority group members are not truly invited to participate in the organization as valuable members of the all-inclusive *we*. . . . Until we relativize our smaller cultural identities and adopt a common ingroup identity, our diversity initiatives are doomed to failure because we will never fully appreciate our diverse brothers and sisters and they will not feel appreciated.[12]

7. Miroslav Volf, *Exclusion and Embrace: A Theological Exploration of Identity, Otherness, and Reconciliation* (Nashville: Abingdon, 1996), 67–68, rightly notes that passing a judgment need not be thought of as necessarily leading to exclusion. In fact, making appropriate judgments that recognize difference is the first step in fighting against "exclusionary judgments" (68).

8. Michael O. Emerson and Christian Smith, *Divided by Faith: Evangelical Religion and the Problem of Race in America* (New York: Oxford University Press, 2000), 135–51.

9. Emerson and Smith, *Divided by Faith*, 145–46.

10. Christina Cleveland, *Disunity in Christ: Uncovering the Hidden Forces That Keep Us Apart* (Downers Grove, IL: InterVarsity Press, 2013), 87–88.

11. Cleveland, *Disunity in Christ*, 44–65. See also Richard Beck, *Unclean: Meditations on Purity, Hospitality, and Mortality* (Eugene, OR: Cascade Books, 2011).

12. Cleveland, *Disunity in Christ*, 184–85.

This exaltation of individual ethnic identity was presumably the basis for Paul's dispute with Peter in Antioch (Gal 2:11–14). Peter's decision to withdraw from eating with the Gentile Christians was a failure to "walk in a straight line with respect to the truth of the gospel" (Gal 2:14 [my trans.]) because it signified the priority of ethnic identity over God's act in Christ. Paul's letters testify that he often faced the incredible challenge of creating and articulating "a common ingroup identity" that would simultaneously *embrace and yet transcend* the smaller cultural identities of the individuals within his churches. Paul consistently wrestled with this difficulty of embracing difference within the body of Christ without it turning into division and schism. God's act in Christ had brought into existence *one new people comprised of all kinds of people.* How could those who keep kosher and those who do not conform to the same scruples eat together as part of the same church? Could women participate in the same way as men did in the worship assembly? Could the rich and the poor eat and worship together without the poor being shamed? Was it possible for slaves to serve in Paul's mission and in the common worship gathering? Paul is clear that those who have given their allegiance to Christ and have been baptized into Christ are one new people or humanity. And yet their social identities (that is, their gender, ethnicity, socioeconomic status, etc.), while relativized, did not disappear. Unity obviously comes, then, in the midst of diverse social identities.[13] Thus, one of Paul's most significant difficulties was how to enable his churches to find unity and harmony with one another amidst difference. How did Paul do this?

Ultimately, it is God's act in Christ that provides a model of hospitality for us. Paul sought to inculcate within his churches a new identity founded upon God's gracious extension of hospitality in the Messiah for all people, a divine hospitality that produces communities of messianic-shaped friendship and loving regard for the other. Stephen Fowl has claimed, "Friendship with God is our ultimate end because such friendships of love constitute the very life of God, and God will give us nothing less."[14] In other words, cultural, ethnic, status, and even *some level* of theological differences continue in Paul's churches, but the fundamental feature of individual and ecclesial identity, and that which enables the church to see each other as *family and friends,* is their shared experience of divine hospitality, namely, God's gracious extension of welcome and friendship into his family. Again, Fowl says

13. See here, for example, J. Brian Tucker, *"Remain in Your Calling": Paul and the Continuation of Social Identities in 1 Corinthians* (Eugene, OR: Pickwick Publications, 2011).

14. Stephen E. Fowl, *Philippians*, THC (Grand Rapids: Eerdmans, 2005), 209.

it well: "Christian friends do not really choose each other. We are called into friendship with each other *because of our common friendship in Christ* (italics mine).[15] God's act in Christ does not erase or deny social, gender, and ethnic difference and its ongoing relevance, but limits the significance of difference to prevent unity amidst diversity among God's people.[16] David Horrell has stated this well: "I suggest that corporate solidarity in Christ implies, for Paul, neither the *erasure* of previous distinctions nor merely their *encompassing* within a new sphere of belonging, but rather their *relativisation* or revaluation, with real social implications."[17] Given, then, that divine hospitality is the singular act that qualifies people to share in this new family, these differences are not a barrier (nor are they some type of benefit) to full inclusion into God's people and participation in the worship assembly. Further, since divine hospitality has been enacted in the self-giving, other-regarding, and loving act of Jesus's death, these characteristics now form the primary ethic for how members in Paul's churches are to treat one another. Again, divine hospitality results in human hospitality, love, and friendship with and for one another.

In what follows, we'll look primarily at 1 Corinthians, Romans, and Philippians to see the way in which Paul appeals to the church's experience of divine/messianic hospitality as the foundation for the church's primary identity, an identity that transcends social distinctions and enables the church (so Paul hopes!) to have unity amidst difference and diversity. Paul will argue that those who have experienced God's hospitality extended to them in the saving death of Christ are called upon to lay down their rights, privileges, and preferences as a means of loving and welcoming their fellow brothers and sisters in Christ.

The Hospitality of God in Corinth

Paul did not have to work hard to convince his Corinthian church that the risen Lord was powerfully present within the Corinthian assembly. In almost

---

15. Fowl, *Philippians*, 216.

16. I would obviously want to affirm, however, that the gospel does change and transform the sinful tendencies or dispositions that I may have a result of my socio-cultural location, for example, tendencies toward individualism, consumption, and the use of coercive power to achieve my ends.

17. David G. Horrell, *Solidarity and Difference: A Contemporary Reading of Paul's Ethics*, 2nd ed. (London: Bloomsbury T&T Clark, 2015), 138.

every section of the first letter, the logic of Paul's argument presumes that the Corinthians believed that the Spirit of the risen Messiah enlivened their worship, their knowledge, their enactment of spiritual gifts, and their very bodies (see, for example, 1 Cor 1:4–6; 2:10–16; 5:3–6; 6:15–19; 12:1–14:40).[18] Indeed, Paul says that God brought the Corinthian community into existence for the purpose of bringing them "into fellowship [*eis koinōnian*] with his Son Jesus Christ our Lord" (1 Cor 1:9b [my trans.]). The language of fellowship or, perhaps better, partnership indicates a real participation and communion between the church and God's Son. While Paul uses a variety of metaphors to describe the fellowship and union the church experiences with the risen Lord, one powerful and central image Paul sets forth is that of the risen Lord as the divine host who presides over a sacred and celebratory meal that binds the host (the risen Lord) and the guest (the Corinthian church) together as a sacred family. The sacred meal structures both the church's relationship with the divine (the church is the recipient of the Lord's meal) and with one another (the meal is a *communal* celebration).

In the ancient Mediterranean world, including Jewish communities, the worshippers approached the deity through offering sacrifices at the temple of the deity and then sharing a communal meal celebrated in honor of the god. The god was the host and provider who invited his or her worshippers to celebrate a festive meal that honored the deity and brought the worshippers into communion or fellowship with each other *and* with the god.[19] In fact, many texts indicate that tables, couches, and dining ware were used in the sanctuaries of the deities where it was believed the gods and the worshippers would fellowship with one another over the sacrificial meal. Public festivals of *theoxenia* (hospitality to a deity) were held in which the gods were invited to a table complete with food and couches.[20] Notice that the god was the host of the meal and that the communal eating and drinking of this sacrifice in honor of the deity were seen as creating some type of bond or fellowship between the god and his worshippers. In fact, communal fellowship (*koinōnia*) is a shared feature of all meals celebrated

---

18. On which see Luke Timothy Johnson, "The Body in Question: The Social Complexities of Resurrection in 1 Corinthians," in *Contested Issues in Christian Origins and the New Testament*, NovTSup 146 (Leiden: Brill, 2013), 295–315.

19. See the examples given by Dennis E. Smith, *From Symposium to Eucharist: The Banquet in the Early Christian World* (Minneapolis: Fortress Press, 2003), 81–85.

20. David Gill, "*Trapezometa*: A Neglected Aspect of Greek Sacrifice," *HTR* 67, no. 2 (April 1974): 117–37, esp. 120–23; cf. Jipp, *Divine Visitations and Hospitality to Strangers in Luke-Acts*, 88–90.

by intentional groups and communities of worshippers.[21] Thus, when Paul's churches came together to share a meal in celebration of the Lord Jesus they were engaging in a form of worship that was a religious practice common to ancient worshippers.[22] What is of particular interest for us is the way in which the early Christian meal transformed the character of this ritual into fellowship between the Lord Jesus as host and his worshippers as his guests.[23]

Paul depicts Israel's history as a period in which it experienced divine hospitality in 1 Corinthians 10:1–13; here Paul draws an analogy between Israel's wilderness generation and the Corinthian church in order to warn the latter to avoid idolatry with pagan deities: "Therefore, my beloved, flee from idolatry" (10:14). Israel experienced God's beneficence and provision in marvelous ways that parallel the Corinthians' experience of Christ.[24] Paul speaks of God's hospitality and provision for Israel as something mediated to them through the Messiah. Just as the Corinthians have their own spiritual food and drink, which they are consuming at the Lord's Supper (10:16–21; 11:23–26), so the Israelites "all ate the same spiritual food, and all drank the same spiritual drink" (10:3–4a).[25] Paul is probably alluding to those Israelite traditions that refer to God's provision of manna, quail, and water as deriving from God's character as divine host to his people (see, for example, Pss 78:24–28; 105:37–42; see also Ps 23), but what is interesting here for our purposes is Paul's claim that "the rock was Christ" (1 Cor 10:4b). Paul makes the remarkable claim that *Christ* was the provider of the sacramental drink to Israel in the wilderness. Paul creates as close an analogy as he possibly can between the Israelites and the Corinthian church by speaking of Christ as Israel's gracious host who provided this spiritual drink for their nourishment and for fellowship between Israel and God.

21. Luke Timothy Johnson, *Religious Experience in Earliest Christianity* (Minneapolis: Fortress Press, 1998), 163–68.

22. Andrew B. McGowan, *Ancient Christian Worship: Early Church Practices in Social, Historical, and Theological Perspective* (Grand Rapids: Baker, 2014), 31–33.

23. Johnson, *Religious Experience in Earliest Christianity*, 168.

24. David Horrell, "Theological Principle or Christological Praxis? Pauline Ethics in 1 Corinthians 8.1–11.1," *JSNT* 67 (1997): 83–114, here, 96: "So just as all of the Corinthians have been baptized in the name of Jesus Christ (1 Cor 1.13–14; 12:13), and all share in the Lord's supper (1 Cor 10.16–17; 11.17–34), so *all* of the Israelites also shared in the rituals of membership and belonging."

25. One illuminating and helpful treatment of Paul's interpretation of Israel's history in 1 Cor 10:1–13 is Francis Watson, *Paul and the Hermeneutics of Faith* (London: T&T Clark, 2004), 356–74.

Despite Israel's experience of divine hospitality and the fellowship created between them and God through the divine provision of deliverance, baptism, food, and drink (1 Cor 10:1–4), the Israelites were filled with evil cravings (10:6b). Their idolatry and apostasy from God are exemplified in turning away from God's hospitality to improperly eat and drink as they celebrated a sacrificial meal in the presence of the Golden Calf: "the people sat down to eat and drink, and they rose up to play" (1 Cor 10:7b; Exod 32:6). The meaning of "to play" is difficult to define, but it likely refers to the cultic sexual activities that accompanied Israel's celebration of a sacrificial banquet in honor of the image of the Golden Calf and explains Paul's prohibition of fornication in 10:8 (see 1 Sam 18:7; 2 Sam 6:5, 21; 1 Chr 13:8; 15:29).[26] Here Paul reminds the Corinthians of Israel's fornication with the Moabite women where "these [women] invited the people to the sacrifices of their gods, and the people ate and bowed down to their gods" (Num 25:2; see 1 Cor 10:8). Paul's point to the Corinthians is that they must not be like Israel, who experienced God's beneficent provision of spiritual food and drink but turned away from God and ate idolatrous meals and practiced sexual immorality in worship of pagan gods. Paul interprets these scriptural stories, however, by speaking about the Corinthian church's allegiance to Christ.[27] Paul's focus upon *Christ as the Lord of the Corinthian meal* leads him to once again insert Christ into the story of Israel: "let us not test the Messiah, *just as some of them did* and were destroyed by snakes" (1 Cor 10:9 [my trans.]). Paul's exhortation alludes to Numbers 21:5–6 and Psalm 78:18–19, texts which speak of Israel as *testing God* and asking whether "God is able to prepare a table for us in the wilderness." Paul reads Israel's history as contained in the Scriptures "typologically" (10:6, 11) and as providing "instruction" for the church in Corinth, as they contain images that correspond to the situation of the church in Corinth.[28] Israel's history of idolatry takes place with respect to food, namely, with a preference for sacrificial banquets and meals in honor of pagan deities *instead of the nourishment and fellowship provided by the God of Israel.*

---

26. Watson, *Paul and the Hermeneutics of Faith*, 365, says: "Paul's selection of this brief quotation from Exodus 32 serves to emphasize that what he and his fellow-Jews call 'idolatry' is associated not just with specifically cultic actions but also with feasting, singing and dancing—that is, with communal celebration. That is why its allure is so powerful."

27. See here especially Chris Tilling, *Paul's Divine Christology*, WUNT 2.323 (Tübingen: Mohr-Siebeck, 2012), 95–96.

28. See Matthew W. Bates, *The Hermeneutics of the Apostolic Proclamation: The Center of Paul's Method of Scriptural Interpretation* (Waco, TX: Baylor University Press, 2012), 145–47.

Israel's experience of divine hospitality in the wilderness and their turn from God to pagan deities provide the context for Paul's argument that when the Corinthians eat the Lord's meal it is a real *"fellowship* in the blood of Christ" and *"fellowship* in the body of Christ" (10:16 [my trans.]).[29] This is true for the Corinthians even as it was for the Israelites who "when they eat become participants in the sacrifices of the altar" (10:18b [my trans.]; see Lev 7:6; Deut 14:22–26).[30] The language of "fellowship/partnership" (*koinōnia*) resonates with his earlier reminder that God had called the Corinthians into existence for the purpose of having fellowship with God's Son (1:9). Paul makes the meaning of this statement of fellowship explicit in 11:20–26 where, drawing upon earlier Christian tradition (similarly Luke 22:14–20), Paul identifies the church's fellowship with one another as grounded in the remembrance of Jesus's hospitality enacted in his cruciform death. Thus, by connecting the "Lord's meal" with Jesus's Passover meal with his disciples, Paul establishes that the risen Christ is the host of the church's community meal. As we have seen in Luke's Gospel, Jesus associates his saving death with food and drink precisely because his death is the means whereby Jesus enacts the divine hospitality that creates a family that belongs to and worships the risen Lord. This meal that the Corinthian church celebrates is "the *Lord's* table" (10:21b) and "the *Lord's* supper" (11:20) over which the powerful risen Lord presides as the host. That Paul sets forth the Lord as the host of this meal is clear in that the Lord provides the food and drink for the meal *and* in that the meal is an opportunity to "remember" and "proclaim" the saving death of the Lord until his return (11:25–26).[31] Paul believes that when the Corinthian church comes together in the name of Jesus to eat this meal (5:4; 11:33), they are nourished on the spiritual food and drink (10:3–4) of their crucified and risen Lord (11:24–25) who was not only remembered and celebrated but was powerfully present with them at their meal (10:16–17). Paul is at pains to make

29. I understand this *real participation and communion* in the Lord as a reality that is mediated by the powerful presence of the Spirit who comes from Christ. On which, see Grant Macaskill, *Union with Christ in the New Testament* (Oxford: Oxford University Press, 2013), 201–12.

30. See here Richard B. Hays, *1 Corinthians*, Interpretation (Louisville: Westminster John Knox Press, 1997), 167–68.

31. See James C. Walters, "Paul and the Politics of Meals in Roman Corinth," in *Corinth in Context: Comparative Studies on Religion and Society*, ed. Steven J. Friesen, Daniel N. Schowalter, and James C. Walters, NovTSup 134 (Leiden: Brill, 2010), 343–64, here, 362–63: "Moreover, the phrases 'drink the cup of the Lord' and 'partake of the table of the Lord' suggest that for Paul whatever food and drink might have been provided by those with relatively greater resources for the poorer members of the community should not highlight their generosity, but Christ's."

it clear that the meal that the church eats establishes an *exclusive relationship* between Christ and his people. This is why the Corinthians cannot "participate in the Lord's table and the table of demons" (10:21b).[32]

But Paul is also clear that the church's celebration of Christ's hospitality has important social entailments as well. Fellowship with the Lord, ritualized through his meal, is the foundation for communal fellowship with one another.[33] The Lord's Meal, or divine hospitality as I have been calling it, is the foundation for unity, friendship, and voluntary self-abasement that pursues the good of the other within the church. *Since* the meal is a participation in Christ's body and blood, and "*since there is one loaf*, we who are many are one body, for we all participate in the one loaf" (10:17 [my trans.]). Paul's statement corresponds to the similar claims that ground the church's unity and common fellowship in the one Lord (John 10:16–17; Eph 4:4–6).[34] The sacrificed *body* of Christ (10:16), ritualized in the sharing of the meal, is now seen visibly in the Corinthian church as "the one body" (10:17). Those who eat from this bread are in fact Christ's body, and this is why the divisions running along the lines of wealth and status are so problematic.[35] Jerome Murphy-O'Connor states it this way: "Since all share in the one drink that is Christ and in the one bread that is Christ, Christ (to put it very crudely) becomes a passion that all hold in common, and are thereby forged into unity."[36] The crucified Jesus Christ is both the gift and the giver who provides the foundation for the unity and friendship of the "many" within the church. If the church, then, is the visible incarnation of Christ's sacrificed body, it is almost impossible that the church should be broken by division, conflict, and inhospitality toward each other.

We have seen that meals functioned as opportunities for both the initiation and creation of social bonding among friends, family, and colleagues, but as such, they also provided the public opportunity to advertise social ranking and hierarchy. In Corinth it seems likely that the Lord's Supper was celebrated in the homes of (relatively) wealthy homeowners who acted as the

---

32. Nicely articulated by Larry W. Hurtado, *Lord Jesus Christ: Devotion to Jesus in Earliest Christianity* (Grand Rapids: Eerdmans, 2003), 146.

33. Tilling, *Paul's Divine Christology*, 99.

34. Markus Barth, *Rediscovering the Lord's Supper: Communion with Israel, with Christ, and among the Guests* (Atlanta: John Knox Press, 1988), 35.

35. Ronald P. Byars, *The Sacraments in Biblical Perspective*, Interpretation (Louisville: Westminster John Knox Press, 2011), 216.

36. Jerome Murphy-O'Connor, *1 Corinthians*, NTM (Wilmington, DE: Michael Glazier, 1979), 97.

hosts of the meal (11:22, 33).[37] The hosts almost certainly provided not only the household space but also the food and drink for the celebratory meal (see Rom 16:23). Thus, when the Corinthian church "comes together" (11:17, 18, 20, 22, 33, 34) to celebrate the meal, the church suffers from "divisions" and "factions" (11:18, 19; cf. 1:10) as the wealthy homeowners and their friends shame the poor (the "have-nots," 11:22) by either reserving the best portions of the meal for themselves or consuming the food before the poor arrive to eat (11:21).[38] By treating the Lord's Supper as simply another occasion to reaffirm the social hierarchy by eating "one's own" meals (*to idion deipnon*, 11:21), Paul says the hosts are despising and shaming "the have-nots" (11:22). The basic problem is social inequality and inequity in terms of the meal as one participant goes hungry while another is satiated and drunk (11:22).[39] Paul is essentially declaring that the Corinthians have failed to recognize the particular character of social fellowship and bonding demanded by the celebration of this meal in *the Lord's* honor. The contrast between "each one devouring his *own meal*" (11:21a) and "the *Lord's* Meal (11:20b) functions as a critical reminder of the one they celebrate and proclaim when they come together to eat. Paul's rhetorical strategy, then, is to establish *the Lord Christ* as the singular host of the supper and *not the wealthy Corinthian patrons*.[40] When the church comes together to share in this meal, they are feasting upon the body and blood of Jesus Christ that has been given *for them* (11:24–26). They celebrate that God's hospitality has been extended to them in Christ's saving death and confess that the resurrected and living Jesus is present in their midst as they remember him by proclaiming the Lord's death until his return (11:26).[41] The true character of this meal is its celebration of what the Lord has done for others. The meal is the tangible expression of Paul's consistent call to give up their rights for the good of others (1 Cor 8:11–13; 9:1–18; 10:24, 33; 11:1).[42] Using this meal to proclaim the Lord's death means that the

37. Gerd Thiessen, *The Social Setting of Pauline Christianity* (Edinburgh: T&T Clark, 1982), 151–53.

38. The phrase *prolambanei en tō phagein* may mean "to eat beforehand" but is much more likely to mean simply "to eat a meal." See Bruce W. Winter, *After Paul Left Corinth: The Influence of Secular Ethics and Social Change* (Grand Rapids: Eerdmans, 2001), 144–48.

39. See Smith, *From Symposium to Eucharist*, 191.

40. See Walters, "Paul and the Politics of Meals in Roman Corinth," 359–63.

41. See Peter Lampe, "The Eucharist: Identifying with Christ on the Cross," *Interpretation* 48 (1994): 36–49.

42. Beverly Roberts Gaventa, "'You Proclaim the Lord's Death': 1 Corinthians 11:26 and Paul's Understanding of Worship," *Review and Expositor* 80, no. 3 (Summer 1983): 377–87, here, 383–84.

church is a herald or messenger of the Lord's table-practices with sinners and outcasts (see Luke 7:34; 15:1–2; 19:1–10). In other words, the identity of the Corinthian church is established by the divine hospitality manifested in Jesus's saving death *extended to all kinds of people* (see 1 Cor 1:26–31). But ironically it is precisely those for whom Jesus died and whom God called who are being treated unjustly.[43] The primary exhortation that Paul gives to the church comes in 11:33: "so then my brothers and sisters, when you come together to eat *extend hospitality to one another [allēlous ekdechesthe]*." The Greek phrase that I have translated "extend hospitality to one another" may have the double valence of "show hospitality" and simply "wait for one another," that is, wait until everyone has arrived before you eat the meal.[44] Richard Hays has stated this nicely:

> Paul is telling the Corinthians not just to wait for one another but to *receive* one another as guests (cf. Rom 15:7) when they come together. . . .
> On this reading, Paul is calling the more affluent Corinthians not merely to preserve a public appearance of unity in the celebration of the Supper but actually to break down the barrier of social status and to receive the poorer members as guests in their homes, sharing their food with those who have none.[45]

Paul's recounting of the tradition of Jesus's Last Supper and his meal-practices in verses 23–26 is for the purpose of reminding the church of the ethical and social entailments of the divine hospitality that was extended to them through the death of Jesus. The church is called to remember and to imitate Jesus' hospitality practices. When Paul recounts the words of Jesus "Do this in remembrance of me" (11:24b) and declares that the Lord's Supper is a "proclamation of the Lord's death until he comes" (11:26b [my trans.]), Paul is declaring that the Corinthians are committing themselves to give of themselves and their resources for others *just as Christ had done for them in his death.*[46] At the least, Paul is calling for the church to prioritize the meal

---

43. Michael J. Gorman, *Becoming the Gospel: Paul, Participation, and Mission* (Grand Rapids: Eerdmans, 2015), 244.

44. John Koenig, *New Testament Hospitality: Partnership with Strangers as Promise and Mission* (Eugene, OR: Wipf and Stock, 2001), 70.

45. Hays, *1 Corinthians*, 202–3.

46. See here especially Suzanne Watts Henderson, "'If Anyone Hungers . . .': An In-tegrated Reading of 1 Cor 11.17–34," *NTS* 48, no.2 (April 2002): 195–208, here, 203: "In other words, if Paul's driving concern is the community's imitation of Jesus' self-giving table act, it

as the Lord's meal in such a way that it will function as a time of unified
coming together, which depends upon the meal functioning as an occasion
for friendship and equality between all those who eat the meal (11:17, 20, 33,
34).[47] But his concern that the rich not shame the have-nots and his statement that "if anyone is hungry, let him eat in the house" (11:34 [my trans.];
see 11:22a) encourage the church to extend welcome and friendship to the
poor precisely by using the meal as a way to remember Jesus's hospitality
as an opportunity for inclusivity, rejection of hierarchy, and opportunities
to feed the hungry.[48] Paul may in fact allude to Isaiah 58:6–7, 10 where God
makes clear his demand upon Israel:[49]

> Is this not the fast that I choose? . . . Is it not to share your bread with
> the hungry, to bring the poor and homeless into your house, to clothe
> the naked when you see him, and not to ignore your own flesh and
> blood? . . . If you offer yourself to the hungry, and satisfy the needs of the
> afflicted one, then your light will shine in the darkness and your night
> will be like noonday.

Markus Barth articulates the way in which divine hospitality elicits human
hospitality:

> If the acts of sharing, eating, and drinking natural products are to be a
> proclamation of Christ's death, then the efforts directed toward properly
> rewarded production, adequate distribution, fair prices, and sufficient
> provision of daily bread must not and cannot be excluded from a gen-
> uine celebration of the Lord's Supper. Rather, social responsibility and
> action are the essence of the meal that Christ has instituted. Without
> . . . the breaking of bread in favor of the hungry, there is no communion
> with Christ. . . . [50]

---

becomes increasingly problematic to suggest that he would deliberately separate the 'social'
issue of real-life hunger from a 'sacramental' meal 'proclaiming the Lord's death.'"

47. Smith, *From Symposium to Eucharist*, 196–97.

48. Henderson, "'If Anyone Hungers . . . ','" 205–7. Winter, *After Paul Left Corinth*,
151: "By receiving one another they share their resources with those who 'have not' and thus
alleviate the acute embarrassment felt by those who came without food to the Lord's Dinner.
They also respond to one another in precisely the same way Jesus responded to the needs of
everyone present in his body given 'for you' (11:24)."

49. Henderson, "'If Anyone Hungers . . . ','" 207.

50. Barth, *Rediscovering the Lord's Supper*, 56. Also helpful here is Luise Schottroff,

Paul's cryptic statement that those who eat and drink without "discerning the body" actually eat and drink "judgment for themselves" (11:29) does not concern lack of introspection over one's sins, nor does it refer to some doctrinal error; rather, failure to discern the body is a warning to those who would celebrate the Lord's meal in a way that fails to enact love, honor, and friendship to the poor.[51] The failure is that of shaming the poor, despising the church, and discriminating against the so-called lesser members of the community. This is why some among the Corinthians have even become sick and experienced judgment due to their abuse of the table. John Koenig states it well: "But if Christ is *not* welcomed by his people in one another, that is, if barriers are erected to obscure or prevent this hospitality, then he comes to the supper as a judging host whose food and drink have the effect of punishing his guests."[52] Those who eat of the Lord's Supper and thereby remember the divine hospitality received from the Lord's loving and saving death also commit themselves to pursuing the pattern of love, equality, unity, and friendship within the church.

Messianic Hospitality in Rome

Again, in his letter to the Romans Paul employs the language of hospitality and characterizes Christ as extending welcome to the entire church as a means of eradicating divisions and disputes within the church. Christ has become a servant to both "the circumcised" and "the Gentiles" in order to create a multiethnic and worldwide family who together with one voice give praise to God (Rom 15:7–13). The social and religious characteristics that would potentially divide and create disputes between Jew and Gentile within Paul's churches are legion, but Paul insists that the welcome of the loving Messiah to both Jew and Gentile functions as the basis for the unity and friendship of the church in Rome.

The exact cause of the dispute (or whether Paul's argument is even preemptive) and whether it ran along ethnic lines is not easy to determine, but it seems clear that the locus of difficulty is the church's common meal with

---

"Holiness and Justice: Exegetical Comments on 1 Corinthians 11.17–34," *JSNT* 23, no. 79 (January 2001): 51–60.

51. Francis J. Moloney, *A Body Broken for a Broken People* (San Francisco: HarperCollins, 1997), 165–68.

52. Koenig, *New Testament Hospitality*, 69.

each other.[53] And this is why Paul draws upon the language of hospitality and friendship to resolve the tensions that are arising from their table fellowship. It seems likely that some community members or households believed all food to be clean and therefore the Jewish food laws to be inconsequential. After all, didn't Jesus declare "that nothing is unclean in itself" (Rom 14:14; see Mark 7:15)? But others, perhaps concerned with the relationship between foodstuffs and pagan sacrifices or with the Jewish food laws, believed it important to abstain from certain foods *and* to observe religious holidays. As Paul says, "one person supposes he can eat anything, while another eats only vegetables" (14:2) and "one person judges one day above another, while another considers each day to be the same" (14:5). Stanley Stowers argues that the fundamental problem here "comes when the weak and the strong will not accept one another into the relation of mutual aid and friendship indicated by *proslambanein* [hospitality/friendship]."[54] When Paul says that "the kingdom of God is not about food and drink but righteousness and peace and joy in the Holy Spirit" (14:17 [my trans.]) he is by no means devaluing the church's common meal; rather, he is arguing that the common meal is not about what one does or does not eat, but instead the meal is to provide the opportunity for mutual partnership with one another.[55]

Paul's fundamental exhortation is not to the so-called "weak" but to those who believe they have the rights and freedoms to abstain or not abstain. Paul bookends his treatment of the problem with the exhortation: "*Let us welcome* [*proslambanesthe*] anyone who is weak in faith, not for the purpose of passing judgments with respect to doubtful matters" (Rom 14:1).[56] And again, in Romans 15:7: "So then welcome one another [*prolambanesthe allēlous*], just as the Messiah welcomed you [*kathōs kai ho Christos proselabeto hymas*] to the glory of God" (15:7). Tangibly this will be demonstrated in refusing to judge, look down upon, or discriminate against one another (14:3a). Again, Paul reminds the church that their welcome of each other

53. See especially Mark Reasoner, *The Strong and the Weak: Romans 14:1–15:13 in Context*, SNTSMS 103 (Cambridge: Cambridge University Press, 1999), 187–216. See also Smith, *From Symposium to Eucharist*, 214–15. Also important is John M. G. Barclay, "'Do We Undermine the Law?': A Study of Romans 14:1–15:6," in *Paul and the Mosaic Law*, ed. James D. G. Dunn (Tübingen: Mohr-Siebeck, 1996), 287–308.

54. Stanley K. Stowers, *A Rereading of Romans: Justice, Jews, and Gentiles* (New Haven, CT: Yale University Press, 1994), 323.

55. Koenig, *New Testament Hospitality*, 56.

56. I have discussed this in more detail in Joshua W. Jipp, *Christ Is King: Paul's Royal Ideology* (Minneapolis: Fortress, 2015), 70–75.

is predicated upon the fact that "God has welcomed [them]" (*ho Theos gar auton proselabeto*, 14:3b).[57] Thus, the hospitality that Paul demands to be extended to the weak is grounded christologically in the very welcome they have received from the Messiah. Messianic hospitality elicits human hospitality and welcome to one another. John Barclay has stated it this way: "They are to be welcomed to meals not just *in the same way* as Christ has welcomed them, but also *because* they stand before God on the basis of Christ's welcome alone (15:7)."[58] The Messiah's hospitality finds concrete expression in his willingness to become "a servant" both for those of "the circumcision" and for "the Gentiles" in order that there might be one unified people of God (Rom 15:8–9).[59] This is further indicated by Paul's prefacing his treatment of the issue with a call to take on the virtue and character of Christ: "clothe yourselves with the Lord Jesus Christ" (13:14 [my trans.]). And perhaps *the* fundamental aspect of Christ's character in Romans is his love and regard for the other. Thus, the strong must accommodate and refrain from insisting upon their rights lest it harm a brother (14:15; 15:1–3). Christ dies for the weak and for sinners (5:6, 8); his death reveals God's love (5:5, 8). The Messiah's death releases us from any eschatological anxiety that might separate us from "the love of the Messiah" (8:35). Christ is "the one who loved us" (8:37). In fact, within Romans 13:8–15:13 we find numerous echoes of Jesus's own teaching to his disciples that asks them to be careful they do not place any stumbling blocks or hindrances before their weaker brother (see Rom 14:13, 20–21 and Mark 9:42–50; Matt 18:6–9).[60]

In fact, Paul's frequent use of the sibling language "brother/sister" (14:10, 15) to describe the members of the church suggests that Paul is attempting to get the members of the church to see one another as part of the same kinship group.[61] If the Messiah has loved his neighbor supremely, has welcomed the weak and the ungodly, and has extended hospitality to Jew

57. Koenig, *New Testament Hospitality*, 55 is right that the "him" probably "applies to both sides; it is God's prior welcome that ennobles all potential guests."

58. John M. G. Barclay, *Paul and the Gift* (Grand Rapids: Eerdmans, 2015), 512.

59. On which, see J. Ross Wagner, "The Christ, Servant of Jew and Gentile: A Fresh Approach to Romans 15:8–9," *JBL* 116 (1997): 473–85; Bates, *The Hermeneutics of the Apostolic Proclamation*, 289–304.

60. See Michael Thompson, *Clothed with Christ: The Example and Teaching of Jesus in Romans 12.1–15.13*, JSNTSup 59 (Sheffield: JSOT, 1991), 121–40; James W. Thompson, *Moral Formation according to Paul: The Context and Coherence of Pauline Ethics* (Grand Rapids: Baker, 2011), 169–79.

61. Reidar Aasgaard, *"My Beloved Brothers and Sisters!": Christian Siblingship in Paul*, ECCon 265 (New York: T&T Clark, 2004), 209–11; Horrell, *Solidarity and Difference*, 121–26.

and Gentile alike, then how could those within the churches in Rome fail to extend hospitality to each other![62]

Christ's hospitality is exemplified in 15:3 where Paul's statement "even the Messiah did not please himself" (15:3 [my trans.]) is set forth as the loving and cruciform model for the strong (15:1). Christ's refusal to please himself, a clear reference to his sacrificial suffering and death for others, is the ground for Paul's appeal to the strong: "we who are strong ought to bear the weakness of those without strength and not please ourselves. Let each one of us please his neighbor for the good of building up the neighbor" (15:1b–2). The depiction of Christ pleasing his neighbor instead of himself means that Christ is the one who, in the first instance, fulfills Paul's statement: "the one who loves the other has fulfilled the law" (Rom 13:8b [my trans.]). The parallel between "you shall love your neighbor as yourself" (Rom 13:9b) as the fulfillment of the Torah and Christ as the one who pleased his neighbor (Rom 15:2–3) indicates that the Messiah fulfills the Torah through his loving hospitality enacted toward his neighbor.

As Christ perfectly loved and welcomed his neighbor, so Paul calls the church to the same pattern and to "walk according to love" in imitation of Jesus's self-abasing death for others (Rom 14:15). The result of "welcoming one another just as Christ welcomed you" (Rom 15:7) is that the church will be able to pursue the things that make for peace, harmony, and edification (14:19). The church will "have the same mind toward one another according to the standard of Jesus Christ" and this will lead to a church marked by unity that praises God *together with one voice* (Rom 15:5–6 [my trans.])—with the Messiah himself leading the choir in praise to God (Rom 15:9b–12)![63] The hospitality and love of the Messiah is the pattern or way of thinking that controls how Christians act toward one another and enables them to put into practice the earlier friendship exhortations of extending hospitality to one another (12:10), weeping with those who weep and rejoicing with those who rejoice (12:15), and having the same mind toward one another (12:16).[64] This unified friendship that embodies the Messiah's hospitality will, we can

---

62. Similarly, see Stowers, *A Rereading of Romans*, 323.

63. See here again Bates, *The Hermeneutics of Apostolic Proclamation*, 298–300.

64. Commenting on Romans 15:1–6, Douglas A. Campbell, "Participation and Faith in Paul," in *"In Christ" in Paul: Explorations in Paul's Theology of Union and Participation*, ed. Michael J. Thate, Kevin J. Vanhoozer, and Constantine R. Campbell, WUNT 2.384 (Tübingen: Mohr-Siebeck, 2014), 37–60, here, 49, rightly states: "Given that Christ loves it would then follow even more obviously that Christians love because they possess the loving mind of Christ."

presume, find its tangible outworking in both the weak and the strong finding a way to accept one another *and eat together at the same table.*[65]

Friendship in Christ in Paul's Churches

Given Paul's belief that God had acted to extend divine hospitality and friendship to humanity, one of Paul's tasks was to create communities of messianic-shaped friendship. God has reconciled humans to himself through the death of Christ, thereby converting hostile enemies and adversaries of God into God's friends (Rom 5:9–10; Col 1:20–22). Paul is an ambassador for the Messiah who is entrusted with God's message of reconciliation that humanity's transgressions and hostilities have been eradicated (2 Cor 5:18–21). God makes the first move to erase humanity's sin and hostility through the saving death of the Messiah and enables divine blessings of righteousness (2 Cor 5:21), future salvation from divine wrath (Rom 5:9–11), the gift of the Spirit (Rom 8:7–9), and peace (Eph 2:14–18; Col 1:20). The eradication of enmity between humanity and God, namely reconciliation, justifies speaking of God extending friendship *in* Christ *through* Paul *to* Paul's churches. John T. Fitzgerald is right, then, to describe God as one who has "transformed Paul into his friend and entrusted him with the task of bringing God's gift of friendship to others."[66] As Wesley Hill has suggested, the New Testament authors reconfigure friendship language into the language of spiritual kinship such that true friendship is elevated to "a way of speaking about the bonds between Christian siblings."[67] I suggest, then, that one of Paul's agendas is forming his churches into communities that embody the reality of divine friendship.

Paul's creation of churches that embody God's friendship in Christ is seen most clearly in his letter to the Philippians. Numerous scholars have

65. Smith, *From Symposium to Eucharist*, 216.

66. I rely here on the work of L. Michael White, "Morality between Two Worlds: A Paradigm of Friendship in Philippians," in *Greeks, Romans, and Christians*, ed. David L. Balch, Everett Fergusson, and Wayne A. Meeks (Minneapolis: Fortress, 1990), 201–15; Wayne Meeks, "The Man from Heaven in Paul's Letter to the Philippians," in *The Future of Early Christianity: Essays in Honor of Helmut Koester*, ed. Birger Pearson (Minneapolis: Fortress, 1991), 329–36; and John T. Fitzgerald, "Paul and Friendship," in *Paul in the Greco-Roman World: A Handbook*, ed. J. Paul Sampley (Harrisburg, PA: Trinity Press, International, 2003), 319–43, here, 337.

67. Wesley Hill, *Spiritual Friendship: Finding Love in the Church as a Celibate Gay Christian* (Grand Rapids: Brazos Press, 2015), 60.

recognized Paul's use of friendship terminology in order to form the church into a community of friends patterned on Christ's model of humility and self-abasement (Phil 2:5–8). Paul exhorts them to act in a manner that is worthy of their heavenly citizenship so that Paul will find them standing firm "in *one spirit and with one soul,* working together for the faith of the gospel" (1:27 [my trans.]). The church is to implement the pattern of moral and practical reasoning oriented around Christ that enables them to "think the same way, have the same love, share the same soul, and think together on one goal" (Phil 2:2 [my trans.]). And this unity of thinking is predicated upon the pattern of other-regarding love that has been embodied in Christ Jesus (Phil 2:5). In addition to Paul's imitation of Christ's self-abasing pattern of thinking that considers Christ and others ahead of himself (3:2–17), Paul sets forth his friends Timothy and Epaphroditus, who do not strive to satisfy their own self-interests but rather set their minds on pleasing Christ, Paul, and the Philippians (2:19–30). These examples of Christ-shaped moral and practical reasoning, Paul hopes, will enable "Euodia and Syntyche to think the same thing in the Lord" (4:2 [my trans.]).

Similarly, in 1 Corinthians Paul seeks to inculcate a pattern of thinking that considers the good of the church member ahead of her own rights precisely because that member is a fellow brother or sister. Paul hopes that the Corinthians will view themselves as members of one unified family, brought into existence through the cross of Christ, and that this will be the foundation for considering each other's needs ahead of oneself (1:10–12).[68] This is displayed most clearly in 1 Corinthians 8:11–13 where Paul intentionally repeats the word "brother" four times in order to call the one who thinks his knowledge provides him with the right to eat idol-meat to consider first the good of *his brother for whom Christ died* (see Rom 14:10–13).[69] To wound the conscience of one's brother is, Paul declares, to sin against Christ (1 Cor 8:12). Similarly, Paul scolds the Corinthians for fellow brothers taking each other to court (1 Cor 6:6) and for doing wrong and defrauding their fellow *brothers* (1 Cor 6:8).[70]

---

68. That 1 Corinthians is deliberative rhetoric employed by Paul in order to create unity and harmony within the church has been argued convincingly by Margaret M. Mitchell, *Paul and the Rhetoric of Reconciliation: An Exegetical Investigation of the Language and Composition of 1 Corinthians* (Louisville, KY: Westminster John Knox Press, 1992).

69. Horrell, "Theological Principle or Christological Praxis?", 89–90, refers to this as "christologically based relational concerns" and notes that "here the foundation for ethical action is the status of each fellow believer as a brother or sister in Christ."

70. Aasgaard, *"My Beloved Brothers and Sisters!"*, 217–36.

Paul's frequent use of family metaphors for God, Christ, and his churches should also be seen as his broader discourse where the church is portrayed as God's family. Family metaphors were frequently used as a means of describing *fictive kinship* groups in the ancient world and in Paul's churches.[71] Also, Paul consistently refers to his churches as fellow brothers and sisters of one another (1 Cor 1:11, 26; 2:1; 3:1; 2 Cor 2:12–13; Gal 4:12–20; Phil 2:25; 1 Thess 2:17–3:8), as sons or children of God (Rom 8:9–17; Gal 3:26; 4:5–7), to Jesus as "God's Son" (Col 1:13) or "the firstborn son" (Rom 8:29; Col 1:15, 18), and to God as "Father" (Rom 1:7; 6:4; 8:15; 15:6; 1 Cor 1:3; 8:6; 15:24; Gal 1:1, 3, 4).[72] The family language encapsulates the particular Christian narrative whereby the *Father* of Jesus Christ sends forth his *firstborn Son* who saves a community of brothers and sisters for himself. Thus, it makes sense that Paul would speak of the church as "the household of faith" (Gal 6:10; see throughout 1 Timothy).

Hospitality and Mission in Paul's Churches

Paul further employs friendship language in order to facilitate and encourage the advancement of his missionary endeavors by providing material resources both for his mission and for churches in need. For example, family language pervades Paul's exhortations to the church in Corinth to share their resources with the poor in Jerusalem (2 Cor 8:1, 18, 22, 23; 9:3, 5; see Gal 2:1–10). Paul is also thankful that the Philippian church has renewed their interest and concern about him (Phil 4:10), such that they have even become "fellow participants" (*synkoinōnēsantes*) in his trials (4:14). This renewal of their friendship is true to the Philippians' character, for they had "shared" themselves and their resources with Paul from the beginning (4:15–16). Thus, their consistency and refusal to forget about Paul in his times of difficulty are confirmation of their friendship with Paul and co-sharing in the propagation of the gospel.[73] In fact, Paul speaks of their contribution to his needs as the means whereby they receive the joy of participating in the advance of the gospel (1:12; 4:16).

Paul expects that his churches will extend hospitality to one another and particularly itinerant missionaries precisely because they are a commu-

---

71. See here Wayne A. Meeks, *The First Urban Christians: The Social World of the Apostle Paul* (New Haven, CT: Yale University Press, 1983), 85–94.

72. See here Joseph H. Hellerman, *When the Church Was a Family: Recapturing Jesus' Vision for Authentic Christian Community* (Nashville, TN: B&H Publishing, 2009), 76–96.

73. Fitzgerald, "Paul and Friendship," 334.

nity of God's friends.[74] Thus, Paul hopes the Roman Christians will welcome him and provide the support and means he needs in order to evangelize in Spain (Rom 15:22–25). As a preliminary to this end, he expects that the Roman churches will "welcome [Phoebe *our sister*] in the Lord" and that they will provide for all of her needs (Rom 16:1–2). Similarly, the church in Corinth must welcome Timothy and hospitably provide for his needs as he comes to Paul "with the brothers" (1 Cor 16:10–11). Paul also alerts the church that soon he will come to Corinth—a matter of no little contention! (2 Cor. 1:12–23)—and informs them of the hospitality he anticipates from the church (16:5–9). We have no information about the particular occasion, but Paul can command the church in Colossae—like Rome, not a church established by Paul—to welcome John Mark if he should come to them (Col 4:10–11). Paul also expects that Philemon will prepare a guestroom for him when he makes his visit (Phlm 16–18). The fact that Paul commands hospitality for himself and his fellow itinerant missionaries suggests that Paul's churches did conceptualize themselves as family and friends in Christ. More examples could be given, but the simple point is that Paul attempted to instill a worldwide family-friendship identity within his congregations as a means of facilitating household networks that advance Paul's missionary ends.[75] The hospitality to traveling itinerants enabled the gospel to spread to new lands, and hospitality between friends and family was intrinsic to the success of Paul's mission.

Ecclesial Hospitality amidst Diversity in Our Churches

Paul clearly believed that ecclesial unity even amidst great diversity was possible, and the differences that Paul's churches faced do not seem to have been any less challenging than what we face today. Christian friendships formed between Jew and Gentile, slave and free, male and female, rich and poor testify clearly to God's ability to create unity and friendship amidst great diversity. Paul's strategy was to articulate how God's hospitality in Christ created a common identity for all his churches, a welcome that transformed them from enemies and outsiders into friends and family—both with God and with one another. And if God has welcomed us in Christ as his friends and family while we were enemies and outsiders, how can we

---

74. See Koenig, *New Testament Hospitality*, 64–65.

75. Andrew Arterbury, *Entertaining Angels: Early Christian Hospitality in Its Mediterranean Setting*, NTMon 8 (Sheffield: Sheffield Phoenix Press, 2005), 100–9.

not respond with hospitality and friendship to our own Christian friends and family with whom we may differ on the level of our cultural and social identities?

While ethnic, gender, social-status, and cultural differences continue and are not erased through this act of divine hospitality, the church's adoption of a shared identity as family and friends is what enables, or so Paul hopes, the church to do away with divisions (not difference!) based on social, ethnic, and gender differences within the church. As Fowl states: ". . .because Christian friendships are bound up in a common friendship with Christ, we should not seek to build churches around socio-economic, racial, or ethnic similarities."[76] If the church is called into existence out of the hospitality of God, then one of the core mandates for the church is that it be a "befriending community that not only welcomes all who come to it but also offers them a place where the grammar of intimacy and friendship can be learned."[77] We have seen that the core practice that ritualizes God's hospitality to us in Christ and enables friendship is the shared table of our Lord Jesus. Peter Slade has told the story of how the movement called Mission Mississippi worked to create friendships between white and black churches in a state marked by racial and denominational segregation.[78] The founders of the movement hoped to change the racial divisions in their state "through the power of new relationships, made possible by the reconciling work of Christ."[79] While not without serious difficulties, what enabled whites and blacks to create and grow in friendships with one another were weekly prayer breakfasts, which provided the context for them to privilege their shared identity as God's friends and family over their cultural identities that had functioned as barriers from one another. Slade recounts how one white, older participant explained his experience of eating and praying together across racial divides: "[When] someone is on your behalf praying to the Lord, and you are praying to the Lord, there is a meet[ing] there—just the commonality right there and you are bonded in Christ. I don't know how to describe that but that is where the reconciliation is. That moment you are one in Christ. You are of one mind, one heart, and one soul."[80] The testimony

76. Fowl, *Philippians*, 217.

77. Paul J. Wadell, *Becoming Friends: Worship, Justice, and the Practice of Christian Friendship* (Grand Rapids: Brazos Press, 2002), 53.

78. Peter Slade, *Open Friendship in a Closed Society: Mission Mississippi and a Theology of Friendship* (New York: Oxford University Press, 2009).

79. Slade, *Open Friendship in a Closed Society*, 39.

80. Slade, *Open Friendship in a Closed Society*, 170.

encapsulates perfectly how the privileging of shared friendship in Christ enables a unity that does not erase but does transcend racial divides.

These kinds of friendships are possible only when we recognize that the primary feature of our identity is that God has welcomed us in Christ, and this divine embrace and gift of friendship have come to us apart from any preexisting notions of social worth that would be based upon our cultural or social identities.[81] Hans Reinders makes a similar argument with respect to those with physical disabilities, though his comments can be applied more broadly: "Difference can be celebrated only because it has no theological significance: in the eyes of God, human beings are equally worthy of his loving kindness, no matter what differences the bodies of these human beings may exhibit. This is the sameness that is true of all of us, which is why difference in the widest possible variety can be celebrated."[82]

Again, this is not to say that our social and cultural differences are unimportant! But, for Paul, they are emphatically not the basis for our individual or communal identity, our moral reasoning and behavior, or the corporate constitution of our churches. Thus, to privilege men over women, or married over single, or one ethnicity over another within the church is to fail to heed the social significance of Christ's welcome and friendship as the ground of the church's identity. In fact, Paul consistently asks those with privileged status to demonstrate love for their neighbor by sacrificing and giving up their "presumed" rights! Regardless of our particular differences, our primary communal identity as those who have received and experienced God's hospitality and received his friendship is *friends and family*.[83] Wesley Hill has made a powerful plea for the recovery of Christian friendship that transcends biological ties and social and cultural preference: "The story of Jesus' self-giving for the sake of sinners

---

81. In some ways my argument is similar here, though his focus is on the language of grace and gift and not hospitality, to John Barclay's *Paul and the Gift* (Grand Rapids: Eerdmans, 2015).

82. Hans S. Reinders, *Receiving the Gift of Friendship: Profound Disability, Theological Anthropology, and Ethics* (Grand Rapids: Eerdmans, 2008), 284; a similar argument has been made with respect to race and hybridity by Brian Bantum, who argues that Christian baptism "ushers in a radical transformation of the relations based upon racial and cultural assertion which now must be radically overturned." One's identity is now constituted by one's relationship to God; therefore, one's cultural, racial, and biological markers "are not hidden, but are now marked with new political possibilities." See Brian Bantum, *Redeeming Mulatto: A Theology of Race and Christian Hybridity* (Waco, TX: Baylor University Press, 2010), 147–48.

83. Reinders, *Receiving the Gift of Friendship*, 285–92.

inevitably exerts pressure on our understanding of friendship, pushing us out beyond comfortably narrow boundaries of affection and expanding our love to include others whom, previously, we would have left outside our charmed circle."[84]

Pursuing this vision of friendship demands embracing (and being embraced by) those outside of our natural kinship/friendship group. Hill is particularly concerned with the contemporary church's exaltation of the nuclear family and the intractable difficulties and stigmatization that thereby accompany the unmarried and transgendered individuals who are looking for deep and meaningful friendships inside the church.[85] Ephraim Radner, among many others, has observed that close same-sex, especially male, friendships "are today often suspect or given over to intrusive deconstruction by observers."[86] In my own teaching context in the North Shore suburbs of Chicago, I have seen the multiple challenges many single adults face in integrating into and forming deep friendships inside of the "family-friendly" churches.[87] Sadly, many single students training for pastoral ministry feel pressure to find their spouse quickly, lest their unmarried status reflect poorly upon them and prevent them from finding a ministry position. My attempts to convince my students that Paul was right in 1 Corinthians 7 that the unmarried "does better" have (understandably!) not been met with much (if any) success. Hill's challenge to the church to recover the practice of spiritual friendship, however, is infused with hope as he recounts numerous personal stories of married couples and singles sharing deep friendship together and creating "habits of hospitality" that enabled his church to create a space into which more and more people were invited in order to grow in friendship.[88] Married couples whose lives are often so focused upon "the pressing demands of generative existence" are not simply the givers or the hosts, however, but often are those who are

---

84. Hill, *Spiritual Friendship*, 58–59.

85. See further Julia Duin, *Quitting Church: Why the Faithful Are Fleeing and What to Do about It* (Grand Rapids: Baker, 2009); Mark A. Yarhouse, *Understanding Gender Dysphoria: Navigating Transgender Issues in a Changing Culture* (Downers Grove, IL: InterVarsity Press, 2015), 145–61.

86. Ephraim Radner, *A Time to Keep: Theology, Mortality, and the Shape of a Human Life* (Waco, TX: Baylor University Press, 2016), 178.

87. See also Christina Cleveland, "A Liberation Theology for Single People," April 11, 2016, accessed September 1, 2016, http://www.christenacleveland.com/blog/2016/4/a-liberation -theology-for-single-people.

88. For example, Hill, *Spiritual Friendship*, 113–15.

able to learn about true friendship and openness from single persons who often understand (even if sometimes implicitly) their vocation as "friendship cultivators."[89]

Further, given that God's extension of friendship to us has taken place in the other-regarding and self-abasing act of Christ's humiliation and death on the cross, built into our shared identity is the willingness to hold loosely to our own personal, cultural identities and preferences and to consider the good and the edification of one another—and precisely those with whom we may disagree—*above our own good and preferences*. We have seen that this often means that Paul will ask those with power and the majority of influence to curb their so-called rights for the good of their other family members in Christ. Pursuing unity based on our shared identity in Christ is undoubtedly frequently painful, as it entails the posture of lessening our grip on our cultural identities and adapting ourselves to others for *our* common good. Part of the difficulty, however, is that those of us who comprise the so-called majority culture do not always know—and perhaps do not always really care—how our use of power may negatively impact and marginalize others.

Despite the popularity of multi-racial/ethnic congregations, we are still in further need of the creation of ecclesial spaces where transformational worship can take place in such a way that allows all kinds of people to negotiate and contest the dominant majority culture's attempt to force or expect assimilation.[90] It should not occasion any great surprise that most multiethnic congregations seek to integrate diverse groups into patterns of worship, liturgy, and congregational life that have already been established by the dominant ethnic group.[91] Thus, my argument that Paul articulates a shared group identity as recipients of divine hospitality must not lead to calls for the ethnic and cultural minorities to simply adapt to majority culture. Sandra van Opstal speaks of the way in which the practice of hospitality is a necessity for the worship leader: "As long as our worship makes people feel excluded or in constant visitor status, we are not accomplishing the ministry

---

89. Radner, *A Time to Keep*, 185–89.

90. Thanks to TEDS colleague Peter Cha and Pastor Sandra van Opstal for impressing this point upon me.

91. This is in large part what motivates the strong criticism of multiethnic congregations and notions of racial reconciliation by Jennifer Harvey, *Dear White Christians: For Those Still Longing for Racial Reconciliation* (Grand Rapids: Eerdmans, 2015), esp. 67–81; see also, Korie L. Edwards, *The Elusive Dream: The Power of Race in Interracial Churches* (Oxford: Oxford University Press, 2008).

of biblical hospitality. . . . However, when we are creating an inclusive table in which there is room for all, the meal and experience will represent all who sit at the table. . . . In a multiethnic community no members should be made to feel like perpetual guests."[92] This will be possible, of course, only if those in the privileged majority are truly willing to forgo some of their own preferences and share their own power with the vulnerable and marginalized.[93] And this is only possible when leaders are able to recognize "the reality of white privilege and power in society."[94] Addressing the ways in which power and privilege undergird social divisions "often involves the higher-status group's voluntarily abdicating its higher status. These are both difficult and potentially painful processes that require individuals to examine closely the ways in which their social identities (such as race, gender, economic status, education level) influence the status, power, privilege and mobility that society affords them."[95] But of course, this extension of love, regard for the other, and restriction of one's supposed "rights" for the good of the other is *the* hallmark virtue of Christ's extension of hospitality and friendship to us (see, for example, 1 Cor 8:11–13; 10:24; Rom 15:1–7).

Study Questions

1. What are the causes of irreconcilable differences among followers of Jesus in your community? Describe any personal experiences you have with irreconcilable differences between you and a fellow Christian(s).

2. Is it possible to have real difference and diversity in our churches without this leading to division? Why or why not? Are there limits to the amount of difference and diversity our churches are able to handle? Why or why not?

3. How can churches successfully pursue unity without forcing those who are different to assimilate to majority culture?

92. Sandra Maria van Opstal, *The Next Worship: Glorifying God in a Diverse World* (Downers Grove, IL: InterVarsity Press, 2015), 63.

93. Soong-Chan Rah, *The Next Evangelicalism: Freeing the Church from Western Cultural Captivity* (Downers Grove, IL: InterVarsity Press, 2009).

94. Soong-Chan Rah, *Many Colors: Cultural Intelligence for a Changing Church* (Chicago: Moody, 2010), 124. See the entire sixth chapter in particular here.

95. Cleveland, *Disunity in Christ*, 166–67.

4. What do you think of Paul's strategy for seeking unity in his churches? Would it work today?

5. What are the social and ecclesial implications of the Lord's Supper in your own thinking and in your own church? Why is it that many churches have focused almost solely on the "vertical" implications of the Lord's Supper to the exclusion of the "horizontal" implications?

6. In what ways does your church conform or not conform to Paul's call for the church to be a context for Christian friendship and family?

CHAPTER 3

The Meaning of Human Existence and the Church's Mission in the Gospel of John

Humans are inherently creatures of desire, filled with love, longing, and affection. Humans invariably love what it is they believe will satisfy their longings and desires.[1] And so we order our desires and affections (even if unconsciously and implicitly) in such a way as to aim at our vision of human flourishing and what we think constitutes the good life.[2] In other words, humans order their desires, emotions, and loves to what they think will result in life, joy, and human flourishing. James K. A. Smith has presented a powerful Augustinian account of anthropology in his *Desiring the Kingdom* that privileges the notion of humans as lovers and desiring creatures. He says: "It's not what I think that shapes my life from the bottom up; it's what I desire, what I love, that animates my passion. To be human is to be the kind of creature who is oriented by this kind of primal, ultimate love—even if we never really reflect on it."[3] Or again, "I *long* for some end. I *want* something, and want it ultimately. It is my desires that define me. In short you are what you love."[4] Furthermore, for many this quest for life and flourishing includes a missional component. Jean Vanier has said that every community wants to share the "universal truth that they have discovered," whether it be love, peace, truth, the meaning of life, or beauty. Humanity, it would seem, is

---

1. See throughout Brent Strawn, ed., *The Bible and the Pursuit of Happiness: What the Old and New Testaments Teach Us about the Good Life* (Oxford: Oxford University Press, 2012).

2. See Charles Taylor, *A Secular Age* (Cambridge, MA: Harvard University Press, 2007), 16.

3. James K. A. Smith, *Desiring the Kingdom: Worship, Worldview, and Cultural Formation*, vol. 1, *Cultural Liturgies* (Grand Rapids: Baker, 2009), 51.

4. James K. A. Smith, *You Are What You Love: The Spiritual Power of Habit* (Grand Rapids: Brazos, 2016), 9.

imbued with a quest for life and the missional desire to extend and share that life with others.[5]

And yet it is worth pondering whether our desires and loves are accurately aimed at what will satisfy our craving for life. As we will see, the Gospel of John indicates that we were created for life and transcendence, and yet humans in North America suffer today more than ever due to isolation, loneliness, lack of friendship, narcissism, and meaninglessness. Humans are inherently social creatures in need of meaningful social connection. Humans need friendship, in other words, in order to flourish. Aristotle has said that even the wealthiest, most virtuous, and self-sufficient man would be unhappy if he lived without friends.[6] And yet loneliness and isolation mark our society, as it is estimated that in the United States alone more than sixty million people "feel sufficiently isolated for it to be a major source of unhappiness in their lives."[7] Increased technological capacities, the dominance of work in self-identity, and lack of stable roots have contributed to the decline of friendship and meaningful human relationships.[8] More people than ever—whether due to forced migrations, economic hardships, urban poverty, or the anonymity that often characterizes the wealthy urban elite—experience a sense of rootless homelessness or alienation from *home*.[9] Christian Smith's interviews with emerging adults ages 18 to 23 in North America document extensively the ways in which the practices of many young adults—including shopping, intoxication through alcohol and drugs, and frequent sexual encounters—*self-admittedly* do not satisfy their own desires.[10] The direction of human love and desire, it would seem for at least many, is misdirected and disordered as the object of love—whether it be the material satisfaction of the desires of a consumer, recreation and entertainment, ideologies of power and prestige, or sexual gratification—and fails to make good on humanity's quest for life.[11]

5. Jean Vanier, *Community and Growth*, 2nd ed. (New York: Paulist Press, 1989), 85.

6. See Aristotle, *Nicomachean Ethics* 1155a1–10. See further David Konstan, *Friendship in the Classical World* (Cambridge: Cambridge University Press, 1997), 72–78.

7. John T. Cacioppo and William Patrick, *Loneliness: Human Nature and the Need for Social Connection* (New York: W. W. Norton & Company, 2008), 5.

8. Gilbert C. Meilaender, *Friendship: A Study in Theological Ethics* (Notre Dame, IN: University of Notre Dame Press, 1981), 1–2.

9. On which see Steven Bouma-Prediger and Brian J. Walsh, *Beyond Homelessness: Christian Faith in a Culture of Displacement* (Grand Rapids: Eerdmans, 2008), 7–12.

10. Christian Smith, *Lost in Transition: The Dark Side of Emerging Adulthood* (Oxford: Oxford University Press, 2011).

11. Paul J. Wadell, *Becoming Friends: Worship, Justice, and the Practice of Christian Friendship* (Grand Rapids: Baker, 2002), 123–24.

Perhaps more powerfully than any other New Testament composition, the Gospel of John raises the questions of human existence, desire, and the meaning of life. In particular, John's Gospel is oriented around the question of revelation, that is, how can humans who are alienated from the God *of life* come to know God and thereby have life?[12] The answer to this question is literally a matter of life and death, for John is emphatic that God alone is the author and giver of life. God alone has life within himself. Therefore, to know God is to have life and to be alienated from God is death. But the Gospel of John is equally clear that God created humanity *to have life*. This is the mission of Jesus: to make God known to broken, lonely humans who are alienated from God and from one another and to thereby give the life of God—the life that is shared between the Father and the Son—to humans who are longing for life. Jesus's mission is neatly encapsulated in his statement: "I have come so that they might have life and in abundance" (John 10:10b [my trans.]). And this life is shared by virtue of Jesus's revelation of the Father (1:18).

The Gospel of John states that knowledge of God requires an act of God to mediate this divine knowledge to humans. God and his Son belong to the heavenly world from above, whereas humans belong to the world below and this means that humans are epistemologically and relationally alienated from God (8:23–24). John uses a variety of metaphors and images that highlight the relational and epistemological gap between God and humanity. Light and darkness are in implacable opposition, for example, and when the former invades the latter, most of humanity prefers to stay in the dark lest their evil deeds be exposed and judged (3:18–21). Humanity's opposition to all that stems from God is stated compactly in the prologue: "he was in the world, and the world was made through him, but *the world did not know him*" (1:10 [my trans.]). Humanity's opposition to God is amplified, then, in the prologue's claim that "he came to his own, but his own did not welcome him" (1:11 [my trans.]). But the consequences of humanity's alienation from God are enormous. Humanity was created for life, but the author of the Fourth Gospel is clear that life can be found only in God and his Word: "in him was life, and the life was the light of all people" (1:4). In fact, the Gospel claims to have been written with a missionary purpose, namely, so that by believing in Jesus people may come to have fullness of life (20:30–31). Craig

---

12. John Ashton, *Understanding the Fourth Gospel*, 2nd ed. (Oxford: Oxford University Press, 2007), 305–29; Christopher W. Skinner, *Reading John*, Cascade Companions (Eugene, OR: Cascade Books, 2015), 8–31.

Koester has said that for John, "People do not have life in themselves. They must receive life from an outside source. The idea that human beings are created in this way means that they have an inescapable need for the life that comes from God."[13]

Jesus, the Stranger from Heaven

If God is from above and God alone can give humans life, then how is it that humans can come to know this God and receive life? The Gospel of John presents Jesus as the heavenly stranger who through the incarnation shares divine knowledge and presence with alienated humans by enabling them to partake of the hospitality of God.[14] The mission of Jesus is "one of life-giving. He came to give life and to give it abundantly. He came to take away all the blockages that prevent the flow of life."[15] Jesus is able to mediate divine hospitality to humans precisely because he has existed with God, as the Logos, from the beginning (1:1–3) and by taking on human flesh and making his home on earth reveals God to humanity (1:14).[16] The Son makes his dwelling with God as "the unique God who is in the bosom of the Father" (1:18 [my trans.]). He created the world and all that is in it (1:3, 10). And yet despite Jesus's coming to his own creation and to what belongs to him, "his own people did not welcome [ou parelabon] him" (1:11b [my trans.]). The Word takes on human flesh and makes its home, or better, "tabernacles" (eskēnōsen) on earth with humans in order to reveal the glory of God to humans (1:14). Thus, John gives us a portrait of Jesus as a stranger who leaves his natural heavenly habitat with God in order to make his temporary abode on earth with humans.

Jesus trades his original habitat, however, precisely in order to mediate divine and heavenly knowledge to alienated humans. John frequently

---

13. Craig R. Koester, *The Word of Life: A Theology of John's Gospel* (Grand Rapids: Eerdmans, 2008), 56.

14. That John depicts Jesus as the "heavenly stranger" was articulated clearly by two classic studies. See Wayne A. Meeks, "The Man from Heaven in Johannine Sectarianism," in *The Interpretation of John*, ed. John Ashton (Philadelphia: Fortress Press, 1986). This originally appeared as Wayne A. Meeks, "The Man from Heaven in Johannine Sectarianism," *JBL* 91 (1972): 44–72. And also, see Marius de Jonge, *Jesus, Stranger from Heaven and Son of God: Jesus Christ and the Christians in Johannine Perspective* (Missoula, MT: Scholars Press, 1977).

15. Vanier, *Community and Growth*, 87.

16. See Dean Flemming, *Why Mission?*, Reframing New Testament Theology (Nashville: Abingdon, 2015), 54.

speaks of Jesus in this capacity as the Son of Man who functions as the link between heaven and earth and, therefore, as "the Stranger *par excellence*."[17] After amazing Nathanael with his remarkable insights, Jesus predicts that Nathanael will experience in Jesus something greater than Jacob's ladder: "you will see heaven opened up and God's angels ascending and descending on the Son of Man" (1:51 [my trans.]; see Gen 28:12). Jesus is able to speak to Nicodemus about heavenly realities because he alone comes from above, and: "no one has ascended into heaven except the one who descended from heaven, namely, the Son of Man" (3:13 [my trans.]). Only the heavenly stranger knows the secrets of God and is able to reveal them to humanity.[18] Jesus is not from this world, but as the Son of Man he has come from heaven to earth in order to do the Father's work of revealing God to alienated humans (6:30–40; 8:23–24). He is God's bread that has "come down from heaven" (6:33). Only Jesus knows "where I came from and where I'm going" (8:14 [my trans.]). Jesus repeatedly speaks of having come from God and of returning or ascending to the Father (1:9; 3:19; 9:39; 12:46–47; 16:28; 18:37).

Jesus's heavenly origin as the Son of Man puts the characters' frequent questioning of Jesus's origins in a consistently ironic light, for despite protestations to the contrary, Jesus's opponents emphatically do not know where Jesus has come from. Jesus's descent from heaven is a stumbling block for the Jews as they ask: "Is not this Jesus, the son of Joseph, whose father and mother we know? How can he now say, 'I have come down from heaven'?" (6:42). Or Jesus's descent from heaven is misunderstood and ignored by those confused about his heavenly identity: "Can it be that the authorities really know that this is the Messiah? Yet *we know where this man is from*; but when the Messiah comes, no one will know where he is from" (7:26b–27). John's irony is heightened in the episode where the religious authorities admit their ignorance about Jesus's heavenly identity: "We know that God has spoken to Moses, but as for this man, we do not know where he comes from" (9:29). The highest point of the irony comes when Pilate explicitly asks Jesus: "Where are you from?" (19:9) with Jesus maintaining silence in response (19:9b–10). Jesus's heavenly origins result in conflicts between Jesus and the authorities, and the narrative bears out the prologue's anticipatory claim: "he came to his own, but his own did not welcome him" (1:11 [my trans.]).

---

17. Meeks, "The Man from Heaven in Johannine Sectarianism," 146. On this, see also Skinner, *Reading John*, 68–70.

18. On which, see Meeks, "The Man from Heaven in Johannine Sectarianism," 147–50.

And yet the mission of this heavenly stranger is to reveal God, to make him known to us, and to impart saving relational knowledge of God to humanity. The statement that "his own did not welcome him" (1:11) is matched by "but as many as did welcome him, he gave the right to become God's children" (1:12 [my trans.]). He has "made his home among us" in order to reveal the Father's glory (1:14). So if this is Jesus's mission, then how is Jesus able to impart this saving knowledge of God to humanity?

Jesus, the Life-Giving Host

Jesus uses the primary symbols of hospitality and acts as divine host to humanity as he shares the saving and revelatory presence of God through wine (2:1–11), water (4:4–42), bread (6:1–71), washing his disciples' feet (13:1–20), and providing an eternal home (14:1–6). All of the elements of hospitality symbolize *God's hospitality to humans who, are in need of the revelatory and saving presence of Jesus.* This is one of the means whereby Jesus's identity is revealed, for the basic elements of hospitality function as life-giving symbols that enable alienated humanity to come to a saving knowledge of Jesus's divine identity. Jesus's characterization as the stranger who is transformed into host in his provision of wine, water, and bread is theologically fitting, for one of the primary purposes of the custom of hospitality to strangers is *the revelation of the identity of the guest.* The symbolic hospitality elements of wine, water, bread, foot washing, and home are used to express humanity's deep desire and need for God and the overcoming of that which separates humanity from God and life.

Jesus performs his first sign in Cana of Galilee as Jesus, who is invited to the wedding along with his disciples as guests (2:2), exchanges the role of guest for host as he provides an abundance of good wine for the rest of the wedding guests. Jesus's mother's statement to Jesus that "they have no wine" (2:3b) provides Jesus the opportunity to reveal his glory to his disciples (2:11) by transforming the water into "the good wine" (2:10). Up to this point in the narrative, Jesus has been identified by John as the Lamb of God (1:29, 36), the anticipated Messiah (1:41, 45), the Son of God (1:49), and Israel's King (1:49), and Jesus's sign confirms people's belief as he reveals his glory to them (2:11; see 1:14). While Jesus is invited to the wedding as a guest, he takes on the mysterious role of the bridegroom by acting as the true beneficent host of the wedding. This depiction of Jesus as the host of the wedding conforms to John the Baptist's self-presentation as "the friend of the bridegroom, who stands and hears him, rejoices greatly at the bridegroom's voice" (3:29).[19] But Jesus is obviously not any ordinary host, for the presence of the Messiah at the wedding banquet, along with the miraculous provision of good wine, recalls the many prophetic texts that envisage God's harmonious relationship with Israel enacted through the eschatological banquet where wine and food are served in abundance.[20]

> On this mountain the Lord of hosts will make for all peoples a feast of rich food, a feast of well-aged wines, of rich food filled with marrow, of well-aged wines strained clear. (Isa 25:6)
> The time is surely coming, says the Lord, when the one who plows shall overtake the one who reaps, and the treader of grapes the one who sows the seed; the mountains shall drip sweet wine, and all the hills shall flow with it. I will restore the fortunes of my people Israel. (Amos 9:13–14a)
> They shall come and sing aloud on the height of Zion, and they shall be radiant over the goodness of the Lord, over the grain, the wine, and the oil, and over the young of the flock and the herd; their life shall become like a watered garden, and they shall never languish again. Then shall the young women rejoice in the dance, and the young men and the old shall be merry. I will turn their mourning into joy, I will comfort them, and give them gladness for sorrow. (Jer 31:12–13)

The good wine that Jesus the Messiah provides at the wedding banquet, then, symbolizes the joy of God's saving presence with his people through Jesus the bridegroom and host of the messianic banquet (see 3:29).[21] But Jesus's words to his mother—who appears again only in John's Gospel at the cross (19:25–26)—in response to her request for the wine, "My hour has not yet come" (2:4; cf. 7:30; 8:20; 12:23–27; 13:1; 16:32) foreshadow that the good wine and the full revelation of Jesus's glory will only take place at the cross. Jesus has provided the good wine, but the full revelation of his glory is still to come at the cross.[22] Craig Koester says it nicely: "Jesus' messiahship would lead to Golgotha, and his glorification would be accomplished through crucifixion

---

19. Jane S. Webster, *Ingesting Jesus: Eating and Drinking in the Gospel of John*, SBLAB 6 (Atlanta: Society of Biblical Literature, 2003), 39.

20. On marriage and the wedding banquet as a symbol for God's relationship with Israel, see Hosea 2:18–20; Isaiah 54:4–8; Ezekiel 16; Revelation 19:7–9; 22:17.

21. See further Joel 3:18; 2 Bar 29:2–7; T. Levi 8:4–6.

22. J. Ramsey Michaels, *The Gospel of John*, NICNT (Grand Rapids: Eerdmans, 2010), 153.

and resurrection. The divine favor revealed by his gift of wine was a prelude to the gift of his own life."[23]

Jesus's encounter with the Samaritan woman follows this same pattern of stranger transformed into divine host (4:4–42). That is to say, the dramatic tension of John 4 concerns the revelation of Jesus's identity, and the hospitality encounter between Jesus and the woman provides the context for Jesus's unveiling of the fact that he is the Messiah (4:26) and Savior of the world (4:42). Jesus, along with his disciples, "had to go through Samaria" (4:4), and because he was "tired out by his journey" Jesus sat down near Jacob's well (4:6).[24] Jesus is further characterized as a needy guest as he sits down beside the well and asks the Samaritan woman for some water to drink (4:7). But Jesus's request troubles the woman since he is a Jewish man and she is a Samaritan woman and "Jews have no relations with Samaritans" (4:9 [my trans.]).[25] Once again, the custom of hospitality provides the context for the unveiling of Jesus's identity, but now the woman finds that the roles are reversed as Jesus takes on the role of the host: "If you knew the gift of God, and who it is that is saying to you, 'Give me a drink,' you would have asked him, and he would have given you living water" (4:10). The woman does not know either "the gift of God" or the identity of the speaker, and this corresponds to Jesus's description of himself both as *the giver* of the living water and *the gift* itself.[26] The living water that Jesus provides is a gift from God (4:10), quenches humanity's thirst forever (4:10, 14, 15), and becomes "a spring of water gushing up to eternal life" from within those who drink of it (4:14).

Later, within the context of a dispute over Jesus's identity where some think he's a good man and others argue that he is a deceiver (7:14–36), Jesus invites the crowd to come to him for living water:

> "If anyone thirsts, let him come to me and drink. For whoever believes in me, just as the Scriptures have said, rivers of living water will flow out of his belly." And he said this about the Spirit which those who believed in him were about to receive; for the Spirit had not yet been given since Jesus hadn't been glorified. (7:37b–39 [my trans.])

23. Craig R. Koester, *Symbolism in the Fourth Gospel: Meaning, Mystery, Community*, 2nd ed. (Minneapolis: Fortress Press, 2003), 86.

24. See Andrew E. Arterbury, "Breaking the Betrothal Bonds: Hospitality in John 4," *CBQ* 72, no. 1 (January 2010): 63–83, here, 76.

25. On which, see Koester, *Symbolism in the Fourth Gospel*, 187–88.

26. Webster, *Ingesting Jesus*, 57.

Jesus's invitation to drink this living water, coming as it does on the last day of the Feast of Tabernacles (7:37a), portrays Jesus as the fulfillment of the feast. Koester has shown the way in which water was associated with the Feast and how it recalled God's provision of water for Israel in the wilderness (Exod 17:1–6; Num 20:2–13) and anticipated God's eschatological provisions for his people in the future (see, for example, Ezek 47:1; Zech 14:8).[27] This living water presumes confession of the crucified and risen Jesus as the Messiah, given that the living water is identified with the Spirit who enables the confession of the believers. Just as in John 4:10–14, the one who drinks of the living water that Jesus offers will also become a source for the flowing waters.[28]

Returning to John 4, we see that the turn in the conversation between Jesus and the woman indicates that this living water is intimately associated with the revelation of Jesus's identity.[29] The conversation between Jesus and the Samaritan woman centers upon the revelation of his identity as she asks him about whether he is greater than "our father Jacob" (4:12–15), is led to aver that his supernatural knowledge of her life must mean he is a prophet (4:19), and speculates about his relationship to the coming Messiah (4:25–26). The climax of the episode takes place when, in response to her claim about the coming Messiah who will declare all the hidden mysteries, Jesus responds: "I am he, the one who is speaking to you" (*egō eimi, ho lalōn soi*, 4:26). Jesus's words "I am" resonate with the God of Israel's self-designation and reinforce Jesus's divine identity (Exod 3:14; Deut 32:39; Isa. 43:25; 45:18–24; 51:12). God's gift of living water that satisfies one's thirst, then, is the experiential knowledge that Jesus is God's Messiah. Again, Jesus is both the giver of the living water *and* its content. The woman leaves behind her water jar to go into the city and proclaim that she *may* have found the Messiah (4:28–29), with the result that many of the Samaritans believe in Jesus "because of the woman's testimony" (4:39b).[30] The woman's abandonment of the jar "suggests that the water she needed was the revelation that Jesus was the Messiah for whom her people had been waiting."[31] Unlike the inhospitable Samaritans in Luke 9:51–56, here the Samaritans welcome Jesus hospitably for two days (4:40–41) with the result that more Samaritans believe that Jesus is the Mes-

---

27. Koester, *Symbolism in the Fourth Gospel*, 198–99.

28. Webster, *Ingesting Jesus*, 56.

29. Arterbury, "Breaking the Betrothal Bonds," 81.

30. The woman appears to be uncertain as she asks: "Come and see a man who told me everything I did; this is not the Messiah, is it?" (4:29).

31. Koester, *Symbolism in the Fourth Gospel*, 190.

siah (4:42). Whereas earlier the woman did not know about the living water (4:10) and the Samaritan people did not know what they worshipped (4:22), now the Samaritans can claim that "we have heard for ourselves, and we know that this is truly the Savior of the world" (4:42).

We have seen Jesus provide good wine (2:1–11) and living water (4:4–42) to symbolize the revelation of his joyous, life-giving, saving presence with his people, and now in John 6:22–71 Jesus offers the bread of life, which he alone can provide as the means by which he will give resurrection life to those who believe in him. Throughout, this discourse contrasts the physical manna that Moses provided for Israel (Exod 16:20–21) and Jesus's offer of bread of life that will never perish but is "the food that endures for eternal life" (6:27). Jesus's miracle of feeding the five thousand with bread has as its purpose the insight that Jesus is able to nourish those who believe with "the true bread that comes down from heaven" (6:32b [my trans.]). The Israelites who experienced God's provision of bread in the wilderness generation died (6:31; see also Exod 16:4, 15; Ps 78:24), but "the bread of God is that which comes down from heaven *and gives life to the world*" (6:33). The parallel between Moses and Jesus breaks down here, for Jesus is not only the one who gives the bread, he also *is* the bread of life for the world (6:35, 48).[32] Jesus is both the host who provides the bread and the content of the gift he provides.[33] Jesus promises that those who taste of this bread will never hunger again, for their desires will be satisfied with eternal life (6:35), and this is directly related to the revelation of Jesus's identity. Jesus is the "bread that came down from heaven" (6:41; see 6:33, 38, 41, 42, 50, 51, 58), and has been sent by the Father (6:38b, 39). Those who "eat" and "munch" on Jesus's crucified body are insured of the presence of life today and the reality of resurrection life on the last day (6:44, 47–48). God's hospitality is made available through the broken body and shed blood of the Son of Man who has come down from heaven to give his flesh "for the life of the world" (6:51b; see 6:53; 19:34). Ingesting Jesus's crucified body and drinking his blood is the means whereby Jesus shares his resurrection life with his people (6:44–48). As Jane Webster has said: "The act of eating Jesus' flesh and drinking his blood internalizes Jesus so that his flesh and blood become a part of the consumer and the consumer becomes a part of Jesus."[34] Jesus says that those who ingest his body and blood "abide in me and I abide in them" (6:56). Throughout this discourse, Jesus uses the

---

32. Koester, *Symbolism in the Fourth Gospel*, 100.

33. Webster, *Ingesting Jesus*, 78–79.

34. Webster, *Ingesting Jesus*, 83.

metaphors of seeing and believing (6:26, 30, 35, 36, 40, 46, 47) as the way in which people consume the body and blood of the crucified Jesus. In other words, to consume Jesus's body and drink his blood is to believe that this crucified one is the source of resurrection life *and* that the crucified one is God himself. The crowd is offended, for example, because they think they know of Jesus's earthly origins stemming from the family of Joseph, and hence they question: "how can he now say 'I have come down from heaven'?" (6:42). Or again, after some declare Jesus's teaching to be difficult (6:60–61), Jesus asks whether they will also be offended when his divine identity is revealed at the cross and they see "the Son of Man ascending to where he was before" (6:62; see also 3:13–15; 8:28). Brant Pitre has stated the force of John 6:62 clearly: "It is only through the mystery of Jesus' divine identity and divine power that he will be able to give his disciples his body and blood under the form of 'real food' and 'real drink' (John 6:55)."[35] We see again, then, that God's hospitality and life-giving sustenance is mediated through the crucified body of Jesus the *heavenly stranger*.

We have seen that one of the primary ways in which Jesus reveals his divine identity as the crucified one who gives his body for the life of the world is by means of the hospitality symbols of wine, water, and bread. These symbols are theologically fitting for the author of the Fourth Gospel as they are inherently associated with life *and* are used to press the connection between the quality of life *and* eating and drinking together with the Messiah. We have seen that each one of these hospitality symbols is connected to the crucified body of Jesus. Jesus's provision of good wine foreshadows the hour when the glory of God and the glorification of Jesus are revealed at the cross (for example 12:27–36). Jesus's provision of water takes place after Jesus is glorified at the cross and sends forth the Spirit (7:37–39; 19:34; 20:19–23). And the bread of life is explicitly and forcefully associated with Jesus's broken body and shed blood (6:53–58). Thus, God's hospitality that gives life to the world *is* the revelation of Jesus's divine identity in his mission to give life to the world through his death. Jesus's greatest and most subversive act of hospitality, the act that insures that his people will have an eternal home (John 14:1–4), is seen in his washing of his disciples' feet in John 13:1–20.

---

35. Brant Pitre, *Jesus and the Jewish Roots of the Eucharist: Unlocking the Secrets of the Last Supper* (New York: Doubleday, 2011), 111. For an understanding of Jesus's teaching in John 6:22–71 within the context of Jesus's promise to give his flesh to his people to eat in the form of eschatological manna from heaven, see Brant Pitre, *Jesus and the Last Supper* (Grand Rapids: Eerdmans, 2015), 193–250.

The climax of John's depiction of Jesus as the heavenly stranger who mediates God's hospitality takes place on an evening before the Passover when Jesus washes the feet of his disciples before his crucifixion.[36] Jesus's act is situated within the context of his impending death, for the narrator clues us in to the fact that Jesus is about to undergo the second stage of his journey as he returns back to the Father. The context for Jesus's act is the Passover meal, and therefore the meal scene contributes to the emphasis on the fellowship, intimacy, and friendship between Jesus and his disciples.[37] Twice the narrator tells the reader that the heavenly stranger is about to return to the Father: "his hour had come in order that he should leave the world and go back to the Father" (13:1b [my trans.]; see 2:4; 7:6-7, 30; 8:20) and "knowing that the Father had placed all things into his hands and that he had come from God and was journeying back to God" (13:3 [my trans.]). But Jesus's act of washing his disciples' feet is also set within the context of the cross as Jesus's display of love for his disciples: "having loved his own who were in the world, he loved them to the end" (13:1b). This description of Jesus's loving his disciples *to the end* is the narrator's way of telling his readers that Jesus's manner of love is an unimaginably perfect love that he will reveal for his disciples at the cross where he will declare "it is finished" (*tetelestai*, 19:30).[38] At the supper, Jesus "takes off" his outer garment and "takes up" his towel and wraps it around himself (13:4). The language of *taking off* and *taking up* is reminiscent of the language Jesus has used earlier to describe his death and resurrection: "For this reason the Father loves me, because I lay down [i.e., take off] my life in order to take it up again" (10:17; see 10:11, 15, 18).[39] Jesus's washing of his disciples' feet is "thus an extension of his action as the Good Shepherd, who lays down his life for the sheep (10:17–18), and ties in with the love command he will offer shortly."[40] Thus, even the lan-

---

36. On the importance of Jesus's act as occurring within the context of a meal scene, see Webster, *Ingesting Jesus*, 103–5.

37. On the meal scene as the context for the creation of friendship between Jesus and the disciples, see Martin M. Culy, *Echoes of Friendship in the Gospel of John*, NTMon 30 (Sheffield: Sheffield Phoenix Press, 2010), 142.

38. Koester, *Symbolism in the Fourth Gospel*, 132; Francis J. Moloney, *Love in the Gospel of John: An Exegetical, Theological, and Literary Study* (Grand Rapids: Baker, 2013), 105; Webster, *Ingesting Jesus*, 107.

39. The same term is used to describe Peter's willingness to lay down his own life (13:37–38).

40. Jason S. Sturdevant, "The Centrality of Discipleship in the Johannine Portrayal of Peter," in *Peter in Early Christianity*, ed. Helen K. Bond and Larry W. Hurtado (Grand Rapids: Eerdmans, 2015), 109–20, here, 113.

guage the narrator uses to describe Jesus's assuming the role of servant-host reminds the attentive reader of Jesus's impending death on the cross where he voluntarily lays down his own life for his people.

Arland Hultgren has rightly referred to Jesus's act of washing his disciples' feet as "a symbolic act of eschatological hospitality."[41] That is to say, the act symbolizes the love that Jesus will display for his disciples at the cross whereby the disciples will be fully transformed into God's friends and family. Both Jewish and Greco-Roman texts frequently speak of the provision of water for the washing of feet as a constituent component of the host's responsibility for caring for guests (Gen 18:4; 19:2; 24:32; 43:24; Judg 19:21; 1 Sam 25:41; Homer, *Odyssey* 19.308–319; 1 Timothy 5:10).[42] Richard Bauckham states the importance of footwashing clearly: "Footwashing appears in the literature most often as preparation for a meal, and also as a duty of hospitality, either to expected guests or to passing strangers, who needed both to be refreshed after their journey and to be properly prepared for sharing a meal with the host."[43] But rarely does one find a depiction of the host, unless it is actually a slave or servant, doing the actual washing of the feet of the guests as Jesus does when he assumes the form of a servant-host and washes the feet of his disciples (13:4–5).[44] Jesus's taking on the role of servant-host and thereby voluntarily lowering himself is obviously surprising and offensive to Peter who, from one vantage point, rightly understands that this is "an astonishing breach of social convention" since a student is not greater than his teacher or a slave greater than his master (13:16).[45] Peter will have to accept Jesus's voluntarily enacting the service of a slave if he will embrace the saving death of Jesus who will die the death of a slave on the cross.[46] But Jesus's washing of his disciples' feet is the proleptic sign of divine hospitality that Jesus will enact at the cross, and this event is

---

41. Arland J. Hultgren, "The Johannine Footwashing (13.1–11) as Symbol of Eschatological Hospitality," *NTS* 28, no. 4 (October 1982): 539–46.

42. John Christopher Thomas, *Footwashing in John 13 and the Johannine Community*, JSNTSup 61 (Sheffield: JSOT Press, 1991), 35–40, 46–50; Hultgren, "The Johannine Footwashing (13.1–11) as Symbol of Eschatological Hospitality," 541–42.

43. Richard Bauckham, *The Testimony of the Beloved Disciple: Narrative, History, and Theology in the Gospel of John* (Grand Rapids: Baker, 2007), 192.

44. See Ruth B. Edwards, "The Christological Basis of the Johannine Footwashing," in *Jesus of Nazareth: Lord and Christ: Essays on the Historical Jesus and New Testament Christology*, ed. Joel B. Green and Max Turner (Grand Rapids: Eerdmans, 1994), 367–83, here, 368.

45. Koester, *Symbolism in the Fourth Gospel*, 130.

46. Bauckham, *The Testimony of the Beloved Disciple*, 194.

soteriologically necessary for the disciples, for Jesus tells them "unless you are washed you have no share with me" (13:8b [my trans.]).[47]

This statement is of one accord with Jesus's other *unless* statements that present a necessary qualification for salvation: unless you are born from above (3:3-5), unless you eat the flesh of the Son of Man (6:53), unless you believe that I Am (8:24). Thus, Jesus's enactment of loving hospitality at the meal is the necessary symbol of Jesus's love at the cross that will result in their cleansing and purification. And having a share in Jesus's identity and destiny presumably indicates that Jesus's disciples will follow Jesus in his journey back to his heavenly Father (see 13:1-2; 14:1-4).[48] The similarities with the transformative ritual of Christian baptism are obvious (esp. 3:3-5; see also 1 Cor 6:11; Eph 5:26; Heb 10:22).[49] Further, Jesus is clear that the washing of their feet needs to happen only once (13:10), and is thus a transformative ritual that moves the disciples to a state of purification and cleanness (13:10-11). Thus, Jesus's washing of his disciples' feet is not merely a remarkable display of service and humility, but also foreshadows the incredible love whereby he saves his people by voluntarily embracing the cross and revealing his divine identity in his journey back to the Father. Remarkably, Jesus declares that while they do not understand what he is doing now, later at the cross ("when *it* happens") the disciples "will believe that I Am [*hoti egō eimi*]" (13:19b). The divine identity of Jesus is revealed in Jesus's washing of his disciples' feet, the act that symbolizes his unimaginable love on the cross for his people. As Moloney states: "In these gestures of loving self-gift, anticipating the cross, Jesus makes known the love of God."[50] In fact, the Gospel of John bears out the notion that Jesus and the Father are depicted as friends as a result of the unity, intimacy, and love that are shared between Father and Son (1:18; 3:35; 5:20; 10:17; 14:31; 17:1-2, 6-11, 24). Love, trust, and making known secret knowledge about the identity of God—all of these virtues resonate with ancient (and modern) notions of friendship. And John is clear that the Son's relationship with the Father is the foundation for Jesus's extension of friendship to his disciples.[51]

Jesus's act of hospitality cleanses his disciples so that they are able to

---

47. Moloney, *Love in the Gospel of John*, 106.

48. Webster, *Ingesting Jesus*, 111-12. More broadly, see G. C. Nicholson, *Death as Departure: The Johannine Descent-Ascent Schema* (Chico: Scholars Press, 1983).

49. Thomas, *Footwashing in John 13 and the Johannine Community*, 97-106; Andrew B. McGowan, *Ancient Christian Worship: Early Church Practices in Social, Historical, and Theological Perspective* (Grand Rapids: Baker, 2014), 175-82.

50. Moloney, *Love in the Gospel of John*, 109.

51. Culy, *Echoes of Friendship in the Gospel of John*, 129.

be welcomed into the house of Jesus's father (14:2).[52] As Mary Coloe has said, "The gesture of welcome in the washing of feet points ahead . . . to the crucifixion as the creation of God's household."[53] Jesus is the agent of the Father's gracious hospitality whose loving act of washing enables the disciples to follow in Jesus's trajectory. Jesus's journey back to his Father, in fact, is for the purpose of preparing dwelling places in the Father's mansion for his disciples to reside (14:3). Jesus's act of washing his disciples' feet is a "sacrament of friendship" as it is the basis for Jesus's statement "you are my friends" (15:14).[54] Jesus has laid down his life for his friends. Jesus has shared all things with his disciples. He has made known all of the secrets of the Father as he revealed the identity of God to them in full: "I said you are friends, because everything that I have heard from the Father I have made known to you" (15:15). Ambrose, bishop of Milan, in the latter part of the fourth century, said this about Jesus's friendship with his disciples: "Therefore a friend hides nothing, if he is true: he pours forth his mind, just as the Lord Jesus poured forth the mysteries of his Father."[55]

Jesus's washing of his disciples' feet is not only a soteriological act, but it also defines the mission of Jesus's disciples. The disciples' call is to *participate in, to share in* this love and mediate it to the world. Just as they have experienced the loving hospitality of Jesus the servant-host, so Jesus declares: "I have given to you an example, that just as I have done for you so you also may do" (13:15 [my trans.]). This explains Jesus's cryptic comments about a student not being greater than his teacher and a slave not greater than his master (13:13, 16). If Jesus has humbled himself to display sacrificial loving service to his disciples, then the disciples also must follow his example by "washing the feet of one another" (13:14b). This is the means whereby the rest of the world will continue to see the revelation of Jesus's divine identity (13:19). Later Jesus will declare that his act of love is the basis for a new kind of friendship between himself and his disciples. The greatest act of love imaginable is the love of a friend who gives his life for the sake of his friends, and since Jesus is about to enact this love for his disciples he is able to say: "you

---

52. Hultgren, "The Johannine Footwashing (13.1–11) as Symbol of Eschatological Hospitality," 542.

53. Mary L. Coloe, "Welcome into the Household of God: The Foot Washing in John 13," *CBQ* 66, no. 3 (July 2004): 400–415, here, 414–15. Though I do not think Jesus's act should be interpreted as one of his signs.

54. Gail R. O'Day, "I Have Called You Friends," *Christian Reflection* (2008): 20–27, here, 25–26.

55. Ambrose, *On the Duties of Ministers*, 3.22.135.

are my friends if you do what I command you" (15:14). The command or stipulation is that they prove themselves friends of Jesus by continuing to "love one another as I have loved you" (15:12). Friendship is rooted in the divine love and friendship shared between Jesus and the Father ("as the Father has loved me, so I have loved you," 15:9), and now Jesus's disciples are included with this friendship.[56] Gail O'Day says it well: "Jesus has been the ultimate friend—he gave his life in love for us. Now it is our turn to be Jesus's friend, which means that we love one another as he has loved us."[57] The mission of the church is set in motion by love that is displayed by Jesus at the cross, the love that transforms slaves into friends of God, the act of love that reveals the very identity of God. As the disciples continue to love as Jesus has loved, they make known the presence of God to the world.

The Meaning of Human Existence and the Mission of the Church

The mission of the church is to participate in God's hospitality whereby Jesus extends life and redemption to humans who are alienated from God and each other. We have seen that in the Fourth Gospel, Jesus's mission is to make God known by offering God's hospitality to humans so that they might have life. This is one of the fundamental themes of the Gospel of John, namely, the Father's plan to give life to humanity through Jesus. God's mission is stranger-centered theology as Jesus, the heavenly stranger, leaves his home and journeys to earth in order to make his home and live among humans who are alienated from God and life.[58] Jesus intentionally enters into a variety of hospitality scenarios—as a guest at a wedding, as a Jewish stranger initiating conversation with a Samaritan woman drawing water at a well, as the host who satisfies the hunger of the great crowd with bread and fish, and subversively by taking the form of a slave and washing the feet of his disciples—in order to share God's hospitality with hungry and thirsty humans. Smith again states this well when he notes that the "incarnational

56. John T. Fitzgerald, "Christian Friendship: John, Paul, and the Philippians," *Interpretation* 61, no. 3 (July 2007): 284–96, here, 284–86.

57. O'Day, "I Have Called You Friends," 24. Also see Jürgen Moltmann, "Open Friendship: Aristotelian and Christian Concepts of Friendship," in *The Changing Face of Friendship*, ed. Leroy S. Rouner (Notre Dame, IN: University of Notre Dame Press, 1994), 35.

58. So Amos Yong, *Hospitality and the Other: Pentecost, Christian Practices, and the Neighbor* (Maryknoll, NY: Orbis, 2008), 131. See also Dean Fleming, *Why Mission? Reframing New Testament Theology* (Nashville: Abingdon, 2015), 69–70.

impulse to provoke our response is continued in his body in the tangible ways he nurses and nourishes our faith, giving us bread, wine, and water along the way."[59] The sharing of the tangible hospitality elements creates the possibility for strangers to eat, drink, and enter into the space whereby they might encounter true life. The elements of hospitality that Jesus offers to humans—wine, water, bread, home, and friendship—are tangible and necessary components of human life. No one has life apart from food, drink, home, and friendship. But the hospitality of God that Jesus provides satisfies humanity's deeper craving for transcendence and ultimate meaning—for life with God. When we experience God's hospitality, the "insatiability of human desire is absorbed by the abundance of God's grace in the consumption of Jesus' body and blood."[60] Experiencing God's hospitality certainly includes *knowledge about* God, but John's vision of God's hospitality presses the audience to an experiential, relational knowing of God and the Son as living persons. This is why John speaks of God's hospitality as mediated through the life-giving, experiential realities that all of humanity craves and needs in order to flourish: water, wine, bread, home, and friendship.[61]

The Gospel of John suggests that one way to conceptualize the church's mission is by inviting others into experiencing God's hospitality just as Jesus enters into hospitality scenarios and provides the opportunities for evangelism whereby people may experience life through almost every element of hospitality practices. In other words, if we have experienced the wine, the living water, the bread, and friendship with Jesus as the life-giving saving presence of Jesus, then perhaps Jesus is calling us to think about how we might share divine hospitality with those who long for life by inviting them to experience wine as the new covenant wine, bread as the bread of life, water as the living water, service as the service of the host who would give his own life, and home as an anticipation of our heavenly home. Those who have experienced the hospitality of God through Jesus are then transformed into agents of God's hospitality who share this hospitality with others who are searching for life. We have seen this clearly already in John 13 where Jesus washes the feet of the disciples as an "example" for the disciples who, as his emissaries, extend God's hospitality to others by following Jesus's pattern of

---

59. Smith, *You Are What You Love*, 112.

60. William T. Cavanaugh, *Being Consumed: Economics and Christian Desire* (Grand Rapids: Eerdmans, 2008), 54.

61. The frequency with which John's Gospel uses the five senses to express humanity's experience of the Incarnation is impressive. See Dorothy Lee, "The Gospel of John and the Five Senses," *JBL* 129, no. 1 (Spring 2010): 115–27.

sacrificial love (13:20). We have seen that John uses this act to portray the ritual transformation of the disciples from slaves and students into friends. And this friendship with Jesus enables the disciples to extend friendship to others.[62] This is stated clearly by Christine Pohl and Christopher Heuertz: "Jesus offers us friendship, and that gift shapes a surprisingly subversive missional paradigm. A grateful response to God's gift of friendship involves offering that same gift to others—whether family or strangers, coworkers or children who live on the street."[63] The writings of Jean Vanier and the ministry of L'Arche – a worldwide ministry of residential communities where both the developmentally disabled and their caregivers live together as friends in community – testify to the way in which Jesus' love and gift of friendship creates a *community of friends* who are bound together in a covenant of unconditional love, service, and friendship.[64] In the communities of L'Arche, men and women who have come from "asylums, psychiatric hospitals and other situations of rejection and total abandonment . . . [experience the movement from] death to resurrection, from anguish to trust, from loneliness to community, from despair to hope." Likewise, the assistants experience life and joy through the discovery of love, friendship, and their own vulnerabilities and needs in relationship with the weak, wounded, and vulnerable.[65] This vision of place, friendship, mutuality, and service that is embodied in residential communities all over the world is rooted in the belief that Jesus's gift of friendship and love creates new and surprising forms of friendship between those who would otherwise be alienated from one another.[66]

One of the consistent themes of John 13–17 is that the church shares in the mission of the Son.[67] And if the Son has shared the saving knowledge of God that results in life by means of the hospitality elements, then we should trust that hospitality relationships with others, a friendship witnessed to in the L'Arche communities, is a faithful and fruitful way of sharing God's

---

62. O'Day, "I Have Called You Friends," 26.

63. Christopher L. Heuertz and Christine D. Pohl, *Friendship at the Margins: Discovering Mutuality in Service and Mission* (Downers Grove, IL: InterVarsity Press, 2010), 30.

64. On the importance of John 13–15 for L'Arche, see Jean Vanier, *The Scandal of Service: Jesus Washes Our Feet*, L'Arche Collections (Toronto: Novalis, 1998).

65. This theme permeates Vanier's writings, but see here, Jean Vanier, *An Ark for the Poor: The Story of L'Arche* (Toronto: Novalis, 1995), 109.

66. Vanier, *Community and Growth*, 93–95.

67. See here especially Andreas J. Köstenberger, *The Missions of Jesus and the Disciples according to the Fourth Gospel: With Implications for the Fourth Gospel's Purpose and the Mission of the Contemporary Church* (Grand Rapids: Eerdmans, 1998).

saving presence with others. Those who have experienced God's hospitality are invited by John's Gospel to look for those with whom we can share meals and hospitality encounters, invite them to share in our lives as those who have encountered God's hospitality, be attentive to ways in which we might explain the true meaning of bread, wine, water, home, and service—that others will encounter God's saving hospitality. In other words, the Gospel of John encourages a form of missional hospitality whereby we open up our lives and homes *as well as* our worship, ecclesial spaces, and liturgy for the purpose of extending God's life-giving hospitality to outsiders.[68] It is through the church's worship, liturgy, and sacraments that "we learn that our highest possible excellence is a life of being loved by God and loving God, a life of seeking God's good and delighting in God's beauty just as God seeks our good and delights in us."[69] It is also a place where we can learn friendship. We have seen that the early church in Acts was committed to a form of evangelistic hospitality where it was through the church's devotion to the teaching of the apostles and the breaking of bread that God added new believers to the church's number each day (Acts 2:42–47). Paul Wadell has suggested that the goal of Christian friendship is to create a space where worshippers of God embody and proclaim God's kingdom and thereby continue the mission of God.[70]

If the church is the place where the bread of life, the living water, and divine friendship are now experienced, then those committed to evangelistic hospitality will seek to extend these life-giving realities through opening up our spaces of worship to visitors and outsiders.[71] The church is the community that has both experienced the life-giving, transformative, revelatory presence of Christ *and* been commissioned by the risen Jesus to continue his mission of making the Triune God known to the world. The church is where our habits, desires, longings, and knowledge are reshaped toward the Triune God who has life in himself.[72] Despite its brokenness and imperfections, then, the church should expect that Christ's hospitality is manifested in its public life of worship–the music, confession, communion, the proclaimed word–and should therefore look for ways in which the church's public life

---

68. See here especially Patrick R. Keifert, *Welcoming the Stranger: A Public Theology of Worship and Evangelism* (Minneapolis: Fortress, 1992); Robert E. Webber, *Celebrating Our Faith: Evangelism through Worship* (San Francisco: Harper and Row, 1986).

69. Wadell, *Becoming Friends*, 27.

70. Wadell, *Becoming Friends*, 15–37.

71. Yong, *Hospitality and the Other*, 134–38.

72. See here Smith, *You Are What You Love*, 57–81.

reveals God's hospitality to non-Christians. If being human means, in part, that we are longing, loving, desiring creatures who are in search of life, then John's Gospel calls us to the belief that it is in the public life of the church—its rituals, liturgy, and word—where our desires are turned away from the false promises of life and joy in consumerism, entertainment and leisure, or wealth and are instead reordered toward the true life that is found only in God's hospitality and friendship.[73]

Study Questions

1. Toward what are your desires ordered? What brings you meaning, joy, and satisfaction?

2. If you successfully and fully attained whatever it is that you most deeply desire, do you think it would truly make you happy? Explain why or why not.

3. What is the meaning and purpose of human life according to John's Gospel?

4. Why does Jesus use tangible and physical elements like bread, water, wine, friendship, and home to reveal his identity?

5. If one of the purposes of the Gospel of John was mission and evangelism (John 20:30–31), then how might the Gospel encourage us to engage in evangelistic hospitality?

73. On worship reordering our desires, see Mark Labberton, *The Dangerous Act of Worship: Living God's Call to Justice* (Downers Grove, IL: InterVarsity Press, 2012), 37–40.

PART TWO

Human Hospitality

CHAPTER 4

Hospitality and the World: Overcoming Tribalism

One danger in practicing hospitality that some of you may have experienced or even objected to in my arguments up to this point is the false belief that we are the hosts and others are merely guests. In other words, for those with a sense of power and privilege, we may be tempted to feel as though others are always the beneficiaries of our hospitality, and this can allow us to retain a false sense of superiority. Amy Oden describes this danger clearly: "The feeling of pity and the desire to better the lives of others is a good thing, often inspired by God in one's heart. But it is seductive, even dangerous, for the host to view herself as the helper. The would-be act of hospitality becomes an act of condescension and failure to see, either one's own need or the true identity of the stranger as Christ."[1] But the Bible frequently indicates that God's people are not only hosts but also guests—sometimes guests of one another and always guests of God. Both this chapter and the next will explore how the Scriptures mandate that God's people embody the role of a good guest, as both one who learns, receives, and condescends in the presence of strangers *and* one who is constantly dependent upon the hospitality of God as God's guest.

In surveying the religious dynamics at work in the world today, Martin Marty suggests that "the conflict of faith communities who regard each other as monstrous has become the most volatile and often militant spiritual, or anti-spiritual, eruption in the world. Around the globe people gather into convulsive movements in which they define themselves over against others,

---

1. Amy G. Oden, *And You Welcomed Me: A Sourcebook on Hospitality in Early Christianity* (Nashville: Abingdon, 2001), 109.

usually in the name of God."[2] Frequently the religious other is viewed as undermining one's culture and society, as a threat to one's religious allegiances and values, and often as a potential agent of violence. In fact, we are often told that intense religious devotion is causally connected to wars, violent extremism, and global terrorism.[3] And distinct religious communities face very real difficulties in navigating how to relate to one another. Religious commitments are often (at least in part) responsible for many of the world's civil and external wars.[4] Whether we think of Israel and Egypt, early Christianity and imperial Rome, or Christians and Muslims during the Crusades, the conflicts and threats faith communities have posed to one another are notoriously widespread. Thus, the challenge of loving, engaging in friendships, and showing hospitality to the religious other is, perhaps, one of the most daunting situations facing Christians today. Can Christians engage in real friendships with adherents of other religions? Do Christians have anything beneficial to offer our broader society and world? These questions depend on an even more fundamental set of questions: *should* Christians even pursue intentional friendships with people of other faiths? Similarly, are Christians and churches called to benefit and serve the world at large? Do the Scriptures encourage Christians to draw limits and boundaries with respect to their offer of hospitality and friendship when it comes to the secular world or the religious other?

The New Testament authors frequently encourage Christians to do good to outsiders, to refrain from retaliation, to pursue peace, and to have a good reputation before all people (for example, Luke 6:27–36; Rom 12:14–13:7; 1 Cor 10:32; Gal 6:10; 1 Thess 3:12; 5:15; 1 Pet. 2:12; 3:13–17). The frequent refrain, found especially in Paul, to *do good to all people* would seem to presume that all people have *some level* of shared ground or common values over right and wrong, good and bad. But one of the challenges and potential barriers to engaging in meaningful friendships with religious others is mutually incompatible beliefs, especially with respect to the person of Jesus. From its very beginnings, the Christian faith has been charged with accusations of intolerance and exclusion. Any form of religious pluralism would seem to be strictly prohibited by the exclusive claim "Jesus is Lord" (Rom

2. Martin E. Marty, *When Faiths Collide*, Blackwell Manifestos (Malden, MA: Blackwell, 2005), 6.

3. See, however, William T. Cavanaugh, *The Myth of Religious Violence* (New York: Oxford University Press, 2009).

4. See here Philip Jenkins, *The Next Christendom: The Coming of Global Christianity* (Oxford: Oxford University Press, 2002), 163–90.

10:9–10; 1 Cor 8:4–6), and Jesus's statement that "I am the way, and the truth, and the life. No one comes to the Father except through me" (John 14:6). The Acts of the Apostles tells the story of the Christian encounter with the religious other in such a way as to highlight the conflict and sometimes even violence that occurs when the early Christian characters proclaim Jesus is Lord or challenge pagan belief about the gods (Acts 12:20–23; 14:8–18; 16:16–18; 19:1–40).[5] Additionally, the persecution experienced by the recipients of Peter's first letter is unsurprising, given that they view themselves as having been ransomed "out of the worthless way of life inherited from your ancestors" (1 Pet 1:18 [my trans.]; see also 1:6; 4:1–4). Peter's reference to the Gentiles' former way of life in pagan religion as "worthless" no doubt accurately reflects the exclusive contrast the early Christians saw between those in Christ and everyone else (see, for instance, 1 Cor 6:9–11; Eph 2:1–3, 12; Col 3:5–8), but the description is no less harsh for the way it portrays those who remained committed to their ancestral customs and religion.[6] The early Christians read a Greek translation of Psalm 96:5 (LXX 95:5) that claimed that "the gods of the nations are *demons*" (the Hebrew has "idols"), and as Luke Johnson has shown, this effectively placed "all pagan religion neatly into the realm of the demonic."[7] The translation almost certainly influenced Paul who, in 1 Corinthians 10:19–21, regards pagan sacrifices as offered to demons.

Our exclusive allegiance to Christ and confession of him as the full revelation of God are commitments that must not be compromised or watered down. But does confession of Jesus alone as Lord necessarily lead, then, to tribalism, to "religious tribalism," to a form of hostile rejection of non-Christians?[8] Is it actually possible to do good to all people when we have such different visions of ultimate reality? Is it appropriate to engage in meaningful *friendships* with those outside of the Christian faith, perhaps even sharing intimate forms of hospitality and table-fellowship with one another? If so, how do we engage in deep friendships *and* simultaneously

5. See here Susan Garrett, *The Demise of the Devil: Magic and the Demonic in Luke's Writings* (Minneapolis: Fortress Press, 1989).

6. On the importance of the distinction between Paul's churches and outsiders and its use in his ethical exhortations, see David G. Horrell, *Solidarity and Difference: A Contemporary Reading of Paul's Ethics*, 2nd ed. (London: Bloomsbury T&T Clark, 2016), 147–82.

7. Luke Timothy Johnson, *Among the Gentiles: Greco-Roman Religion and Christianity*, ABRL (New Haven: Yale University Press, 2009), 2.

8. On which see Martin E. Marty, *The Public Church: Mainline-Evangelical-Catholic* (New York: Crossroad, 1981).

navigate our different religious commitments and values? Are friendships with the religious other only an opportunity for covert evangelism?

Amos Yong has argued that "the Christian mission is nothing more or less than our participation in the hospitality of God."[9] By this, Yong means that God's mission embodies the hospitality of God such that God sends his Son as a stranger to reconcile enemies and strangers to himself. As a result, Christians embody this "divine hospitality that loves strangers" even "to the point of giving up our lives on behalf of others as to be reconciled to them, that they might in turn be reconciled to God."[10] We have seen that in the Gospel of John, Jesus's mission is to make God known to lost, hungry, and thirsty people by extending divine hospitality to them so that they might have life. And in the Gospel of Luke, we have seen that Jesus shares meals with sinners, outcasts, and the marginalized as a means of welcoming them into God's kingdom. So too, I suggest, we have a portrait of Paul who intentionally enters into the role of the guest of religious others as a means of embodying and extending God's hospitality to religious others. In this chapter, I take as my starting point two texts, one from the Acts of the Apostles and one from Paul's first letter to the church in Corinth. These two texts, among others, I believe, encourage the Christian to enter into the role of *guest with non-Christians* and thereby call for friendship, relational engagement, and mission with those who do not share our Christian faith. The New Testament encourages Christians to pursue meaningful friendships and beneficial other-regarding relationships with the religious other *for their own sake* as well as with *the hope that they will encounter the life-giving presence of Jesus*. While I am not equipped to make proposals for how to eradicate inter-religious strife, I do suggest that the Christian is called to engage in the risky, difficult, *and rewarding* task of both showing hospitality to *and receiving hospitality from* the religious other.

Friendship and Hospitality with Religious Others in Acts 27–28

Three distinct interactions between Paul and Gentile characters provide a window into the impression of Paul that Luke wishes to leave his readers.[11]

9. Amos Yong, *Hospitality and the Other: Pentecost, Christian Practices, and the Neighbor* (Maryknoll, NY: Orbis, 2008), 131.

10. Yong, *Hospitality and the Other*, 131.

11. For this section of my argument I have adapted a portion of an earlier argument from "Philanthropy, Hospitality, and Friendship," *Christian Reflection* (2015): 65–72, here, 67–71. I

The character portrait of Paul, within which Luke concludes his work, is of one who benefits the religious other, who engages in friendship and meaningful relationships with non-Christians, and who not only extends but also receives hospitality from non-Christians.

The first named character Paul encounters when he is taken on board the ship traveling to Rome is "Julius a Roman centurion of the Augustan Cohort" (27:1 [my trans.]). Mention of a Roman military figure entrusted with transporting prisoners *may have* activated the stereotypes of the brave soldier and faithful citizen, but nearer at hand may have been the stereotypes of the Roman soldier as violent, brutish, and willing to use force to keep the prisoners in order—as the soldiers are, for example, more than ready to suggest the use of violence in order to prevent the prisoners from escaping when the ship wrecks (27:42; see also Luke 23:11).[12] But Luke's characterization of the centurion is anything but violent. In fact, it is instead glowingly positive. To be sure, Luke says, "Julius showed philanthropy to Paul by allowing him to be cared for by his friends" (27:3 [my trans.]). Not violent, brutish, or greedy, the military man embodies the prized virtue of *philanthropia*. Philanthropy—often translated as kindness, love for humanity, or generosity —was considered to be one of the premier Hellenistic virtues and was often associated with the making and maintenance of friendships through acts of mercy, kindness, hospitality, and clemency. To show philanthropy was the mark of the educated, virtuous, and civilized person such that the term was often applied to rulers who showed philanthropy through the provision of benefactions to their subjects.[13] Later the centurion shows more kindness to Paul when he saves Paul's life by disrupting the plan of the soldiers who want to kill all the prisoners when the ship wrecks on Malta (27:43). The motivation for the centurion's kindness to Paul is left unexplained, and yet this account of a military man's philanthropy toward Paul the vulnerable prisoner "unsettle[s] the authorial audience's expectations" as it casts this Gentile man as favorable to Paul and as showing acts of mercy toward the vulnerable.[14]

---

have provided a detailed discussion of what follows in Joshua W. Jipp, *Divine Visitations and Hospitality to Strangers: An Interpretation of the Malta Episode in Acts 28:1–10*, NovTSup 153 (Leiden: Brill, 2013).

12. On stereotypes of soldiers and their relevance for understanding Luke's positive depictions of the Roman centurions, see Laurie Brink, *Soldiers in Luke-Acts: Engaging, Contradicting, and Transcending the Stereotypes*, WUNT 2.362 (Tübingen: Mohr-Siebeck, 2014).

13. See further Mikeal C. Parsons, *Acts*, PCNT (Grand Rapids: Baker Academic Press, 2008), 367–70.

14. Brink, *Soldiers in Luke-Acts*, 124.

Paul is not only *a recipient* of philanthropic kindness from Julius, but he is also a prophetic agent from God who secures the salvation of all of his shipmates. On three occasions, Luke portrays Paul as offering prophecies, exhortations, and encouragements that provide safety to those on board the ship. He frequently warns the leaders of the ship to refrain from immediate continuation of the journey due to the dangerous sailing conditions (27:9–11), and his prophecy comes to fruition when the typhoon threatens to destroy the ship (27:18–20). Later, after "all hope of our being saved was at last abandoned" (27:20), Paul receives a message from God's angel that God will see to it that Paul makes it safely to Rome *and* that God also "will freely give to [Paul] all those sailing with you" (27:24b [my trans.]). Paul is God's prophetic instrument for the salvation of his shipmates, and, as God's prophet, Paul encourages everyone on board with the angel's message (27:25–26). When some of the ship's crew try to escape due to fear that the ship would break apart against the rocks, Paul is able to advise the centurion to keep the soldiers on board: "unless these men stay in the ship, you cannot be saved" (27:31). As Richard Pervo notes: "Paul is the cause of their deliverance and thus their savior."[15] On six occasions Luke uses forms of "to save" in order to refer to the salvation or safety of the shipmates and Paul (27:20, 31, 34, 43, 44; 28:1),[16] and given that one of Luke's primary themes is God's salvation for all people it may be that Luke intends the reader to view God's rescue of the crew through Paul as a metaphor for the salvation of the Gentiles.[17]

Paul initiates a meal with his shipmates and takes the lead as host (27:33–38), thereby mediating salvation for his shipmates in a striking manner. Twice Paul exhorts everyone to "share in the nourishment" of the meal together (27:33, 34). Paul's actions whereby "he took bread; and giving thanks to God in the presence of all, he broke it and began to eat" (27:35) clearly mimic Jesus's sharing of meals with all people in the Gospel of Luke (see, for example, Luke 9:11–17; 22:14–27; 24:28–35). Just as Jesus's meals were marked by their inclusive character, so is the meal between Paul and his shipmates characterized by the involvement of "everyone" on board the ship (see 27:33, 35, 36, and 37). Luke is clear about the purpose of this meal: "it exists for your salvation" (27:34b [my trans.]). The meal literally does give salvation in that it

---

15. Richard I. Pervo, *Acts*, Hermeneia (Minneapolis: Fortress Press, 2009), 662.

16. See here the fine article by Susan M. Praeder, "Acts 27:1–28:16: Sea Voyages in Ancient Literature and the Theology of Luke-Acts," *CBQ* 46, no. 4 (October 1984): 683–706.

17. On salvation in Luke-Acts, see Luke 1:47, 69, 71; 2:11; 2:30; 3:4–6; 6:9; 7:50; 8:12, 36, 48, 50; Acts 2:21, 40, 47; 4:9, 12; 11:14; 13:47; 14:9; 15:1, 11; 16:30, 31; 28:28.

provides the hungry crew with the needed strength to endure the impending loss of their ship, but Luke may intend his readers to view the meal as mediating divine salvation whereby the prisoners are saved by sharing in divine hospitality. The echoes of Jesus's table-fellowship with sinners in the Gospel of Luke, the reference to "all 276 souls on the ship" (27:37)—which reminds the reader of earlier scenes where Luke had recounted the number of "souls" saved (2:41; 4:4)—as well as the repeated references to salvation throughout the sea-voyage all suggest that "Paul allows the Gentiles to taste God's salvation through his extension of hospitality, and thereby Luke symbolically portrays the Gentiles as being incorporated into God's people."[18]

Paul's prophecy is fulfilled as the ship breaks apart and the crew lands on Malta (27:26; 27:44–28:1). Paul's interaction with non-Jewish peoples continues in Acts 28:1–10 where he receives another remarkable display of philanthropy and hospitality from the Maltese islanders. Paul is a total stranger to the Maltese, and so this is a potentially dangerous situation. Luke refers to the Maltese as "barbarians" (28:2, 4) and thereby activates widespread cultural connotations that associated barbarians with *inhospitality* toward shipwrecked strangers. Odysseus, for example, when encountering a new land and people in his voyages often spoke the phrase: "Alas, to the land of what mortals have I now come? Are they insolent, wild, and unjust? Or are they hospitable to strangers and fear the gods in their thoughts?" (Homer, *Odyssey*, 6.119–121).[19] Luke activates an impending *in*hospitality scenario, however, only to overturn it—"the barbarians showed us no small philanthropy" through their provision of a fire to keep the prisoners warm (28:2). Further, their kindness to the prisoners is, according to prominent Hellenistic moralists, the height of virtue since shipwrecked strangers have no means to reciprocate for hospitality received. Once again, the philanthropy of the barbarians toward the needy and vulnerable demonstrates that the Maltese belong to the same Lukan exemplars of hospitality as Zacchaeus (Luke 19:1–10), Cornelius (Acts 10:1–11:18), and Lydia (Acts 16:11–15).[20]

After Paul's triumphal incident with the viper reveals that he is no ordinary prisoner but rather bears the powerful presence of God (28:3–6), Publius (the first man of Malta) wisely shows hospitality to Paul and his com-

18. Jipp, *Divine Visitations and Hospitality to Strangers*, 256.

19. For further examples, see Jipp, *Divine Visitations and Hospitality to Strangers*, 39–44, 257–59.

20. For a wealth of rich information on hospitality in Luke-Acts and the broader ancient Mediterranean world, see Andrew Arterbury, *Entertaining Angels: Early Christian Hospitality in Its Mediterranean Setting*, NTMon 8 (Sheffield: Sheffield Phoenix Press, 2005).

panions: "he welcomed us and for three days extended friendly hospitality to us" (28:7b [my trans.]). This display of hospitality and friendship to Paul elicits Paul's reciprocation of the gifts of Jesus-like healing of Publius's father (28:8) and the healing of all the sick on the island (28:9). Luke's narration of these healings recalls Jesus's healing of Peter's mother-in-law (Luke 4:39) and his initial healing ministry in Capernaum (Luke 4:40–41) and suggests that Jesus's ministry is continuing to spread to the ends of the earth.

The episode concludes with the Maltese cementing their relationship with Paul: "they bestowed many honors on us, and when we were about to sail, they put on board all the provisions we needed" (28:10). The Maltese "barbarians" are anything but uncivilized or ignorant of the ways of hospitality towards strangers, for they reflect the attributes of ideal hosts by providing a safe conveyance for the next stage of their guests' journey. Luke may, in fact, intend for his readers to view the Maltese as eliciting a formalized guest-friendship with Paul through their hospitality. When two distinct ethnic parties engage in a mutual sharing of hospitality, gifts, and friendship it was often seen as creating a permanent binding relationship—on par with friendship or even non-biological kinship.[21] The Maltese barbarians, then, through their *continued* enactments of hospitality appear to have initiated a binding kinship-like relationship with Paul.

When Paul claims that God's salvation has gone forth to the Gentiles who will provide a listening and receptive audience (28:28), the examples of Julius the Roman centurion, the shared meal between Paul and his shipmates, and the hospitable Maltese barbarians provide good reason for the reader to expect that the legacy and mission of Paul will continue even after his imprisonment and death. Philanthropy, shared hospitality, and friendship have been displayed abundantly between these Gentile characters and Paul throughout his journey to Rome. The sea-voyage, then, provides a lasting and memorable impression of Paul's character and identity as one who was open to fresh encounters with all peoples and a lasting impression of Gentiles as receptive, friendly, and hospitable.

We should take note that Luke portrays Paul entering into the cultural and religious logic of the Maltese.[22] Luke does not present Paul mocking

21. On the relevance of the custom of ritualized friendship (guest-friendship) for understanding Acts, particularly the Peter-Cornelius episode, see Walter T. Wilson, "Urban Legends: Acts 10:1–11:18 and the Strategies of Greco-Roman Foundation Narratives," *JBL* 120 (2001): 77–99.

22. This paragraph has been adapted from Joshua W. Jipp, "Hospitable Barbarians: Luke's Ethnic Reasoning in Acts 28:1–10," *JTS* (forthcoming).

or demonizing the Maltese but, rather, operating within the cultural and religious logic of the islanders. Luke has not projected fantastic stereotypes of the exotic islanders. This is *not* to say that Luke works with a contemporary sanitized, tolerant, pluralist ideology of religious belief; nor is it to say that Luke translates the Christian message into ideas and practices amenable to Greco-Roman paganism (or vice versa).[23] But it *is* to say that Luke does not demonize the religion of non-Jews, and in fact presents non-Jews as capable of rightly responding to the emissaries of the risen Christ *even out of their own Greco-Roman cultural and religious dispositions.* We have already noted that on three separate occasions Luke presents non-Jews showing disinterested "kindness" or "friendliness" to Paul (*philanthrōpōs*, 27:3; *philanthrōpian*, 28:2; *philophronōs*, 28:7). Given the literary function of sharing possessions and showing hospitality to strangers as a highly positive symbolic depiction of one's acceptance of God's visitation of his people in the Lukan writings, it is striking that the Maltese are portrayed exemplarily as engaging in both of these activities (28:2, 7, 10).[24] The important point here is that Paul does not engage in demonizing the religious and cultural logic of the Maltese. Nor does he show them to be superstitious, naïve, fickle, or worthy of being mocked for their inferior rationality. Instead, Luke's Paul is a guest who works within—even as he disrupts their beliefs and allegiances— the cultural and religious logic of the Maltese, a logic that enables them to show kindness to the incarcerated, to recognize the powerful presence of God at work within Paul, to initiate friendship with Paul, and to engage in sharing their possessions with Paul and his crew. I am not claiming that Luke valorizes Greco-Roman religion. He clearly does not, and he presents significant episodes where his characters criticize aspects of Greco-Roman religiosity (for example, 12:20–23; 14:8–18; 19:8–40). He does, however, make abundant use of Greco-Roman religious discourses in order to show that the early Christian movement embodies supremely the superior elements of Greco-Roman religiosity and philosophy. The "Christian" characters, then, disrupt the cultural and religious dispositions of the pagan audience as they call them to exclusive allegiance to Israel's Messiah, *even as* they simultaneously work within their religious and cultural logics.[25]

---

23. See here especially C. Kavin Rowe, "The Grammar of Life: The Areopagus Speech and Pagan Tradition," *NTS* 57, no. 1 (January 2011): 31–50.

24. On the role of sharing possessions in Luke-Acts, see Luke Timothy Johnson, *The Literary Function of Possessions in Luke-Acts*, SBLDS 39 (Missoula, MT: Scholars Press, 1977).

25. I have argued something similar with respect to Paul's speech in Athens in Joshua W.

Proclaiming and Embodying the Gospel as a Good Guest

We have seen Paul function as both host *and guest* in Acts 27 and 28, and in his farewell address to the Ephesian elders, Paul declares that he has proclaimed the gospel both "in public and from house to house" (Acts 20:20). This is no surprise, given how frequently Paul takes on the role of the guest in his missionary work. For example, Paul is the guest of Lydia (Acts 16:11–15, 39–40), the Philippian jailer (16:25–34), Jason (17:1–9), Prisca and Aquila (18:1–4), and Titius Justus (18:7–8), the Maltese (28:1–2, 7–10), and the Roman Jews (28:15). In Paul's journey from Miletus to Jerusalem in Acts 21, Paul is the guest of disciples in Tyre (21:4–5), the brethren in Ptolemais (21:7b), Philip in Caesarea (21:8), Mnason the Cypriote in Caesarea (21:15–16), and finally the brethren in Jerusalem (21:17).

We have important evidence of Paul's self-portrait as a *good guest* in his letters as well. Most notably, in 1 Corinthians 9:19–23 Paul provides us with an autobiographical account of his own understanding of embracing the role of the *good guest who adapts himself to his host* in hospitality contexts in order to share the gospel with all people. In 1 Corinthians 9:19–23, Paul states:

> Because I am free from everyone I have enslaved myself to all people, so that I might win many. I have become a Jew to the Jews, so that I might win Jews; to those under the law as one under the law (though myself not under the law), so that I might gain those under the law; to the lawless as one lawless (though myself not apart from God's law but in the law of Christ), so that I might gain the lawless; I have become weak to the weak, so that I might win the weak; I have become all things to all people, so that I might in every way save some. I do all things for the sake of the gospel, so that I might become a fellow-sharer in it. [my trans.]

Five times Paul says he has adapted himself ("I have become . . .") to a particular group of people *in order that* he might win that particular group of people to the Lord. This raises at least two questions. Why does Paul set forth his behavior as a good thing, as something praiseworthy and virtuous? We might be forgiven for supposing that someone who constantly adapts his character, preferences, and likes to his company would be seen

---

Jipp, "Paul's Areopagus Speech of Acts 17:16–34 as *Both* Critique *and* Propaganda," *JBL* 131, no. 3 (2012): 567–88.

as deceptive and having no clear commitments of his own! And, secondly, in what context would Paul's "becoming all things to all people" (1 Cor 9:22b) even be possible? Where would one be able to find a locale that was so monolithic to be composed of only "the Jews," or "those without the law," or "the weak"?

Paul's "I have become" statements make good sense if they are viewed as his description of how he adapts to his host as an ideal guest.[26] This would explain how Paul could be in a context where he would have been exclusively among Jews or Gentiles or those of a socially lower status. Hospitality protocols demanded that guests respectfully submit to the hospitality offered to them by their hosts. Usually this involved enjoying whatever food and drink were provided by the host, engaging in pleasant and meaningful conversation, refusing to insult or shame the host in any way, and respecting the religious and cultural rituals or values of the host. A variety of contextual indicators demonstrates that Paul is speaking of himself as an ideal guest. First, the entirety of 1 Cor 8–10 is held together by the theme of food, and the theme is picked up again, as we have seen, shortly after in 11:17–34.[27] Second, 1 Cor 10:23–11:1 reprises some of the themes in 9:19–23, and here the issue Paul addresses centers explicitly upon an *unbeliever* inviting you to share a meal in a hospitality context (1 Cor 10:27). Third, in 1 Cor 9:1–18 Paul has been giving to the Corinthians an explanation for his refusal to accept payment for his ministry from them and his decision to lower himself voluntarily by working with his hands in order to support his mission.[28] This stretch of text contains an abundance of echoes of the Jesus-tradition that was later incorporated into Luke 10:1–16 where Jesus offers his instructions to the 72 missionaries for how to conduct themselves in their mission.[29] Both Luke 10 and 1 Corinthians 9:1–23 focus on the themes of mission, food, and payment. We can understand Paul's claims better if we take a brief look at

---

26. See here especially, David J. Rudolph, *A Jew to the Jews: Jewish Contours of Pauline Flexibility in 1 Corinthians 9:19–23*, WUNT 2.304 (Tübingen: Mohr-Siebeck, 2011). Also very helpful here on 1 Cor 9:19–23 as Paul's "missionary rule" is Eckhard J. Schnabel, *Early Christian Mission*, 2 vols. (Downers Grove, IL: InterVarsity Press, 2004), 953–60.

27. Peter D. Gooch, *Dangerous Food: 1 Corinthians 8–10 in Its Context* (Waterloo, Ontario: Wilfrid Laurier University Press, 1993).

28. On the social-status of manual laborers, see Ronald F. Hock, *The Social Context of Paul's Ministry: Testimony and Apostleship* (Philadelphia: Fortress Press, 1980); Dale B. Martin, *Slavery as Salvation: The Metaphor of Slavery in Pauline Christianity* (New Haven, CT: Yale University Press, 1990).

29. Dale C. Allison Jr., *The Jesus Tradition in Q* (Harrisburg, PA: Trinity Press International, 1997), 104–19; Rudolph, *A Jew to the Jews*, 188–90.

Luke 10:5-9 where Jesus instructs the missionaries regarding their proper conduct as good guests.[30]

> When you enter into a household, first say, "peace be upon this household." And if there be a son of peace there, let your peace remain upon him, and if not, then let your greeting return to you. And stay in the household *eating and drinking whatever is set before you*; for the worker is worthy of his payment. And do not pass from house to house. And whatever city you may enter into and they welcome you, *eat what is set before you*. And heal the weak/sick in it and say to them, "the kingdom of God has come near to you." [my trans.]

These traveling missionaries are not ordinary guests, for they embody the presence of Jesus as they go before "the Lord" as his emissaries (Luke 10:1, 16). Jesus speaks, then, of the household as a sacred place where God's kingdom is proclaimed and enacted, and its acceptance is demonstrated through the hospitable reception of the emissaries of the gospel.[31] Our familiarity with Luke's Gospel and its depiction of Jesus's eating with sinners and outcasts enables us to see that the emissaries are extending the same kind of open table-fellowship that characterized Jesus's ministry (for instance, Luke 5:27-32; 19:1-10).[32] In other words, just as Jesus practiced an open table by adapting to his hosts, even resulting in the slur that he was a glutton and drunkard because of his table-companions (Luke 7:34), so his emissaries are to be indiscriminate in whom they receive hospitality from and what they are served to eat and drink provided that they are offered a hospitable reception.[33]

So Paul declares that as an apostle he too has "the right to eat and to drink" (1 Cor 9:4 [my trans.]; see also Luke 10:7). Paul has the right to receive payment for his ministry, for "the Lord commanded that those who proclaim the gospel should get their living by the gospel" (1 Cor 9:14; see also Luke 10:7). Paul is no doubt echoing his own practices when he tells the Corinthians that "if one of the unbelievers invites you to eat and you want to go, *eat everything that is set before you* without asking questions because of

---

30. See here especially, David Lertis Matson, *Household Conversion Narratives in Acts: Pattern and Interpretation*, JSNTSup 123 (Sheffield: Sheffield Academic Press, 1996).

31. See especially Matson, *Household Conversion Narratives in Acts*, 47-49.

32. See here David P. Moessner, *Lord of the Banquet: The Literary and Theological Significance of the Lukan Travel Narrative* (Minneapolis: Fortress Press, 1989), 139.

33. Rudolph, *A Jew to the Jews*, 185.

your conscience" (10:27 [my trans.]). In other words, the believer should be a good guest by eating the host's food so as not to give any offense to the host. This helps makes good sense of Paul's claims in 1 Corinthians 9:19–23 that he adapts himself to his host as a good guest who seeks to "give no offense to Jews or to Greeks or to the church of God" (10:32a). In other words, Paul's claim "I have become all things to all people" (1 Cor 9:22) is a reflection of his remembrance of Jesus's hospitality practices as one who proclaimed God's kingdom by eating with women, Pharisees, sinners, and tax collectors. This is why Paul says that, "even though I am free from all people, *I have enslaved myself to all so that I might win many*" (9:19 [my trans.]). In other words, Paul does not make use of his freedoms, though they are absolutely within his right to do so (see 9:1–15a), but voluntarily becomes a *slave of all people*. Paul's voluntary self-abasement and enslavement to all people echoes Jesus's own teaching: "whoever wants to be first *must become a slave of everyone*; for even the Son of Man did not come to be served but to serve and to give his life a ransom for many" (Mark 10:44–45 [my trans.]).[34] Just as Jesus ate with the strictly Law-observant Pharisees (Luke 7:36–39; 11:37–41; 14:1–6), so Paul accommodates to the practices of "those under the law" (1 Cor 9:20). As Jesus ate with those despised by Israel's religious elite (Luke 7:36–50; 15:1–2), so Paul adapts himself to his hosts who are "lawless" (1 Cor 9:21) and "weak" (1 Cor 9:22). Paul embraces weakness as an extension of his imitation of the one who was "crucified in weakness" (2 Cor 13:4; see also 2 Cor 12:9–10). Paul's claim "I have become weak to the weak so that I might win the weak" resonates with those passages where Paul sets forth Christ as one who voluntarily lowers himself, embraces shame, servitude, and sin so that we might share in his wealth and righteousness. Notice the similarity, then, between Paul's self-description in 1 Cor 9:19–23 and the following Pauline "interchange" texts where Christ condescends to humanity:[35]

Who even though he was in the form of God did not consider equal honors with God something to be grasped after, but considered himself nothing, taking the form of a slave, he was born in human likeness. And

34. Very helpful here is Seyoon Kim, "*Imitatio Christi* (1 Corinthians 11:1): How Paul Imitates Jesus Christ in Dealing with Idol Food," *BBR* 13 (2003): 193–226, here, 197.

35. The language of "interchange" is used to explain the dynamic whereby Christ takes on and identifies with our humanity and we share in his glorious benefits. See Morna Hooker, "Interchange in Christ," in *From Adam to Christ: Essays on Paul* (Cambridge: Cambridge University Press, 1990), 13–25. Also see Rudolph, *A Jew to the Jews*, 176–78; Horrell, *Solidarity and Difference*, 242–44.

being found in human form he humbled himself by becoming obedient to death, even death on a cross. (Phil 2:6–8 [my trans.])

Christ redeemed us from the curse of the law by becoming a curse for our sake. (Gal 3:13a [my trans.])

He who did not know sin became sin for us, so that we might become the righteousness of God in him. (2 Cor 5:21 [my trans.])

You know the gift of our Lord Jesus Christ, that even though he was rich he became poor for you so that you might become rich out of his poverty. (2 Cor 8:9 [my trans.])

Thus, Christ voluntarily *became* man, *became* a slave, *became* obedient to death, *became* a curse, *became* sin, and *became* poor. So Paul, referring five times to "the weaker" church members in 1 Cor 8:7–13, calls the church to imitate the condescension of Christ by voluntarily giving up their rights and to consider those for whom Christ has died.[36] So also Paul adapts himself as a good guest to *all of his hosts*. This explains why Paul rejects the Corinthian financial support as it attempts to transform Paul into something of a client or dependent upon those with financial resources.[37] Instead, Paul does not seek his own good, but instead he seeks "to please all people in all things . . . so that they might be saved" (10:33). Paul forgoes any rights, privileges, or preferences of his own and, instead, voluntarily adapts to people of every stripe—even the weak and lawless—so that all people might enter into Paul's life. And this life, of course, is nothing less than the life of Christ, for as Paul exhorts the church: "*Become* imitators of me, just I also imitate Christ" (1 Cor 11:1 [my trans.]). In fact, this may be all we need to understand Paul's unexplained phrase that he is "in the law of Christ" (1 Cor 9:21 [my trans.]), namely, his imitation of Christ's character and extension of loving others and divine hospitality to all people.[38]

36. Margaret Mitchell shows how many early Christian authors understand 1 Corinthians 9:19–23 as Paul's description of mirroring the rhetorical technique of divine condescension. See Margaret M. Mitchell, "Pauline Accommodation and 'Condescension' (συγκατάβασις): 1 Cor 9:19–23 and the History of Influence," in *Paul beyond the Judaism/Hellenism Divide*, ed. Troels Engberg-Pedersen (Louisville: Westminster John Knox Press, 2001), 197–214.

37. See here Joshua Rice, *Paul and Patronage: The Dynamics of Power in 1 Corinthians* (Eugene, OR: Pickwick Publications, 2013); Peter Marshall, *Enmity in Corinth: Social Conventions in Paul's Relations with the Corinthians*, WUNT 2.23 (Tübingen: Mohr-Siebeck, 1987).

38. I have written in more detail about the phrase "the law of Christ" as it pertains to Galatians, 1 Corinthians, and Romans in *Christ Is King: Paul's Royal Ideology* (Minneapolis: Fortress Press, 2015), 43–76.

Hospitality, the World, and Friendships with Non-Christians

We can learn much about engaging in intentional friendships with religious others from Paul's willingness to embrace the role of guest in his relationships with non-Christians. For example, those who read Acts 27:1–28:10 as Christian Scripture are challenged to bestow (as hospitable hosts) and receive (as receptive guests) the kind of hospitality and kindness that would result in the creation of friendship with non-Christians. In this text, the gifts of God—table-fellowship, the salvation/safety of the shipmates, and healing—are not hoarded or held back as the exclusive property of Paul but are shared liberally and freely with those not belonging to Paul's own family network or religious community. They are, furthermore, shared without requiring or asking for a response. Paul demonstrates no hesitation in receiving kindness from a Roman military man, happily and freely shares a meal with prisoners, and shows no fear to stay in Publius's home and receive his hospitality. Thus, Luke leaves his readers with a portrait of Paul as entering into host and guest relationships with outsiders as a means of extending God's salvation to all people. Luke seems, in fact, to even make a point of invoking cultural stereotypes—Roman centurions, prisoners, and barbarians—only in order to overturn them specifically to show the church that these are the people to whom God's salvation has been and will be extended, and that they are not only worthy of receiving but are supremely capable of practicing and initiating friendship, hospitality, and philanthropy.

Churches today who would continue to embody the same message and values should reflect upon where and how their gifts and resources may be put to use in service of the larger world. Likewise, churches who seek to hear and be shaped by God's Word in Acts 27–28, might reflect upon whether they are intentionally seeking opportunities to bestow divine hospitality and create friendship relationships with so-called outsiders. Perhaps the church would do well to reflect upon whether soldiers, prisoners, and the ethnically "other" *still* represent some of the same cultural stereotypes needing to be overturned.

The church that would take seriously the message of Acts 27–28 would, however, not *only* reflect upon how and to whom they should dispense hospitality, but it would also seek ways in which they might receive, learn, and experience the gifts from others who are not part of their friendship-family network. This is, in fact, what we see Paul doing in 1 Cor 9:19–23 and calling Christians to do in 1 Cor 10:23–11:1. The church can learn much from Paul's willingness to adapt to his host in hospitality contexts. Christians who have some level of power and privilege may be tempted to imagine that they always play the role of the host, namely, the one who gives and provides the hospitality. But this can be a form of consolidating power that forces one's guest to adapt, while you retain the power and thereby are not forced to accommodate to someone else's different home, customs, rituals, language, leadership, and worship practices. In conclusion, here are some brief suggestions for how embracing the role of host *and especially guest* with non-Christians can facilitate Christian mission in and to the world.

1. Pursuing Interfaith Hospitality and Friendships

One way in which Christians can share in God's mission in and to the world is by embracing the posture of *guest* in one's intentional pursuit of friendships with followers of other religions. We have seen from Acts that Paul was blessed and ministered to as a guest of the Maltese islanders and Publius, and we have seen from 1 Corinthians that Paul adopts the role of a guest—rooted in the teaching and ministry of Jesus (for instance, Luke 10:1–16)—in order that by rejecting his own rights and preferences he might embody and proclaim the good news of the gospel to all people. Paul's embrace of the role of guest is consistent with the broader biblical witness that we have seen, namely, that Christians are guests of God and guests in the world. So what can we learn from Paul the guest about our own relationships and friendships with religious others?

First, it is worth stating the obvious: Paul was not afraid that the religious other would pollute or contaminate him *by virtue of their mere presence.* Going so far as to adapt himself to the particular culture, food, and rituals of the homes of the religious other and offering the advice "if an unbeliever invites you and you want to go, then eat everything set before you" (1 Cor 10:27a [my trans.]) demonstrates that Paul follows Jesus's practice of extending the gospel through entering into intimate relationships and friendship with non-Christians. Undoubtedly, occasions for limiting hospitality exist. Paul's flexibility, for example, emphatically does not extend to Christians engaging in sacrifices to pagan deities (1 Cor 10:19–21) or having sexual relations with prostitutes (1 Cor 6:13–20)! But the biblical witness mandates "hospitable openness [that] means interacting with rather than isolating ourselves from neighbors."[39] Christians should look for op-

---

39. Yong, *Hospitality and the Other*, 125.

portunities to engage in personal encounters where they can both share their own stories and listen to the stories and experiences of non-Christian neighbors.[40] This hospitable openness can perhaps best take place in one another's homes where hospitable interaction with the religious other can entail offering clear and sensitive explanations of one's own faith commitments and religious practices. If hospitality is making room for the other by welcoming the stranger into one's own space, then hospitality to the religious other will not hide or refrain from sharing his Christian beliefs and practices.[41] And vice versa, the Christian should receive with gratitude the opportunity to learn from her non-Christian friend about her beliefs, rituals, and practices.[42]

Paul's embrace of the role of a good guest almost certainly involved his intentional attempt to understand and enter into the particular culture, rituals, and even religious logic and practices of his hosts. On the one hand, Paul develops explicit boundaries and limitations to Christian involvement in non-Christian religious practices (see, for example, 1 Cor 6:12–20; 10:19–21); and, yet, on the other hand, he clearly indicates that he adapted himself to some of the particular cultural and religious practices of *non-Christians in their home* (1 Cor 9:19–23). No doubt giving up one's comfort and power in order to be the guest of religious others involves risk. This entails receiving their hospitality, enjoying their gifts, and learning from them about their faith, rituals, and food.[43] Alternatively, it means looking for opportunities to explain in word and in practice the meaning of the Christian faith in terms that make sense to one's host. Certainly, the landscape of religion in America is changing in profound ways, and this has proved to be especially unsettling to many.[44] While I am not arguing that Christians should compromise their biblical commitments, Christians in North America must assume a posture of guest as means of learning about many of those deeply religious non-Christians in our own communities.[45] Lamin Sanneh has argued that Christianity, while maintaining its foundational commitments (monothe-

40. Marty, *When Faiths Collide*, 145.

41. See here especially Lesslie Newbigin, *The Gospel in a Pluralist Society* (Grand Rapids: Eerdmans, 1989).

42. Helpful here again is Marty, *When Faiths Collide*, 128–32.

43. Yong, *Hospitality and the Other*, 133: "Hence, Christian missionaries . . . should be of the mentality that they are not only givers but also receivers of the gifts borne by those in other faiths."

44. See here especially Robert P. Jones, *The End of White Christian America* (New York: Simon and Schuster, 2016).

45. On which see Peggy Levitt, *God Needs No Passport: Immigrants and the Changing American Religious Landscape* (New York: The New Press, 2007).

ism, the deity of Jesus, etc.), destigmatized non-Jewish culture in such a way that any and every culture was (and is) a potential conduit for God's revelation. In other words, "all cultures have cast upon them the breath of God's favor, thus cleansing them of the stigma of inferiority and illegitimacy."[46] John Flett similarly describes the necessity of Christian proclamation embracing the local: "Conversion demands significant continuity with the local cultural heritage and leads to an expansion in the Christian tradition itself. To speak of Jesus Christ in another cultural milieu is to open that message to the range of questions, resources and idioms found in that culture, including those in the political and religious spheres."[47] So also Paul (as well as the Christian missionary) embodies, proclaims, and transmits the gospel precisely through appropriate adaptation to the practical forms of *the guest culture and/or household*.[48] This adaptation of the gospel to the particular cultural and religious forms of the guest culture can already be seen in the New Testament, for example, when John identifies Jesus in light of the (*both Hebraic and Greek*) concept of "the logos" (John 1:1-3, 14). One sees this again in Luke's description of the resurrected Jesus's appearance to the two disciples on the Emmaus road in light of the well-known Greco-Roman stories of the visitation of disguised deities (Luke 24:13-35). I suggest that Paul, too, was engaging in mission through translation. His "becoming all things to all people" is a form of sharing the gospel as a guest, as he adapts the gospel to the particular cultural and religious distinctives of each household. This entails a willingness to listen to and understand the religious other, as well as an ability to sympathetically and critically enter into the cultural and religious logic of one's host as a means of embodying the gospel.

Paul saw his willing acceptance of the role of guest as the means whereby he embodied the character of Christ, who also enslaved himself and gave up his own rights for the good of those he came to serve. In other words, in his role as guest Paul intentionally rejects his own rights and preferences in order to grant proper respect and power to his hosts in their own home. Paul's missional strategy of embodying the self-giving, power-rejecting pos-

46. Lamin Sanneh, *Translating the Message: The Missionary Impact on Culture*, 2nd ed. (Maryknoll, NY: Orbis, 2009), 54; See also Lamin Sanneh, *Disciples of All Nations*, Pillars of World Christianity (Oxford: Oxford University Press, 2008), 25-56; Andrew F. Walls, *The Missionary Movement in Christian History: Studies in the Transmission of Faith* (Maryknoll, NY: Orbis, 1996), 26-42.

47. John G. Flett, *Apostolicity: The Ecumenical Question in World Christian Perspective* (Downers Grove, IL: InterVarsity Press, 2016), 261.

48. Sanneh, *Translating the Message*, 57-60.

ture of Christ is significant for contemporary evangelism and mission. The biblical witness, thus, encourages missionaries and evangelists to embrace the marginality and ambiguous nature of guest and stranger of one's host (or host culture).[49] Anthony Gittins states it this way:

> [I]f missionaries were more willing to allow *themselves* to be contextualized as *strangers*, rather than trying to position themselves as controllers, dictators, initiative-takers or proselytizers, then perhaps mutual relationships would be more conducive to a responsible and creative sharing of stories—and thus authentic evangelization—than has so often been the case.[50]

Thus, one aspect of embodying the hospitality of God is through respecting and seeking to understand the cultural and religious protocols of our hosts. This almost certainly entails forms of cultural and linguistic learning and adaptation in order to share friendship with others. This means that, as "The Cape Town Commitment" declares, "Christians are to speak sincerely and respectfully; they are to listen in order to learn about and understand others' beliefs and practices, and are encouraged to acknowledge and appreciate what is true and good in them."[51] Harold Netland has rightly noted that this means that Christians must portray religious others with respect and fairness, that they refuse to demonize the religious beliefs and practices of others, and they resist and critique statements that would promote fear and hatred of non-Christian religious neighbors.[52] Thus, one should not reject the incredible importance of engaging in sympathetic interreligious dialogue as a means of growing friendships and learning about and from the religious other.[53] I expect, further, that Christians who intentionally take on the role of guest in building friendships with non-Christians will find they learn something of significance about *their own faith*. What does it say to us if *Samaritans*, the premier religious other to Jews in the first century, are held up as the embodiment of those who fulfill the merciful demands of *Israel's*

---

49. Anthony J. Gittins, *Gifts and Strangers: Meeting the Challenge of Inculturation* (New York: Paulist Press, 1988).

50. Gittins, *Gifts and Strangers*, 115.

51. Quoted from Harold A. Netland, *Christianity and Religious Diversity: Clarifying Christian Commitments in a Globalizing Age* (Grand Rapids: Baker Academic, 2015), 239.

52. Netland, *Christianity and Religious Diversity*, 239.

53. So Gerald McDermott and Harold A. Netland, *A Trinitarian Theology of Religions* (New York: Oxford University Press, 2014), 277–83.

Torah (Luke 10:25–37) and if *barbarians* are the noble hosts who practice care for the stranger as well as anyone in Luke-Acts (Acts 28:1–10)? At the very least, it may suggest that people of other religions may be used by God to teach us something fresh about our own faith commitments.[54]

2. Sharing the Gifts of God with the World

In our pluralistic society, one important way Christians can embody God's hospitality is by actively looking for ways to share the gifts of God with the world at large. This embodiment of divine hospitality can be seen in pursuing the good of society at large through, for example, caring for the weak and vulnerable, visiting the imprisoned, and providing food for the poor. We have seen, for example, that Luke depicts Paul benefiting and contributing to the safety, encouragement, and sustenance of the 276 incarcerated non-Christians on the ship as well as the sick Maltese islanders, and that the early Christians included all kinds of people in their shared meals as one of the means whereby "day by day the Lord added to their number those who were being saved" (Acts 2:47b).

One of the ways the early Christians shared the gifts of God liberally with the world was in the tangible forms of caring for prisoners and offering aid to the sick and the dying. Rodney Stark has even suggested that one of the factors that facilitated the rapid growth and spread of Christianity in the first five centuries of the Common Era was the response of the Christians to *all* those affected by the plagues and epidemics in the third and fourth centuries.[55] Eusebius describes the indiscriminate care given by the Christians during a plague in the eastern part of the empire (around 312 CE) (*Ecclesiastical History* 9.14):

> [T]he fruits of the Christians' limitless enthusiasm and devotion became evident to all the pagans. Alone in the midst of this terrible calamity they proved by visible deeds their sympathy and humanity. All day long some continued without rest to tend the dying and bury them—the number

---

54. Yong, *Hospitality and the Other*, 103.

55. Rodney Stark, "Epidemics, Networks, and the Rise of Christianity," *Semeia* 56 (1992): 159–75. See also Hector Avalos, *Health Care and the Rise of Christianity* (Peabody, MA: Hendrickson, 1999); Helen Rhee, *Loving the Poor, Saving the Rich: Wealth, Poverty, and Early Christian Formation* (Grand Rapids: Baker Academic Press, 2012), 128–31; Henry Chadwick, *The Early Church* (Harmondsworth, UK: Penguin, 1967), 56–58.

was immense, and there was no one to see to them; others rounded up the huge number who had been reduced to scarecrows all over the city and distributed loaves to them all, so that their praises were sung on every side, and all men glorified the God of the Christians and owned that they alone were pious and truly religious: did not their actions speak for themselves?

In *The Life of Cyprian* Pontius describes how, during the "plague of Cyprian" in 250 CE, the bishop of Carthage exhorted the congregation to show mercy and benevolence in their care for both Christians and pagans (*Life of Cyprian* 9):

> Then afterwards he subjoined, that there was nothing wonderful in our cherishing our own people only with the needed attentions of love, but that he might become perfect who would do something more than the publican or the heathen, who, overcoming evil with good, and practicing a clemency which was like the divine clemency, loved even his enemies, who would pray for the salvation of those that persecute him, as the Lord admonishes and exhorts. God continually makes His sun to rise, and from time to time gives showers to nourish the seed, exhibiting all these kindnesses not only to His people, but to aliens also.

The deadly plague began in Ethiopia and spread throughout the Empire, lasting at least fifteen years, and leading to an incredible death rate. The text is remarkable for its description of the church's extension of care to the sick as indiscriminately including both pagans and Christians. Both rich and poor Christians are called upon to undertake an organized effort to give care to the plague's victims. Bishop Dionysus (describing the effects of the plague in Alexandria around 260 CE) describes the care the Christians gave to the sick in the following glowing terms (*Ecclesiastical History* 7.22):

> Most of our brother Christians showed great love and loyalty, never sparing themselves and thinking only of each other. Heedless of the danger, they took charge of the sick, attending to their every need and ministering to them in Christ, and with them departed this life serenely happy; for they were infected by others with the disease, drawing on themselves the sickness of their neighbors and cheerfully accepting their pains. . . . With willing hands they raised the bodies of the saints to their bosoms; they closed their eyes and mouths, carried them on their shoul-

ders, and laid them out; they clung to them, embraced them, washed them, and wrapped them in grave-clothes. Very soon the same services were done for them, since those left behind were constantly following those gone before.

In the ancient world, health care was largely left to the individual and was not seen as a public concern. The Christian belief in "love," and "philanthropy," and care for one's enemies "introduced into the classical world the concept of social responsibility in treating epidemic disease."[56] Given the society's general lack of public or private charitable care for the poor, it is likely that the "number of Christians increased during the plagues as a result of the . . . creation of new bonds between surviving pagans and Christians, resulting in large numbers of conversions."[57] The church's care for the sick was also just as significantly rooted in Jesus's healing ministry. Amanda Porterfield has stated this well: "[C]are for the sick was a distinctive and remarkable characteristic of early Christian missionary outreach. Early Christians nursed the sick to emulate the healing ministry of Jesus, to express their faith in the ongoing healing power of Christ, and to distinguish Christian heroism in the face of sickness and death from pagan fear."[58] Christian care for the poor did not respect the wealth, social status, or virtue of the persons in need. In fact, early Christian care for the sick was "simple, not complex. Faith and prayer were efficacious. The Christians' health care was free—in contrast to all the other systems. There were no access problems."[59]

The church's indiscriminate concern for the poor was one of the major factors that led to the creation of institutions such as "poorhouses" that supported widows, the sick, and the poor, as well as hospitals, which were "in origin and conception, a distinctively Christian institution, rooted in Christian concepts of charity and philanthropy."[60] Important resources in

56. Gary B. Ferngren, *Medicine and Health Care in Early Christianity* (Baltimore: The Johns Hopkins University Press, 2009), 118.

57. Ferngren, *Medicine and Health Care in Early Christianity*, 121.

58. Amanda Porterfield, *Healing in the History of Christianity* (Oxford: Oxford University Press, 2005), 47.

59. Willard M. Swartley, *Health, Healing and the Church's Mission: Biblical and Moral Priorities* (Downers Grove, IL: InterVarsity Press, 2012), 150.

60. Ferngren, *Medicine and Health Care in Early Christianity*, 124. Also, see Susan R. Holman, *God Knows There's Need: Christian Responses to Poverty* (Oxford: Oxford University Press, 2009), 56–57, 60–62; Peter Brown, *Poverty and Leadership in the Later Roman Empire*, The Menahem Stern Jerusalem Lectures (Hanover, NH: University Press of New England, 2002), 33–43.

our Christian history can encourage us to think about how we might extend God's hospitality and gifts to those outside of the church today.

In addition to the early church's practice of visiting prisoners and caring for the sick and diseased, I think, for example, of Peter Maurin and Dorothy Day, influenced by Jesus's teaching in Matthew 25:31–46 that acts of mercy and hospitality offered to "the least" are actually done to Christ (that is, the poor are Jesus), and their development of Hospitality Houses, which have served (and continue to serve) *anyone* in need of refuge, care, and food.[61] I think of ministries of compassion and welcome, such as the Charis Pregnancy Center, to teenage mothers facing the challenges of unplanned pregnancy and parenthood—often alone (apart from the friends they make through these ministries). I think of Dolores Mission and Homeboy Industries and their work to provide employment, compassion, and gang-rehabilitation for youth.[62] I think of ministries, such as Safe Families, that care for families in distress and connect volunteer host families with under-resourced parents without social connections and seek to host and care for their children for a short time until the children are returned to their parent(s).[63] Parents voluntarily seek aid from Safe Families for a variety of reasons—loss of job, medical treatments, incarceration, abusive relationships, substance abuse rehab, and/or financial difficulties. Volunteer families with Safe Families simply seek to host and care for their children in the short term and to develop meaningful relationships with children *and* parents.

I began this chapter by noting that Paul shares freely without measure the gifts of God with those incarcerated on the ship as well as with the Maltese islanders. God's gifts and the church's resources are used in service of the larger world apart from their response, repentance, or Christian virtue. The events related in Acts 27–28, Jesus's ministry of healing, the early church's incorporation of all kinds of people into its common meals (Acts 2 and 4), the belief that acts of kindness and mercy to the poor and outcast are done to Jesus (Matt 25:31–46), Jesus's parable of the Samaritan who fulfills the Torah

---

61. Christine Pohl, *Making Room: Recovering Hospitality as a Christian Tradition* (Grand Rapids: Eerdmans, 1999), 190–91; Gary Dorrien, *Social Ethics in the Making: Interpreting an American Tradition* (Malden, MA: Wiley-Blackwell, 2011), 366–68.

62. See the description of this ministry and the powerful set of stories by the founder, Gregory Boyle, *Tattoos on the Heart: The Power of Boundless Compassion* (New York: Free Press, 2010).

63. Safe Families for Children, "Safe Families for children—the beginning" (flash video), December 9, 2015, accessed September 4, 2016, https://vimeo.com/148396998.

through his compassionate acts of hospitality to the half-dead man (Luke 10:25–37), the early church's care and medical provision for the sick and dying—all of these examples and many more suggest that one of the ways the church continues the legacy of biblical hospitality is by seeking creative ways to share God's mercy and gifts with the world.

Study Questions

1. What are the dangers involved in assuming that "we" are always the hosts and those who offer hospitality? What biblical texts encourage us to assume the role of guest or recipient of hospitality from others?

2. How can Christians engage in deep and meaningful friendships with people of other religions? In what ways have you? If you don't have (m)any significant friendships with people of other religions, what is preventing this?

3. Does the Bible encourage certain limits to the Christian's friendship with people of other religions? If so, what are these limits?

4. Describe an occasion when you were blessed by hospitality from an unlikely or surprising person or community.

5. Describe an experience when someone of another religious tradition taught you (through word or deed) something significant about your own faith.

6. The author suggested at the end of the chapter that the early church often sought to share God's gifts with the world at large. How do you respond to the practice of the early church to give health care to those afflicted by some of the deadly plagues? How does this stimulate your imagination for how churches today might seek to benefit the world?

CHAPTER 5

Hospitality and the Immigrant:
Overcoming Xenophobia

Christine Pohl has said that strangers "are those who are disconnected from basic relationships that give persons a secure place in the world. The most vulnerable strangers are detached from family, community, church, work, and polity."[1] This definition fits perfectly the experience of most immigrants and refugees. Right now somewhere around eleven to twelve million undocumented immigrants reside in the United States; close to half of these are Mexican.[2] It is estimated that worldwide nine million *forced* immigrants (or refugees) have been granted asylum due to such reasons as war, persecution, or famine.[3] While the specific reasons for immigration vary from person to person, anyone who has taken the time to listen to the many stories of these immigrants quickly realizes that most of these people, especially the undocumented or those who overstay their work visas, have left their home, family, friends, and culture due to severe economic hardships.[4] And

---

1. Christine D. Pohl, *Making Room: Recovering Hospitality as a Christian Tradition* (Grand Rapids: Eerdmans, 1999), 13.

2. For a host of information related to international migration, see http://www.migrationpolicy.org/.

3. Khalid Koser, *International Migration: A Very Short Introduction* (Oxford: Oxford University Press, 2007), 16–17.

4. Personal relationships are the best way to hear their stories, but a variety of excellent films also detail the life of immigrants. For example, *Dying to Get In: Undocumented Immigration at the US-Mexican Border*, directed by Brett Tolley (Mooncusser Films, 2007); *Dying to Live: A Migrant's Journey*, directed by Bill Groody (Groody River Films, 2005); *The Visitor*, directed by Tom McCarthy (Overture Films, 2008). See also the important story of the deportation of Elvira Arellano from my city of Chicago and her continuing work for immigration reform, http://chicagoreporter.com/elvira-arellano-undocumented-immigrant-international-activist/#.VKdS62TF9sA.

these economic challenges are almost invariably the result of factors out of the control of the immigrants: namely, corrupt governments, low wages, and growing global disparities in jobs, education, and health care (much of which is the result of public policies developed by wealthy nations).[5] A safe passage to their country of destination is one of the first difficulties facing immigrants. Khalid Koser notes that approximately close to two thousand migrants die each year trying to migrate from North Africa to Europe.[6] With respect to the US-Mexico border, Kristin Heyer estimates that since the 1990s one border crosser dies every twenty-four hours.[7] The challenges they face to cross the border could characterize many migrants: "drowning, suffocation in overcrowded and perilous cargo transport, mutilations from accidental or coerced train injuries, fatal dehydration, high rates of physical violence, detention under inhuman conditions, and precious little recourse to protection or legal representation."[8] The close and often brutal policing of these southern borders in the rugged terrain of the desert has led to what many now term a humanitarian crisis.[9] With respect to migration from Africa to Asia, Gioachinno Campese says that the Mediterranean Sea, which was for centuries "the space of coexistence of civilizations and religions and the crossroad of peoples coming from different continents" has become a "'monster sea' that has already swallowed thousands of immigrants coming from Africa and Asia, a situation that should be a cause of shame for all 'civilized' European nations."[10]

As if these challenges to one's own bodily safety and protection are not difficult enough, once they reach the US, immigrants are often dehumanized through xenophobic rhetoric and actions, as well as unjust legislation. Current legislation regarding immigrants, as well as the history of the US, has "fostered a widespread conception of immigrants as threatening the rule of

5. See Koser, *International Migration*, 28–33.

6. Koser, *International Migration*, 62.

7. Kristin E. Heyer, *Kinship across Borders: A Christian Ethic of Immigration* (Washington, DC: Georgetown University Press, 2012), 8; Daniel G. Groody, "Jesus and the Undocumented Immigrant: A Spiritual Geography of a Crucified People," *Theological Studies* 70, no. 2 (July 2009): 298–316, here, 302–3.

8. Heyer, *Kinship across Borders*, 9.

9. See Miguel de la Torre, *Trails of Terror and Hope: Testimonies on Immigration* (Maryknoll, NY: Orbis, 2009), esp. chapters 1 and 2; Gioacchinno Campese, "'But I See That Somebody Is Missing,'" in *Ecclesiology and Exclusion: Boundaries of Being and Belonging in Postmodern Times*, ed. Dennis Doyle, Pascal D. Bazzell, and Timothy J. Furry (Maryknoll, NY: Orbis, 2012), 71–91, here, 75.

10. Campese, "'But I See That Somebody Is Missing,'" 75.

law, social cohesion, and the nation's economic health."[11] In the US, and in particular in the Southwest, Latinas and Latinos often live their daily lives under the presumption that they are in the US illegally and must, therefore, face constant policing as the result of this assumption.[12] We have all heard the rhetoric and perhaps some of us have believed that many immigrants to the US, documented or otherwise:

- threaten our national security,
- are criminals,
- contribute to environmental problems due to excessive population growth,
- endanger our cultural identity,
- do not pay taxes and thereby threaten our economy,
- adversely affect health care, and
- take away jobs from citizens and drive down wages.

For many it does not matter that these charges are, as John Stapleford and others have shown, either overstated or entirely false and rely upon "poor analysis" and "use of low-quality data."[13] What is at work in the anti-immigrant rhetoric is almost invariably *fear*, fear that the other will contaminate. Susannah Snyder has documented, with respect to the United Kingdom, how this fear centers upon three common threads: fear that the immigrant will corrupt the nation's cultural identity (related to language, religion, laws, and sense of shared history);[14] fear that the immigrant will threaten national security (related to terrorism, violent crime, disease-carrying, and drug trafficking); and fear that the immigrant will harm the economy and national institutions (related to welfare and health care).[15] Immigrants are viewed as disrupting and destabilizing "fixed categories and

---

11. Heyer, *Kinship across Borders*, 17.

12. See here Jennifer Harvey, *Dear White Christians: For Those Still Longing for Racial Reconciliation* (Grand Rapids: Eerdmans, 2015), 183.

13. John E. Stapleford, *Bulls, Bears and Golden Calves*, 2nd ed. (Downers Grove, IL: InterVarsity Press, 2009), 225; M. Daniel Carroll R., *Christians at the Border: Immigration, the Church, and the Bible* (Grand Rapids: Baker Academic, 2008), 49–62.

14. See here especially Samuel Huntington, *Who Are We? The Challenges to America's National Identity* (New York: Simon and Schuster, 2004).

15. Susannah Snyder, "Fright: The Dynamics of Fear within Established Populations," in *Asylum-Seeking: Migration and Church*, Explorations in Practical, Pastoral and Empirical Theology (London: Ashgate, 2012), 85–126. See also Koser, *International Migration*, 61.

stable identities" and are, therefore, incredibly unsettling to many.[16] Fear that the other will pollute the purity of our nation, then, often produces all kinds of irrational ethnic stereotyping and scapegoating as a means of protection from filth and blame for societal problems.[17] The stereotyping can take many forms—We vs. Them, Civilized vs. Barbaric, Moral vs. the Wicked.[18] I agree with Campese that "what should really alarm society and Christian churches . . . is the level of barbarism that the public debate about immigration has reached."[19] The rhetoric is filled with hate, suspicion, anger, and fright. I recently observed some of the ethnic stereotyping and slurs lodged at those seeking to cross the US-Mexican border, many of whom were women and children: "Send the illegals back," "Save our children from diseases," "Take them away from here," and "We pay taxes," and "You're not welcome here; we don't want you; go back home." Fear and ethnic stereotyping, then, result in attempts to exclude the other, whether through expulsion, violence, or dehumanizing legislation.[20] By means of assigning the other the status of inferior, we "make sure that they cannot live in our neighborhoods, get certain kinds of jobs, [and] receive equal pay or honor. . . . "[21] These exclusionary practices are exemplified in the rhetoric "We need to safeguard our country; we need to protect our border." And this can be seen now, both literally and symbolically, through the *violent* tactics used to police the US border. Numerous stories recount how physical and social violence against the immigrant have included bodily attacks on immigrants, treating immigrants as terrorists, and exclusion from social services. This cycle—fear of the other → ethnic stereotyping → exclusion and violence—is played out over and over again. Snyder summarizes the cycle nicely: "The ecology of fear surrounding migrants can be depicted as a vicious circle in which fears of the established population feed negative media discourse, public acts of hostility, and restrictive policies and actions."[22]

Thoughtful Christians who take the Scriptures seriously *can and do* disagree about what is best public policy, but I want to make the simple suggestion that the Old Testament Scriptures call upon God's people to reject xe-

16. Snyder, "Fright," 94.

17. On stereotyping and scapegoating, see Snyder, "Fright," 102–104.

18. See further Miroslav Volf, *Exclusion and Embrace: A Theological Exploration of Identity, Otherness, and Reconciliation* (Nashville: Abingdon, 1996), 57–64.

19. Campese, "'But I See That Somebody Is Missing,'" 78.

20. Volf, *Exclusion and Embrace*, 67.

21. Volf, *Exclusion and Embrace*, 75.

22. Snyder, "Fright," 116.

nophobic exclusion of the immigrant, and rather to demonstrate hospitality to the immigrant-stranger. God roundly condemns societies that oppress the vulnerable stranger, whereas individuals who love the stranger are righteous and loved by God. Certainly, real questions and problems related to responsible policies and legislation regarding immigration abound, and obviously, the Bible is not a book that contains specific policy prescriptions for contemporary Christians, but those who claim Israel's Scriptures as their own must *first listen and respond to what God's Word has to say about how individuals and societies treat the immigrant.*[23] Too often the starting point for most Christians, when it comes to thinking about contemporary migration, is not what the Scriptures have to say about immigrants but, rather, economic and ethnic presumptions. While many citizens of the US have real stories about undocumented immigrants who have committed crimes and even evaded criminal prosecution, still the starting point for Christians must be what the Scriptures have to say. God's people are called upon to reject every instance of xenophobia, and this is predicated upon the fact that God loves the immigrant. Our vocation, as we have seen from Henri Nouwen, is to convert our hostilities into hospitality, welcome, and friendship.[24] God protects, safeguards, and provides for the immigrant. God's love for the stranger is manifested in the way in which he has worked within Israel's history to give his own people a guest-stranger status. Israel's perpetual immigrant identity before God is a constant reminder that God's people are dependent upon God's hospitable welcome of them as his people. Stated another way, divine hospitality elicits human hospitality. In other words, because God is the one who welcomes humans, that is "the other," into relationship with him, humans are called to enact hospitality in their relations with each other. The structure of the divine-human relationship in terms of divine host and human guest is the foundation for hospitable intra-human relationships.

Hospitality and Inhospitality to God: Genesis 18–19

Children of a previous generation, including my own, may remember the fairy tale of Baucis and Philemon, a story passed on by the first-century Roman poet Ovid in his *Metamorphoses* 8.617–724. In the story, the gods Jupiter

---

23. This is one of the many virtues of M. Daniel Carroll R., *Christians at the Border*.

24. Henri J. M. Nouwen, *Reaching Out: The Three Movements of the Spiritual Life* (New York: Doubleday, 1975), 65–77.

and Hermes disguise themselves in human form in order to test whether humans are pious or wicked. Ovid recounts that the gods visited "a thousand homes, looking for rest; a thousand homes were barred against them until, at last, one welcomed them" (8.628–30). The important point here is that when gods come to test humans, the pious response is hospitality to the disguised strangers and the wicked response is inhospitality. The charming story is worth reading in full, but for our purposes it is enough to note that after Jupiter and Hermes receive the extraordinarily kind welcome from the elderly Baucis and Philemon, they reveal their divine identity and bestow rewards and blessings upon the couple: "We are gods, and this wicked neighborhood will be punished as it deserves. But to you shall be given exemption from this punishment" (8.689–92). The moral of the story is simple: the gods love and reward those who are hospitable to strangers; alternatively, the gods hate and punish the inhospitable.

When the author of Hebrews gives the command to his congregation, "Let us not forget to show hospitality to strangers, for by doing so some have even unknowingly shown hospitality to angels" (Heb 13:2 [my trans.]), stories like the one recounted in Ovid form the justification for welcoming the stranger. While the idea may seem strange to us, the belief that the divine—God, angels, and prophets—might take on the disguise of a stranger in order to test human piety was commonplace in the ancient world. In fact, a host of stories often referred to as *theoxenia* or "hospitality to [a] God" can be found in both ancient biblical and non-biblical writings.[25] The stories are invariably moralistic, as they provide *theological* warrant for showing kindness to strangers, but they are also predictable and generally contain three basic literary components:

- the divine takes on some kind of disguise and visits humans to test their piety;
- the humans respond with hospitality or inhospitality; and
- the gods bless or alternatively punish the humans based on their hospitality.

Most contemporary Christians probably most often remember Abraham as the paradigmatic example of the one whom God justified by faith apart from works (Gen 15:6; Rom 4:2–8). But for most ancient Jewish and

---

25. See throughout my *Divine Visitations and Hospitality to Strangers in Luke-Acts*, 59–130.

Christian interpreters, Abraham was primarily remembered as a paragon of hospitality due to the extraordinary welcome he showed to the Lord in the form of three visitors. We have seen that the author of 1 Clement declares that Abraham's faith and hospitality were the reasons that God gave a son to Abraham in his old age (1 Clem. 10:7). And both Philo and Josephus praise Abraham at length for his pious obedience to God that is manifested in his hospitality and philanthropy to the strangers (Philo, *Abraham* 60–116; Josephus, *Ant.* 1.191–200).[26] Israel's Scriptures provide two lengthy stories about hospitality to the God of Israel in Genesis 18–19 that provide the initial framework for understanding the workings of divine and human hospitality, an economy that simultaneously structures humanity's relationship with God and its relationship with others. While Abraham's encounter with the Lord in the guise of the three men who promise to give Abraham and Sarah a son (Gen 18:1–15), Abraham's intercession before God on behalf of Sodom (18:16–33), and God's rescue of Lot from the destruction of Sodom and Gomorrah (19:1–29) are often read as only loosely connected stories, Genesis 18 and 19 are unified at the level of literary artistry and theological purposes. That is to say, the stories are bound together by the common theme of hospitality to strangers, the presence of Abraham and his family, and the divine messengers.[27]

With the narrator's words "the Lord appeared to Abraham by the oaks of Mamre, as he sat at the entrance of his tent in the heat of the day" (Gen 18:1), the reader immediately is clued in to the fact that Abraham's encounter with the three men is, in fact, a divine visit. While the story does not speak of disguises, transformations, or metamorphoses, the appearance of "the Lord" (18:1) in the form of "three men" (18:2) indicates the mysterious and epiphanic nature of the encounter.[28] Abraham's expectation that the men will eat, drink, and continue their journey after they are refreshed and the general plot-line of divine visits wherein the host remains unaware of the identity of the guests

26. See further Andrew J. Arterbury, *Entertaining Angels: Early Christian Hospitality in Its Mediterranean Setting*, NTMon 8 (Sheffield: Sheffield Phoenix Press, 2005), 59–71.

27. Almost all of the commentaries on Genesis note that chs. 18 and 19 are a unity in their final form of the text, and that the stories are bound together by the literary motif of divine visits and hospitality. See especially John Van Seters, *Abraham in History and Tradition* (New Haven: Yale University Press, 1975), 215–16.

28. Literary complexities and mysteries abound with respect to the author's narration of the Lord's visit throughout Genesis 18–19. See especially William John Lyons, *Canon and Exegesis: Canonical Praxis and the Sodom Narrative*, JSOTSup 352 (Sheffield: Sheffield Academic Press, 2002), 151–57.

indicate that Abraham saw the three men as ordinary strangers passing by his tent. Thus the story invites us to consider Abraham's actions and treatment of the men as his typical response to journeying strangers.

The narrator tells the reader three times that Abraham's first action is one of recognition: "He *looked up* and *saw* three men standing near him. When *he saw* them . . . " (Gen 18:2a). The point may seem too obvious to belabor, but notice that the first act of hospitality to the stranger is one of recognition. One cannot provide welcome if one does not first see the stranger in need of hospitality.[29]

After Abraham sees the strangers, he responds with extraordinary hospitality as indicated by the qualities of haste and generosity that characterize Abraham's actions. Seven features of hospitality are set forth in Genesis 18:1–8:[30]

1. Abraham sees the strangers.
2. Abraham immediately runs and greets the strangers.
3. Abraham invites the strangers to receive hospitality.
4. Abraham offers water to drink and to wash the feet.
5. Abraham provides comfort and rest inside his lodging.
6. Abraham gives food and drink.
7. Abraham promises he will not detain his guests from their travels.

The final component of the divine visit—revelation and reward—is seen in verses 9–15 where the men unveil the reason for their visit: "I will surely return to you in due season, and your wife Sarah shall have a son," and "Is anything too wonderful for the Lord? At the set time I will return to you, in due season, and Sarah shall have a son" (18:10a, 14). Abraham's piety, exemplified in his welcome of the three men within his tent, results in God's confirmation to do the impossible for Abraham and Sarah, namely, to give them a child in their old age.

Many Christians may assume they know exactly what the story of Sodom and Gomorrah in Genesis 19 is all about—sexual deviance! But in fact, Genesis 19 provides the negative counterpart to Abraham's hospitality, and it really makes the simple point that God will judge societies and individuals that abuse the vulnerable stranger.

29. This point is emphasized nicely by Amy G. Oden, *God's Welcome: Hospitality for a Gospel-Hungry World* (Cleveland: The Pilgrim Press, 2008), 17–19.
30. See also Arterbury, *Entertaining Angels*, 59–60.

Before the men travel to Sodom, the Lord decides to test and inspect the people of Sodom: "How great is the outcry against Sodom and Gomorrah and how very grave their sin! I must go down and see whether they have done altogether according to the outcry that has come to me; and if not, I will know" (Gen 18:20–21). The word "outcry" is often used in the Old Testament writings to refer to the groaning of the oppressed as they *cry out* to God that he would see the abuse of justice and save them from the oppression of the wicked (Gen 4:9–11; Exod 3:7; Isa 5:7). The Israelites, for example, cry out to God amidst their oppression by the Egyptians.

> The Israelites groaned under their slavery, and cried out. Out of the slavery their cry for help rose up to God. God heard their groaning, and God remembered his covenant with Abraham, Isaac, and Jacob. God looked upon the Israelites, and God took notice of them. (Exod 2:23–25)

It seems quite likely, then, that Sodom's grave sin is related to some type of abuse of social justice.[31] Thus, when the Lord, in the form of two men, visits Sodom in the evening, it is no surprise that none of the Sodomites pay any attention to these apparently vulnerable strangers (19:1a). It is, rather, Lot, Abraham's nephew, who "saw them" and like his uncle goes to meet them in the city square and invites them to receive shelter under his own roof (19:1b–2a). The fact that Lot is himself a "resident alien" (19:9) draws attention to the sin of the Sodomites as they are nowhere to be found when these strangers need welcome. The failure of any citizen within Sodom to offer hospitality to these men already provides the indictment of Sodom.[32] Lot's hospitality is reminiscent of the hospitality offered to the men by Abraham.

1. Lot sees the strangers and "he rose to meet them, and bowed down" (19:1).
2. Lot responds with a polite greeting: "Please, my lords . . ." (19:2)
3. Lot invites them to his home: "Turn aside to your servant's house and spend the night" (19:2).
4. Lot provides water to wash their feet (19:2).

---

31. See further Weston W. Fields, *Sodom and Gomorrah: History and Motif in Biblical Narrative*, JSOTSup 231 (Sheffield: Sheffield Academic Press, 1997), 171–79.

32. Victor Matthews, "Hospitality and Hostility in Genesis 19 and Judges 19," *BTB* 22, no. 1 (Spring 1992): 3–11, here 4.

5. Lot promises he will not detain his guests from their journey (19:2b).
6. The angels enter his house (19:3).
7. Lot prepares a feast for them and they eat (19:3b).

The obvious similarities between Abraham's and Lot's hospitality to the angels demonstrate that the latter's response of hospitality to the divine visitors is virtuous and entirely appropriate.[33] This is not to say that all of his actions are morally commendable, of course, but it is almost certainly his hospitality to the angels that causes the author of 2 Peter to refer to him as "righteous Lot" (2 Pet 2:7).[34]

While the angels are in Lot's dwelling, the narrator says that the men of the city, "the men of Sodom, both young and old, all the people to the last man, surrounded the house" (19:4). The language is purposeful exaggeration, and the effect is to indict the entire city of Sodom with violent inhospitality against the strangers within Lot's home. The mob's command to Lot to cast out the visitors "so that we may know them" (19:5b) is an obvious reference to their desire to violently gang rape the strangers. The portrait of Lot as a hospitable host continues as he places himself between the violent men and the strangers in his home (19:6). Even the offer of his two virgin daughters to the men, morally repugnant to all readers, is his attempt to fulfill the hospitality protocols no matter the personal cost since, he avers, these strangers "have come under the shelter of my roof" (19:8).

The rumors of the wickedness of Sodom have been confirmed through their attempts to violate and abuse vulnerable strangers in need of safety and protection. The entire city of Sodom, save Lot and his family, has violated hospitality protocols. The story itself is complex, but God's actions are fairly simple. The hospitable Lot, along with his family, is saved precisely because he has shown hospitality to the angels (19:12–17), whereas inhospitable Sodom is destroyed because the "outcry against its people has become great before the Lord" (19:13; see also 19:24–25).

Genesis 18 and 19 offer a fascinating window into ancient hospitality protocols within the context of ancient stories of divine visits to unsuspecting humans. But most importantly these chapters provide the religious and theological sanctions for hospitality to strangers, and the point is both important and simple: God loves and rewards the hospitable

---

33. Matthews, "Hospitality and Hostility in Genesis 19 and Judges 19," 4.

34. T. Desmond Alexander, "Lot's Hospitality: A Clue to His Righteousness," *JBL* 104, no. 2 (June 1985): 289–91.

for they are righteous and pious in his sight, but God judges those who abuse and reject vulnerable strangers for they are wicked. Whoever the God of Israel is, this God is one who loves strangers, demands their protection, and warns individuals and societies that would break hospitality protocols.

Corrupt, Degenerate, and Inhospitable Israel: Judges

But the inhospitable Sodomites are, after all, well . . . Sodomites! It might be tempting to read the stories of Abraham, Lot, and Sodom in a self-justifying way and thus conclude that we who are worshippers of the true God are like Abraham and not like the men of Sodom. But the story in Judges 19 presents a warning *to God's people, precisely to those who are religious,* that even amidst religious devotion and worship of God, they may still have the potential to act like the men of Sodom and to abuse the vulnerable stranger through a hospitality that has become corrupted. Do not forget that in a country that is almost entirely composed of immigrants and whose economic growth was dependent upon immigrants, almost two-thirds of white evangelical Christians are in favor of greater restrictions on immigration into the US.[35] And the history of immigration policies in the US has been characterized by *both* welcome and resistance.[36]

One of the ways the author of Judges demonstrates how corrupt Israel has become in the period of the judges is by showing how the civilizing custom of hospitality, ironically, brings harm, violence, and conflict to those who engage in its practice. The stories in Judges are full of surprisingly twisted ethical behavior, as the author seeks to show that a society where "there was no king in Israel; all the people did what was right in their own eyes" (Judg 21:25; see also 17:6; 18:1; 19:1) is a chaotic world of wickedness. One of these stories in particular shows how hospitality is corrupted or improperly executed and thereby results in violence instead of safety, protection, and friendship.

The story of the Levite and his concubine in Judges 19 shows how flagrant abuses of inhospitality and corruption of hospitality protocols lead to the gruesome and violent death of the female concubine.[37] The opening

---

35. Stapleford, *Bulls, Bears and Golden Calves,* 223.
36. Stapleford, *Bulls, Bears and Golden Calves,* 227–29.
37. On which, see Matthews, "Hospitality and Hostility in Judges 4," 13–21.

comment, "In those days, when there was no king in Israel . . ." (19:1a), reminds the reader that this is a world upside-down, chaotic and absurd. The story centers upon a Levite man and his estrangement from his concubine. She flees from her husband and finds refuge with her father in Bethlehem (19:2). When the Levite seeks to reconcile with her, he travels to Bethlehem and is received with hospitality in the home of the concubine's father (19:3). The hospitality cues are evident, as the Levite "remained with him three days; so they ate and drank, and he stayed there" (19:4b). The reader is expected, then, to view the father-in-law's hospitality favorably. His kind reception of the Levite, the food, the drink, the lodging—these are the standard elements of good hospitality. But there is a serious problem. The father corrupts hospitality protocols by detaining his son-in-law and daughter from their journey back home. After three days of hospitality, the Levite tries to leave but his host forcefully detains him: "Fortify yourself with a bit of food, and after that you may go" (19:5b). And then, "why not spend the night and enjoy yourself?" (19:6b). And so the Levite stays another night with his father-in-law (19:7). The next morning, when he is preparing to leave, the scene plays out again with his father-in-law compelling him to stay another night (19:7–8). So the Levite eats and lingers until the middle of the afternoon (19:8b). When the Levite again tries to begin his journey, the man's excessive hospitality has become obnoxious, not only for the Levite but also for the reader: "Look, the day has worn on until it is almost evening. Spend the night. See, the day has drawn to a close. Spend the night here and enjoy yourself. Tomorrow you can get up early in the morning for your journey, and go home" (19:9b). The father-in-law's hospitality here is too enthusiastic, too zealous, and his attempt to detain his son-in-law and daughter has the ironic effect of putting them in a position of danger and vulnerability as they must now begin their journey home as vulnerable nighttime travelers.[38]

Their journey home is horrific. The Levite rejects his servant's suggestion that they look for lodging in Jebus: "We will not turn aside into a city of foreigners who do not belong to the children of Israel" (19:12a). The Levite's assumption is obvious: they can expect proper hospitality from Israelites only. As the sun goes down, they arrive in the Israelite city of Gibeah where "no one took them in to spend the night" (19:15b). The Levite's expectation is

38. On the repetition of night as indicating danger to the travelers, see Weston W. Fields, "The Motif 'Night as Danger' Associated with Three Biblical Destruction Narratives," in 'Sha'are Talmon': Studies in the Bible, Qumran, and the Ancient Near East Presented to Shemaryahu Talmon, ed. Michael Fishbane and Emmanuel Tov (Winona Lake, IN: Eisenbrauns, 1992), 17–32, here, 21–25.

frustrated, and the echoes of Genesis 19 invite us to see Israel as no better in its hospitality than Sodom.[39] But while they are waiting in the city square, an old man from Ephraim approaches them. He too, like Lot, is a resident alien in Gibeah (19:16b), and immediately breaks hospitality protocol by asking them their names and their business *before* offering an invitation of welcome to them (19:17).[40] The Levite testifies to the inhospitality of the Benjamite city of Jebus: "We are passing from Bethlehem in Judah to the remote parts of the hill country of Ephraim. . . . *Nobody has offered to take me in*" (19:18b). The Ephraimite man begs them, again like Lot, to come home with him, and he takes care of the donkeys, gives them food, drink, and water to wash their feet (19:20–21). As the crew is receiving hospitality in the man's home, the story of Lot and Sodom in Genesis 19:1–11 plays out as a group of men surround the house and demand that the Ephraimite alien put the stranger out of his house so they can have sex with him (19:22; see Gen 19:5). The man responds by taking his virgin daughter *and the concubine of his guest* and offering them to the crowd to "ravish them and do whatever you want to them" (19:24). The obvious implication here is that during this period of Israel's history, violations of hospitality and its corruption are the norm. Hospitality may protect men, but it does not protect vulnerable women.[41] That a host, who is responsible for protecting his guests, would give the guest's concubine to a violent crowd and offer the command "rape her" is bizarre and ludicrous. The story ends with the horrible note "they wantonly raped her, and abused her all through the night until the morning" (19:25). Showing the ultimate violation of hospitality protocols, she is found lying dead at the door of the man's house, arms stretched out upon the threshold (19:26–27).

The corruption of hospitality in the period of the Judges serves the author's broader purposes of showing the sin and wickedness of Israel. The narrator allows the reader to draw the necessary and obvious conclusion, and for our purposes the theological and practical lessons are straightforward: a society that violates the vulnerable is a degenerate, wicked society. The allusions to the story of Sodom's inhospitality in Genesis 19 show that through its corruption of hospitality, Israel is no better than wicked Sodom. Dan Block has stated the ironic warning clearly: "When the Israelites look

---

39. See here especially Daniel I. Block, "Echo Narrative Technique in Hebrew Literature: A Study in Judges 19," *WTJ* 52, no. 2 (Fall 1990): 325–41, here, 336–41.

40. See the fine treatment here by Stuart Lasine, "Guest and Host in Judges 19: Lot's Hospitality in an Inverted World," *JSOT* 29 (June 1984): 37–59.

41. On which see especially Phyllis Trible, *Texts of Terror: Literary-Feminist Readings of Biblical Narratives*, OBT 13 (Philadelphia: Fortress Press, 1984), 65–91.

in a mirror, what they see is a nation, which, even if ethnically distinct from the natives, is indistinguishable from them with regard to morality, ethics, and social values."[42]

Subverting the Stereotype: Ruth

Exclusion and inhospitality do not always take the form of violence, deportation, and unjust legislation; rather, exclusion is often mediated through dehumanizing stereotypes that breed fear, suspicion, and anger among citizens. M. Daniel Carroll R. notes the language used to describe Hispanic immigration: "a flood," a "rising tide," "a horde," and "an invasion"—all of which increase popular fears of immigrants among citizens.[43]

The story of Ruth and Boaz illuminates both the vulnerability of the immigrant and how God cares for the stranger when his people (in this instance Boaz) obey God's laws concerning the immigrant. Ruth's vulnerability is obvious to the reader, for *as a widow and a Moabite foreigner living in Israel*, her very life is dependent upon the protection of those with power.[44] The story highlights her need for provision of food and drink as well as protection from sexual attack (2:8–23).

But Ruth is not only a foreigner and a widow; she is particularly a Moabitess. One of Israel's greatest acts of rebellion against God took place when the men of Israel began to have sex with Moabite women (Numbers 25). These Moabite women enticed Israel to commit idolatry and make sacrifices to the Baal of Peor (25:2–3; see Deut 23:3). Thus, when Naomi, who lived during the "days when the judges ruled" (Ruth 1:1a), is said to have had two sons who "took Moabite wives" (1:4), the reader is justified in wondering if this will simply be one more episode in the plot of Israel's spiral into corruption, immorality, and idolatry. And it would seem as though the narrator intentionally evokes the stereotype of the idolatrous Moabite woman, as he consistently refers to Ruth, the story's heroine, as "Ruth the Moabitess" (1:22; 2:2, 21; 4:5, 10), "the young Moabite woman" (2:6), and the "foreigner" (2:10). But Ruth does not conform to the ethnic stereotype of the adulterous, idolatrous Moabite temptress.[45] She is, in fact, a model of virtue and faithful-

---

42. Block, "Echo Narrative Technique in Hebrew Literature," 336.

43. Carroll R., *Christians at the Borders*, 27.

44. See Michael S. More, "Ruth: Resident Alien with a Face," *Christian Reflection* (2008): 20–25.

45. The story of Ruth exemplifies the obvious point that Israel's relationship to foreign

ness. She clings to Naomi, her mother-in-law, and avers faithfulness to her, the God of Israel, and the people of Israel (1:14–17). Ruth is no idolater, for she leaves her own gods in order to worship Yahweh (1:16–17; see Exod 6:7). Later, Boaz praises her for her loyalty to stay with and care for Naomi (2:11). She conforms to the laws of Israel as she follows the protocols regarding the gleaning that made provisions for the poor (2:8–10, 17–23). And she rightly pursues Boaz, rather than a younger man, as her kinsman redeemer (3:6–13). Thus, Boaz states what the reader already knows: "all the assembly of my people know that you are a worthy woman" (3:11b). The narrator shows us, then, that the ethnic stereotype of the idolatrous Moabitess does not fit Ruth in the least. Carroll R. states it well: "The book of Ruth, therefore, is not only a tale of this woman's praiseworthy responses to Naomi and Boaz; it is also a testimony to her admirable attitudes *as an immigrant*."[46]

But the story is of further importance in that it shows how a vulnerable foreign widow receives hospitality and protection through God's laws. In the following section, we will examine this "legislation of hospitality" in Israel's laws in more detail, but here note that Boaz insures that the gleaning laws of the Torah are followed, and this provides both food and protection for Ruth (2:8–10; see Lev 19:9–10; Deut 24:19–22). Boaz himself even provides food and drink for Ruth (2:14). Through Boaz, then, the God of Israel provides refuge, safety, and hospitality for the foreign widow (2:12).

Legislating Hospitality in the Torah

So far we have examined only narrative depictions of hospitality and inhospitality in the Old Testament. But what does the Torah, God's law for Israel, have to say about hospitality, inhospitality, and the stranger? We will see that the narrative depictions of hospitality are in effect codified as commands in the Torah for how God's people are to treat the immigrant who has settled within Israel. Within the Old Testament the term "alien" (*ger*) is generally applied to non-Israelites who have settled within Israel and do not have land, family, or friends.[47] Along with the widow and orphan, the immigrant was

---

nations was often one of exclusion as it sought to protect itself from the idolatry of those nations. See here Daniel L. Smith-Christopher, "Between Ezra and Isaiah: Exclusion, Transformation, and Inclusion of the 'Foreigner' in Post-Exilic Biblical Theology," in *Ethnicity and the Bible*, ed. Mark Brett (Leiden: Brill, 2002), 117–42, here, 120–30.

46. Carroll R., *Christians at the Border*, 75.

47. Carroll R., *Christians at the Border*, 102–4.

especially economically and socially vulnerable. The immigrant was also often viewed with fear and suspicion due to his or her different culture, place of origin, and language or accent. The command to show justice and hospitality to the immigrant is obvious in the following exhortations, but also pay close attention to the sanctions and warrants that provide the motivation.[48]

You shall not wrong or oppress a resident alien, for you were aliens in the land of Egypt. (Exod 22:21)

You shall not oppress a resident alien; you know the heart of an alien, for you were aliens in the land of Egypt. (Exod 23:9)

When an alien resides with you in your land, you shall not oppress the alien. The alien who resides with you shall be to you as the citizen among you; you shall love the alien as yourself, for you were aliens in the land of Egypt: I am the Lord your God. (Lev 19:33–34)

The Lord your God is God of gods and Lord of lords, the great God, mighty and awesome, who is not partial and takes no bribe, who executes justice for the orphan and the widow, and who loves the strangers, providing them food and clothing. You shall also love the stranger, for you were strangers in the land of Egypt. (Deut 10:17–19)

"Cursed be anyone who deprives the alien, the orphan, and the widow of justice." All the people shall say, "Amen." (Deut 27:19)

No Ammonite or Moabite shall be admitted to the assembly of the Lord . . . because they did not meet you with food and water on your journey out of Egypt. . . . (Deut 23:3a, 4a)

An examination, from which I will provide just a sample, confirms God's demand upon his people to care for the vulnerable immigrant.

Render true judgments, show kindness and mercy to one another; do not oppress the widow, the orphan, the alien, or the poor; and do not devise evil in your hearts against one another. (Zech 7:9b–10)

Father and mother are treated with contempt in you; the alien residing within you suffers extortion; the orphan and the widow are wronged in you. (Ezek 22:7)

48. On these texts, see especially Christian van Houten, *The Alien in Israelite Law*, JSOTSup 107 (Sheffield: Sheffield Academic Press, 1991). More briefly, see Matthew Soerens and Jenny Hwang, *Welcoming the Stranger: Justice, Compassion & Truth in the Immigration Debate* (Downers Grove, IL: InterVarsity Press, 2009), 86–90.

God's demand to seek justice, equality, and even love for the immigrant is predicated upon two important facts about Israel. First, Israel must welcome the stranger because, as Deuteronomy 10 makes clear, *God loves the stranger and stands as a safeguard against their abuse.* The Psalmist confirms the portrait of God: "The Lord watches over the strangers; he upholds the orphan and the widow" (Ps 146:9). We already know as much from our examinations of Genesis 18–19 and Judges 4 and 19, namely, that God favors and rewards the hospitable but punishes the inhospitable or those who corrupt hospitality. Still, the statement that God loves the stranger is jarring: the God of Israel is on the side of the immigrant, the vulnerable stranger; therefore, to love and welcome the immigrant is to imitate God. The importance of Israel's laws protecting the immigrant mark God's people out as distinctive, since no comparable particular concern for the immigrant is found in the law-codes of Israel's neighbors.[49]

But second, Israel knows the heart of an immigrant because it has experienced oppression, injustice, and abuse at the hands of the inhospitable Egyptians who enslaved them for four hundred years (Gen 15:13–14). In other words, Israel knows that God loves the stranger *precisely because God has cared for, saved, and watched over Israel—an immigrant people—from the very beginning.* Further, Israel knows from experience that the vulnerability, poverty, and oppression that go hand in hand with being an immigrant are most frequently the results, not of what the immigrant does but of *what is done to the immigrant by the wicked.*[50] The paradigmatic event for Yahweh's salvation of Israel, then, centers upon their experience as oppressed strangers at the hands of Egypt.[51] Numerous texts refer to the enslaved Israelites as immigrants or aliens (for example, Gen 15:13–14; Deut 23:7; Ps 105:23; Isa 52:4). Later Jewish tradition also remembered Israel's enslavement by the Egyptians as an experience of the latter's inhospitality toward God's people. The author of the Wisdom of Solomon maintains that God judged the Egyptians precisely because "they practiced a more bitter hatred of strangers. Others [that is, the Sodomites] had refused to welcome strangers when they came to them, but these made slaves of guests

---

49. See especially Donald E. Gowan, "Wealth and Poverty in the Old Testament: The Case of the Widow, the Orphan, and the Sojourner," *Interpretation* 41, no. 4 (October 1987): 341–53, here, 343.

50. So Gowan, "Wealth and Poverty in the Old Testament," 349.

51. Rightly emphasized by Patrick D. Miller, "Israel as Host to Strangers," in *Israelite Religion and Biblical Theology: Collected Essays*, JSOTSup 267 (Sheffield: Sheffield Academic Press, 2000), 559–62. Still worth reading is E. W. Heaton, "Sojourners in Egypt," *Expository Times* 58 (1946): 80–82.

who were their benefactors" (19:13–14). Philo speaks of Israel as a nation of vulnerable guests who seek safety and protection from the powerful Egyptians. Instead, Pharaoh treated the Israelites not as guests but as prisoners of war. In so doing, he "showed no shame or fear of the God of freedom and hospitality and of justice to guests and suppliants *who watches over such as these*" (Philo, *Moses* 1.36).[52] Thus, the refrain that *"you know the heart of an immigrant"* calls upon Israel to sympathetically remember her own experience as strangers, and to reject the enticements of using power and privilege to exploit the vulnerable and the weak. If not, they will be found to be imitators not of God but of Egypt.

In fact, even a superficial reading of the Pentateuch reveals that Israel *is an immigrant people.*[53] All of Israel's patriarchs were immigrants and at one point or another are referred to as "aliens," beginning when Abraham left land and family in response to God's promise (Gen 12:1–9). Abraham's encounter with Pharaoh in Egypt highlights his vulnerability as a sojourner: "Now there was a famine in the land. So Abram went down to Egypt to reside there as an alien, for the famine was severe in the land" (Gen 12:10). Abram immigrates to a foreign land in order to save his and his wife's lives, and is also forced into an ambiguous situation where he must lie in order to protect his life.[54] A similar story played out in Genesis 20 and 26 highlights the way in which Abraham and Isaac are vulnerable, even with their great wealth, as sojourners in a foreign land.

Thus, Abraham sojourns in Canaan (Gen 17:8), Gerar (20:1), Philistia (21:34), and Hebron (35:27). Isaac and Jacob, likewise, sojourn in Canaan (35:6–7; 37:1) and Egypt (47:4–9; Ps 105:23). God inscribes an immigrant identity upon Israel *even after Israel has entered into the land.* Every year, for example, when Israel offers the tithe of the first fruits it recites this confession in the presence of God:

> A wandering Aramean was my ancestor; he went down into Egypt and lived there as an alien, few in number, and there he became a great nation, mighty and populous. When the Egyptians treated us harshly and

52. On the broader theme of Egyptian inhospitality in Philo, see Sarah J. K. Pearce, *The Land of the Body: Studies in Philo's Representation of Egypt*, WUNT 1.208 (Tübingen: Mohr-Siebeck, 2007).

53. R. J. D. Knauth, "Alien, Foreign Resident," in *Dictionary of the Old Testament: Pentateuch*, ed. T. Desmond Alexander and David W. Baker (Downers Grove, IL: InterVarsity Press, 2003), 27–33; Soerens and Hwang, *Welcoming the Stranger*, 83–86.

54. See Miller, "Israel as Host to Strangers," 553–54.

afflicted us, by imposing hard labor on us, we cried to the Lord, the God of our ancestors; the Lord heard our voice and saw our affliction, our toil, and our oppression. The Lord brought us out of Egypt with a mighty hand and an outstretched arm, with a terrifying display of power, and with signs and wonders; and he brought us into this place and gave us this land, a land flowing with milk and honey. (Deut 26:5–9)

The confession nicely encapsulates the Old Testament's theological vision of hospitality. God loved the stranger, Israel, and when Israel was afflicted, God acted both to judge the oppressors and vindicate the oppressed stranger. The tithe that Israel offers functions, then, as a remembrance of God's hospitality toward Israel, *and* it is a tangible act of hospitality to the vulnerable, as it is to be shared with "the Levites, the aliens, the orphans and the widows, so that they may eat" (Deut 26:12b). God's people experience Yahweh as their hospitable host, for example, when he feeds them with food and drink in the wilderness (Exod 16:4, 15): "He rained down on them manna to eat, and gave them the grain of heaven. Mortals ate of the bread of angels; he sent them food in abundance" (Ps 78:24–25). Even Israel's relationship to the land is a reminder that God is Israel's host and they are his guests: "The land shall not be sold in perpetuity, for the land is mine; *with me you are but aliens and tenants*" (Lev 25:23).[55] Since God is the owner of the land, Yahweh's provision of food and drink for Israel is a constant reminder that they are his guests (Ps 104; Isa 25:6–8; Joel 3:18; Amos 9:13–15).[56] Even the prayers of Israel testify that they are aliens and strangers before God their host (for example, 1 Chron 29:15; Ps 23:5–6; 39:12–13).

What does Israel's hospitable treatment of the immigrant look like in tangible terms? Specifically, it looks like economic justice: fair and just legal verdicts (Deut 1:16–17), fair payment for labor (Deut 24:14–15), intentional economic and food provision (Deut 24:19–22; Lev 19:9–10; 23:22), inclusion in Israel's festivals (Deut 16:11–14; 31:9–13) including the Sabbath (Deut 5:14–15), Day of Atonement (Lev 16:29), and Passover (Exod 12:48–49; Num 9:14). In short, the immigrant and sojourner are to be accorded equal treatment and the same rights as are the citizen and native-born (Lev 24:22; Num 15:15–16). This is encapsulated in the frequent refrain in the Torah that

55. Patrick D. Miller Jr., "The Gift of God: The Deuteronomic Theology of the Land," *Interpretation* 23 (1969): 454–65; Christopher J. H. Wright, *Old Testament Ethics for the People of God* (Downers Grove, IL: InterVarsity Press, 2004), 103–45.

56. See Victor H. Matthews and Don C. Benjamin, *Social World of Ancient Israel: 1250–587 BCE* (Peabody, MA: Hendrickson, 1993), 83.

there must be one law for both the citizen and the immigrant (for example, Exod 12:49; Lev 24:22).[57]

Finally, Israel's kind and hospitable treatment of the stranger would seem to be predicated upon the fact that God will one day act to include the nations as part of his people. Instead of receiving punishment and judgment, God promises that the foreign nations will join Israel.[58]

> And the foreigners who join themselves to the Lord . . . these I will bring to my holy mountain and make them joyful in my house of prayer; their burnt offerings and their sacrifices will be accepted on my altar for my house will be called a house of prayer for all peoples. (Isa 56:6–7)
>
> But the Lord will have compassion on Jacob and will again choose Israel, and will set them in their own land; and aliens will join them and attach themselves to the house of Jacob. (Isa 14:1)
>
> Many nations will join themselves to the Lord on that day, and shall be my people, and I will dwell in your midst. (Zech 2:11a)
>
> On that day Israel will be the third with Egypt and Assyria, a blessing in the midst of the earth, whom the Lord of hosts has blessed, saying, "Blessed be Egypt my people, and Assyria the work of my hands, and Israel my heritage." (Isa 19:24–25)

Other texts, of course, look forward to a day of reckoning for the nations, but many passages anticipate that when God restores Israel he will also transform the nations, even Israel's enemies, in such a way that they are joined to Israel and worship Israel's God. These "visions of peaceful coexistence, and the possibility of including the foreigner among the people of God," as suggested Daniel Smith-Christopher, provide an eschatological witness toward how we might overcome an obsession with the foreign as impure and in need of exclusion.

Welcoming Immigrants and Refugees

Again, the basic argument of this book is that hospitality to strangers is at the heart of the Christian faith just as it is at the heart of the Scriptures. God's demand to welcome the stranger is inscribed in the very identity of Israel as guests,

---

57. Gowan, "Wealth and Poverty in the Old Testament," 345.

58. On these texts, see Smith-Christopher, "Between Ezra and Isaiah," 137–40.

strangers, and immigrants before God. As Christine Pohl has said, the foundations for Israel's hospitality "were tied closely to Israel's special relationship of dependence on and gratitude to God."[59] The identity of Israel's patriarchs as sojourners in a land not their own, Israel's experience of inhospitality at the hands of the Egyptians, Israel's experience of divine hospitality in the form of water and quail and manna in their wilderness wanderings, the tithe of the first fruits given for the vulnerable, the Davidic monarchy's origins in the virtuous Moabite Ruth, and their relationship to God as his guests on God's land insure that Israel conceptualizes itself perpetually as immigrants, sojourners, and guests before God and as people *whose existence is sustained by God's hospitality.* God loves Israel *because* God loves the immigrant. The biblical texts examined above consistently speak of God's love for the stranger and Israel's knowing the heart of the stranger as the warrants for bestowing welcome to the stranger.

It is encouraging that many explicitly Christian organizations have repudiated the popular xenophobic rhetoric that has often characterized the Religious Right through debunking many of the myths about immigrants that produce fear and suspicion, through actively resettling refugees and providing tangible care for immigrants, and through advocating for immigration reform. Many of these denominations and organizations have acted so precisely because they have rediscovered the importance of the biblical tradition of hospitality toward the stranger.

For example, in 2006 The National Association of Evangelicals published "Resolution on Immigration" and asserted: "While we recognize the rights of nations to regulate their borders, we believe this responsibility should be exercised with a concern for the entire human family in a spirit of generosity and compassion (Deut 10:19; Lev 19:34). As evangelicals responsible to love our neighbors as ourselves (Matt 22:39), we are called to show personal and corporate hospitality to those who seek a new life in our nation." Likewise, the United Church of Christ has also issued a call to welcome the immigrant, to pursue immigration reform, and to reject exclusionary practices out of their commitment to the teaching of the Scriptures. "The Bible is unambiguous in calling us to welcome aliens and strangers in our land, and to love them as we love ourselves. In these times, let us listen to the voice of the still-speaking God. We will learn how to respond to these new sisters and brothers residing among us."[60] Examples could be multiplied.[61]

---

59. Pohl, *Making Room*, 29.
60. See http://www.ucc.org/justice_immigration.
61. See the repudiation of the ICE raid on over three hundred Latino immigrants in

Ordinary followers of Jesus can take very tangible and practical steps to enact hospitality to the immigrant. The action steps are set forth *much more fully* in the important books, articles, and testimonies of the practitioners themselves, but I would like to at least briefly highlight three of them. First, Christians should evaluate political rhetoric and candidates running for public office within the framework of what the Scriptures say about the immigrant rather than personal economic, national, and racial ideologies.[62] The ethnic and cultural stereotyping as well as scapegoating techniques that blame society's ills upon migrants should be rejected and called out as non-Christian behavior. Much of the popular political rhetoric surrounding immigration is as emotive as it is patently false. To give one example, despite the popular belief that immigrants take jobs away from citizens, most agree that "world migrants are admitted to fill gaps in the local labour market. . . . Migrant workers are rarely encouraged to enter situations to compete directly with local workers."[63] Koser goes on to explain that a major gap exists between academic research on migration and political and popular rhetoric: "Even where research points unambiguously to the conclusion that immigrants contribute to economic growth, do not compete for jobs, do not lower wages for the native-born, and represent good value in cost-benefit terms, *this is not how they will necessarily be viewed*" (italics mine).[64] The italicized portion of Koser's statement may appear to be grossly understated for those listening to the rhetoric of certain political candidates who ran for the presidency of the United States in 2016. Campese has diagnosed the situation both in Italy and in the US thus: "Instead of responding to the understandable fear and suspicions of natives with rational arguments and initiatives, these politicians nurture that fear by enacting and implementing restrictive and

Postville, Iowa, in 2008 by Bishop John C. Wester of the United States Conference of Catholic Bishops' Committee on Migration. This is set forth in Jean-Pierre Ruiz, *Readings from the Edges: The Bible and People on the Move*, Studies in Latino/a Catholicism (Maryknoll, NY: Orbis, 2011), 34–35. See also Campese, "'But I See That Somebody Is Missing,'" 72.

62. See the treatment of Republican South Carolina governor Nikki Haley by supporters of her own party when, in her response to President Obama's state of the union address (January 2016), she declared that fixing immigration "means welcoming properly vetted legal immigrants, regardless of their race or religion. Just like we have for centuries." Ann Coulter's tweet helped establish the popular hashtag: #DeportNikkiHaley. See further http://www.npr.org/2016/01/16/463036044/-memeoftheweek-the-racial-politics-of-nikki-haley.

63. Koser, *International Migration*, 94. See further, Stephen Castles and Mark J. Miller, *The Age of Migration: International Population Movements in the Modern World*, 4th ed. (New York: Palgrave Macmillan, 2009), 221–44.

64. Koser, *International Migration*, 97.

useless laws and by speaking of immigration and immigrants in terms of invasion, plague, rats, clandestine people, illegal aliens, and so on."[65]

Second, Christians should educate themselves about migration—its causes, legislation, and so on—so that they can advocate for just and equitable legislation regarding national immigration policies.[66] Discovering the stance of state governors, senators, local congress members, and presidential candidates toward immigration policies is one of the easiest and first steps churches and Christians can take as they pursue just and hospitable laws toward migrants. While the Christian must not ignore those passages that call for obedience to the civil government, which has been instituted by God (for example, Rom 13:1–7; Titus 3:1; 1 Pet 2:11–17), the Christian must also reckon with globalization and the recent transformations in the global economy and take seriously the very real consequences the policies of our own country have had upon would-be migrants.[67] It takes work and education to realize how, in our globalized economy, our own lifestyle and consumer choices, as well as our nation's public policy, can create the necessary conditions for those seeking to migrate to the US.

Third, churches and Christians can engage in meaningful relationships with immigrants and refugees by volunteering with programs such as World Relief, Church World Service, Catholic Legal Immigration Network, and more. One can also pursue friendships with immigrants on a more mundane and personal level by initiating conversation with the owners or servers at your favorite restaurant, your local bank teller, or the owner of your laundromat. All kinds of ministry opportunities are available to those who would take the risk of welcoming the immigrant into one's church, family, and home. Many of the immigrants who come to the US are searching for places to worship, for community, and for friendship. Many of them are, in fact, fellow worshippers of Jesus Christ and are, therefore, our brothers and

---

65. Campese, "'But I See That Somebody Is Missing,'" 72.

66. See Soerens and Hwang, *Welcoming the Stranger*, 198–99.

67. Thus, James R. Edwards Jr.'s argument ("A Biblical Perspective on Immigration Policy," in *Debating Immigration*, ed. Carol M. Swain [Cambridge: Cambridge University Press, 2007], 56) strikes me as naïve in failing to reckon with globalization and the consequences of American public policy upon other nations: "We as Americans have a greater and more immediate moral obligation to be concerned with the welfare and quality of life in the United States than in other countries, just as the residents of those countries should be more concerned with what goes on there than in the United States. . . . Each of us has ties to very particularistic communities, and we must all acknowledge the legitimacy of those ties and the special obligation that we all have to direct our immediate attention to the welfare of those very special communities that each of us calls our own."

sisters in Christ. Many North American churches shut themselves off from the vibrant faith of their devout Latino brothers and sisters at their own peril.[68] As Soerens and Hwang say: "The sojourner or stranger, once considered on the 'margins' of society, now through the church can be invited in to experience the fullness of worship together as one body. Churches are realizing through a diverse body of Christ that worship is a celebration of God himself, who made every tribe, language, people and nation to worship him."[69] Powerful personal stories from churches and individuals who have welcomed the immigrant testify to their experiences of enrichment in their own faith as they hear stories and testimonies about God's global work outside of the US.

Study Questions

1. Describe any personal friendships or relationships you have with recent immigrants or displaced peoples. What do you know about their experiences here?

2. In what ways have you witnessed or personally experienced any fears or concerns about welcoming immigrants and consequences for our economy, national security, and/or national identity?

3. Should the Old Testament's teaching on hospitality and the immigrant influence how we think about our country's public policy? Why or why not? How should the Scriptures influence how we think about pursuing immigration policy and reform?

4. What are some practical ways in which you (and/or your church) might respond to the call to show hospitality to the immigrant?

---

68. See here Todd Hartch, *The Rebirth of Latin American Christianity* (Oxford: Oxford University Press, 2014); Carroll R, *Christians at the Border*, 56–62; see the stories of Mexican immigrant spirituality and faith throughout Daniel G. Groody, "Jesus and the Undocumented Immigrant: A Spiritual Geography of a Crucified People," *Theological Studies* 70, no. 2 (June 2009): 298–316.

69. Soerens and Hwang, *Welcoming the Stranger*, 160.

CHAPTER 6

Hospitality and Economy: Overcoming Greed

For those who have begun the journey from xenophobia and tribalism to hospitality, the challenge, for both individuals and communities, of scarce goods and resources to share with others still remains. Dispensing hospitality to strangers almost always requires sharing out of one's own financial resources—food, shelter, money, time, and so on—and the fear of scarcity or simply not having enough can present serious obstacles to bestowing hospitality to those in need. Christine Pohl has said that those who offer hospitality "live between the vision of God's kingdom in which there is enough, even abundance, and the hard realities of human life in which doors are closed and locked, and some needy people are turned away or left outside."[1] In God's economy his people need not anxiously fret about food, drink, and clothes since God knows his people need these things (Luke 12:22–32); they learn to pray to their merciful and giving Father for their daily needs (Matt. 6:11); and God promises to satisfy the poor with food (Luke 1:52–53). But are these kinds of statements grounded in reality? Can we base our lives on a divine economy that, on the face of it, looks entirely out of touch with the way things work in our world? Much of the seemingly sound economic advice we receive (and act on) does not operate according to divine abundance but scarcity. After all, I won't be advising my children (or anyone else's!) to act as if there's no such thing as economic scarcity when it comes time to think about paying for their college education. The tension between God's kingdom economy of abundance and our human economy of scarcity is all

1. Christine D. Pohl, *Making Room: Recovering Hospitality as a Christian Tradition* (Grand Rapids: Eerdmans, 1999), 131.

147

too real. But worries that we will not have enough resources for ourselves can cause us to close our eyes to the prevalent need and opportunities for relationships that are right before us. Those who practice hospitality, then, would be foolish to ignore the reality of limited resources and economic scarcity. If we are left to our own devices and the workings of our own economy, fear of economic scarcity can easily function as a total barrier from sharing what we do have. I imagine most (perhaps all) of my readers live in a situation of abundance, not scarcity. But, as Pohl says, "we often act as if resources are scarce; we fear there won't be enough, even before we begin sharing what we have. The problem may have much more to do with our willingness to respond than with our resources."[2] What Pohl is describing here, one of the primary impediments to extending hospitality to others, is the vice of greed. In other words, it's not that "we don't have enough to share"; it's that we don't think we have enough to share because we are often distracted by and too busy participating in our consumer capitalist economy.

It may be, then, that the problem is not so much worries about scarcity as it is that we love our possessions (or the desire for new possessions); we love the security and opportunities afforded by our wealth; we love buying stuff—maybe not even the stuff itself, but simply the endless cycle of buying and consuming. Our economy operates according to the belief in the scarcity of resources *and the belief* in the anthropological condition of insatiable human desires, wants, and self-interest.[3] Capitalist economies, then, do not view *the individual's* self-interested desires and wants as a vice but, rather, as the central anthropological condition upon which our economy operates.[4] When we couple this anthropological condition of humanity with a certain view of freedom, defined negatively as the freedom of exchange through the market and non-interference from the state,[5] the result is what we see today: humans who find their meaning and identity in the endless cycle of desire, consumption, and detachment.[6] One may argue that this need not be the result, but with-

2. Pohl, *Making Room*, 135.

3. See Bernd Wannenwetsch, "The Desire of Desire: Commandment and Idolatry in Late Capitalist Societies," in *Idolatry*, ed. Stephen C. Barton (New York: T&T Clark, 2007), 315–30, here, 323–26.

4. On the problematic "theological anthropology" of the dominant tradition of capitalism, see D. Stephen Long, *Divine Economy: Theology and the Market* (London: Routledge, 2000), 9–80.

5. See Milton and Rose Friedman, *Free to Choose* (New York: Avon Books, 1980).

6. Long, *Divine Economy*, 270: "To teach us to desire . . . *that* is the role of the contemporary market."

out agreed-upon *collective ends or common goods* then individual self-interest alone is encouraged.[7] In Christian Smith's extensive interviews of eighteen- to twenty-year-olds, he finds three assumptions that undergird the "mass consumerist way of life" of emerging adults. First, they believe individuals fairly earned their money. Second, no society can or should interfere with the desires of individuals. And third, "people are naturally driven by self-interested acquisitive motives, which ultimately cannot be denied or deterred."[8]

But self-interest does not always take the simple form of wealth accumulation or hoarding our stuff; in fact, in North America we more frequently show greed through our detachment from our money and possessions as we consistently buy and discard. Hence, our enjoyment and attachment to our possessions rarely last long, as we are easily dissatisfied and thereby crave something newer, bigger, and better.[9] Contemporary marketing strategies that seek to create new desires and passions within us facilitate our desires, often through the attempt to sell us supposedly better self-identities.[10] In our consumer capitalist society, "material goods and services are less about possession in the sense of 'having' or hoarding and more about the constant and endless acquisition of novelties for the sake of distinguishing oneself, for the sake of appearance, of being recognized as valuable in the eyes of the market, and, hence, in the eyes of others."[11] Our economy, in fact, is dependent upon us not ever being content or pleased with what we have. Economists and theologians alike have suggested that our consumer culture of capitalism functions like a religion or liturgy that demands our allegiance and toward which we orient our desires and longings.[12] The desire for consumption is,

---

7. Daniel M. Bell Jr., *The Economy of Desire: Christianity and Capitalism in a Postmodern World* (Grand Rapids: Baker, 2012), 99–102.

8. Christian Smith, *Lost in Transition: The Dark Side of Emerging Adulthood* (Oxford: Oxford University Press, 2011), 80.

9. On detachment, see especially William T. Cavanaugh, *Being Consumed: Economics and Christian Desire* (Grand Rapids: Eerdmans, 2008), 33–58.

10. See here especially, Wannenwetsch, "The Desire of Desire," 318–20.

11. Bell, *The Economy of Desire*, 120.

12. James K. A. Smith, *Desiring the Kingdom: Worship, Worldview, and Cultural Formation*, Cultural Liturgies, vol. 1 (Grand Rapids: Baker, 2009), 93–103. That economists operate with religious and theological assumptions in their economic thought is argued by Robert H. Nelson, *Economics as Religion: From Samuelson to Chicago and Beyond* (University Park: Pennsylvania State University Press, 2001), xv: "Economists think of themselves as scientists, but as I will be arguing in this book, they are more like theologians." See also Robert H. Nelson, *The New Holy Wars: Economic Religion vs. Environmental Religion in Contemporary America* (University Park: Pennsylvania State University Press, 2010).

in the words of William Cavanaugh, "a type of spirituality. . . . It is a way of pursuing meaning and identity, a way of connecting with other people."[13] And as we will see, given the Bible's depiction of greed as idolatry, that is to say, false worship, mistaking the economy as "God" is not surprising. The similarities between the economy in Western societies and God is eerily set forth by Brian Rosner:

> Like God, the economy, it is thought, is capable of supplying people's needs without limit. Also like God, the economy is mysterious, unknowable, and intransigent. It has both great power, and, despite the best managerial efforts of its associated clergy, great danger. It is an inexhaustible well of good(s) and is credited with prolonging life, giving health, and enriching our lives. Money, in which we put our faith, and advertising, which we adore, are among its rituals. The economy also has its sacred symbols, which evoke undying loyalty, including company logos, product names, and credit cards.[14]

The biblical critique of greed and excessive consumption as idolatry makes good sense in our context today, where the economy dominates virtually every facet of our existence. Consumer societies can thereby distract us and blind us to the needs—physical and relational—of those who are lonely, hungry, and socially alienated from society. We are unable to share our resources, possessions, and lives with others because we do not think that we "have enough" to satisfy our own desires. Further, when *individual* self-interest is coupled together with freedom (negatively defined) as the only end, the result is almost inevitably domination and exploitation of the poor. While globalization, advanced for the purpose of free market exchanges and profits across borders, may have increased wealth in some sectors, the growth often comes, as Bauckham has argued, "at the expense of the poor. It is also at the expense of all other values in human life: face-to-face community, social solidarity, uncommercialized cultural diversity, and the preservation of the environment."[15] Thus, competition is a necessary component to capitalism, for human social

13. Cavanaugh, *Being Consumed*, 36.
14. Brian Rosner, "Soul Idolatry: Greed as Idolatry in the Bible," *Ex Auditu* 15 (1999): 73–86, here, 82.
15. Richard Bauckham, *The Bible in the Contemporary World: Hermeneutical Ventures* (Grand Rapids: Eerdmans, 2015), 67; Steven Bouma-Prediger and Brian J. Walsh, *Beyond Homelessness: Christian Faith in a Culture of Displacement* (Grand Rapids: Eerdmans, 2008), 94–97.

relations are ordered according to conflict as individuals seek to maximize their own individual interests.[16] One result is that virtually everything, including human lives, is turned into a commodity that can be evaluated "by the same criteria as commodities—marketability, profitability, and consumability."[17] The ideology of capitalist consumerism privileges my own individual private choice for how I spend, buy, consume, and discard—regardless of the ramifications this may have, for example, on the workers who produce the goods I consume.[18] And for those who cannot or do not participate in our economy, it is not difficult to discern their marginal social value and worth.

I am not making a cumulative argument here against capitalist economies, labor, production, and markets. In other words, I'm not trying to demonstrate that capitalist exchange is intrinsically vile. Rather, my simple point is that an uncritical acceptance of and participation in our capitalist consumer economy can function as a significant barrier in sharing our resources, possessions, and time with others for hospitable purposes. As Christians we have little choice, of course, but to participate in and make use of the human economies within which we are embedded, but we must guard our minds, bodies, and desires from the danger of becoming conformed to the patterns and orders of these economies (see Rom 12:2). We might say that the city of God has its own economy that teaches us how to make use of our resources and possessions in different ways and for different purposes.[19] Further, the biblical teaching on greed, economy, and hospitality sets forth an important alternative vision for how we use our resources for mercy, hospitality, and solidarity.[20] The New Testament's teaching on the divine economy represents a powerful challenge to both the ancient and contemporary world's *"ordering of things, persons, and patterns of exchange."*[21]

---

16. Michael Porter, *On Competition* (Cambridge, MA: Harvard University Press, 1998).

17. Bell, *The Economy of Desire*, 106. But see here also Dotan Leshem, *The Origins of Neoliberalism: Modeling the Economy from Jesus to Foucault* (New York: Columbia University Press, 2016), 167–70, 177–81.

18. Cavanaugh, *Being Consumed*, 52–53.

19. Augustine's *City of God* is relevant here. See William T. Cavanaugh, *Field Hospital: The Church's Engagement with a Wounded World* (Grand Rapids: Eerdmans, 2016), 140–56.

20. From a theological perspective, see here Kathryn Tanner, *Economy of Grace* (Minneapolis: Fortress Press, 2005).

21. The phrase is from Stephen C. Barton, "Money Matters: Economic Relations and the Transformation of Value in Early Christianity," in *Engaging Economics: New Testament Scenarios and Early Christian Reception*, ed. Bruce W. Longenecker and Kelly D. Liebengood (Grand Rapids: Eerdmans, 2009), 37–59, here, 39.

In what follows, I propose to examine this "divine economy" as we see it in some New Testament writings and the social world within which their teaching is embedded. This examination falls under three headings: a) from greed to acts of mercy; b) from competitive patronage to mutual solidarity; and c) from structural complicity to prophetic critique.

From Greed to Acts of Mercy

The Bible is chock-full of warnings against the vice of greed. Ezekiel's prophetic oracle against the coastal merchant city promises divine judgment against the city for its excessive luxury, wealth, and hubris (Ezek 26–28). In Paul's lists of vices in Ephesians and Colossians he refers to greed as idolatry (Eph 5:5; Col 3:5; see Rom 1:29).[22] Paul warns the church in Rome about his opponents who "do not serve our Lord the Messiah but rather their own bellies" (16:18) and those in Philippi whose "god is their stomach" (Phil 3:19). Similarly, in Luke's Acts of the Apostles the negative characters or antagonists of the faith are frequently portrayed as greedy individuals who make poor use of their possessions. Judas's gory end is due to his rightly receiving "the wage for his unrighteousness," namely, preferring silver to loyalty to Jesus (Acts 1:18). Ananias and Sapphira hold back the proceeds from their field instead of sharing with the community (Acts 5:1–11); Simon Magus tries to purchase the Holy Spirit (8:14–25); Demetrius's devotion to the goddess Artemis is due to his ability to profit from making silver shrines (19:23–27; see 16:16–18); Felix leaves Paul imprisoned, hoping to receive a monetary bribe (24:24–26). It seems as though one of Luke's agendas is to say something about the relationship between greed and lack of devotion to the true God.[23] A list of warnings from the Bible against greed, luxury, and the pursuit of wealth could be extended at great length, but why is the Bible so unrelenting in its insistence on the evil of greed? In what follows, we will examine the destructive effects of greed as well as its antidote by exploring a few of the teachings of Paul and Jesus.

Greed is ultimately an illness, evidence of a disordered desire that supposes life, joy, and security are to be found in the accumulation of wealth

---

22. Brian S. Rosner, *Greed as Idolatry: The Origin and Meaning of a Pauline Metaphor* (Grand Rapids: Eerdmans, 2007).

23. This theme is highlighted throughout Luke Timothy Johnson, *The Literary Function of Possessions in Luke-Acts*, SBLDS 39 (Missoula, MT: Scholars Press, 1977).

and possessions and not in God. Greed is an illness but it is also foolish, for it supposes that things can fulfill our desires for happiness and security. In 1 Timothy 6:6–19, Paul sets forth a theological perspective on the right use of wealth and describes the love of wealth as a deadly disease that does incredible harm to its host *by disordering human desire*. Notice how Paul uses the language of the corruption of desire to describe greed. Those who long for wealth are filled with "many foolish desires that plunge people into ruin and destruction" (6:9).[24] Greed or *love for silver (philargyria)* results in "cravings" that turn people away from God and lead to "piercing themselves with many pains" (6:10). The language Paul uses suggests that "greed" is something that is living and active as it creates an insatiable hunger and desire for more wealth. But greed is a foolish and dangerous craving, for it tricks people and thereby exerts dominance over them. Thus, greed is a "temptation" and a "trap" that "plunges" its prey into ruin and causes them inordinate pains. Paul warns those who are rich "not to be arrogant or to place their hope in the uncertainty of their wealth" (6:17a) lest they be tempted to think that their money can provide security in this world or function as a safeguard for eschatological life in the next world (see Job 31:24–26; Prov 11:28). As Paul says earlier: "we have brought nothing into the world, and we cannot take anything out" (6:7).

So what is the antidote to the destructive and death-dealing vice of greed? Paul advocates grateful enjoyment of the possessions God has given to his people (6:17b; see 4:4–5), contentment with the basic provisions of food and clothing (6:6–8), and pursuit of the virtues of "righteousness, godliness, faith, love, endurance, and patience" (6:11). In other words, Paul advocates for recognizing the divine economy wherein God is the singular giver of every good gift to his people, and wherein God alone is the eternal, sovereign, and immortal ruler who provides hope and security for the future. The description of God as "the blessed and only ruler, the king over kings, the Lord over lords, the only one having immortality" (6:15b–16a) provides the explicitly theological ground for trusting God with one's life and not one's wealth. But Paul also argues that the divine economy sets forth a better way to use our wealth and material resources. Stated simply, opposed to the greedy accumulation and hoarding of possessions is, as David Downs has

---

24. That Paul (or a Paulinist if one prefers) is using common philosophical topoi to describe greed as a passion of the soul, see the excellent articles by Abraham J. Malherbe, "Godliness, Self-Sufficiency, Greed, and the Enjoyment of Wealth: 1 Timothy 6:3–19," in *Light from the Gentiles: Hellenistic Philosophy and Early Christianity: Collected Essays, 1959–2012, by Abraham J. Malherbe*, NovTSup 150, vol. 1 (Leiden: Brill, 2014), 507–57.

recently argued, "the employment of material resources to perform good works, most specifically through the generous and charitable disposal of wealth."[25] In place of trusting in the insecurity of wealth, Paul says that those with riches should enjoy their wealth *in this way*: "by doing good works, by being wealthy in good deeds, and by being generous and sharing" (6:18b). Whatever name one wants to call this—charitable giving, almsgiving, or acts of mercy—Paul suggests that God's economy advocates an enjoyment of wealth that is found in generously using one's possessions for the good of others.[26] Those who use their wealth in this way "store up for themselves a good foundation for the age to come, so that they may grasp the life that is truly life" (6:19). If God alone is the eternal sovereign king, then he is able to pay back with eternal life those who, by sharing their wealth and possessions with others, store up eschatological treasures (see Matt 6:19–21). In short, the antidote to greed is recognizing that in God's economy, God is the giver of all wealth and material resources, that wealth is to be enjoyed through doing good works and sharing generously, and that God will reward those who share their resources by giving them eschatological life.[27]

The Gospel of Luke is filled with Jesus's criticisms of the exploitative, extractive human economy operating in Roman Palestine, along with his call to participate in God's economy through almsgiving, acts of mercy, and grateful trust in God to provide. Jesus's teachings and parables reflect what studies of the ancient economy have taught us, namely, that the economy was primarily oriented around subsistence agriculture, the cities were places of consumption and not production, and wealth was powerfully connected to land.[28] Let's look at one extended passage here that reflects some of these realities—Luke 12:13–34. You may remember the story of the man who asks Jesus to act as a mediator between him and his brother over their dispute about their inheritance of land (Luke 12:13–15). It's likely that the one who came to Jesus was the younger brother who, for all we know, had a legitimate grievance. We may be surprised at Jesus's response, which seems to show a total repudiation of entering into the brother's economic concerns: "who appointed me as a judge or arbiter over you"? (12:14). Underlying this man's desire for land, for

---

25. David J. Downs, *Alms: Charity, Reward, and Atonement in Early Christianity* (Waco, TX: Baylor University Press, 2016), 157.

26. I take the three infinitives in 6:18 as epexegetic to "for our enjoyment" in 6:17b. For a defense of this translation, see Malherbe, "Godliness, Self-Sufficiency, Greed," 550.

27. Downs, *Alms*, 160.

28. The standard work here is Moses I. Finley, *The Ancient Economy* (Berkeley: University of California Press, 1999).

inheritance, for what many might say is rightfully his, Jesus identifies the sin of greed: "Watch out and guard yourself against all greed [*pleonexias*], for one's life does not consist in the superfluities of one's possessions" (12:15). In other words, Jesus is targeting the man's desire for superfluous abundance of possessions.[29] Frequently, the vice of greed combines the insatiable desire for wealth *with* the hunger for advanced social standing, and given that landowners were invariably accorded great degrees of status, this makes good sense here. Notice the antithesis Jesus makes between "life" and "possessions" (12:15b).

Jesus's harsh rebuke of the brother and his warning against avarice leads immediately into the parable of the rich foolish landowner (12:16–21). Presumably, the man thinks that he can make his *life* (note the man's self-reference to his *soul*, vv. 19, 20) secure through the accumulation of possessions.[30] Luke takes the standpoint from below, namely, the peasant economy, and sees the man as a symbol of the wealthy, extractive, consuming, exploitative landowners who could turn a substantial profit should any bad harvest come.[31] If we imagine the way in which the man might have answered his own questions regarding the excess of his crops, "What shall I do?" (12:16, 17), we can easily imagine Jesus (or Paul!) filling in the blank "give it away–all of it"! In an economy filled with peasants, where the poor constantly live at a subsistence level, the man's decision to hoard his possessions is painfully oblivious to the needs of the poor around him. Third, and perhaps most importantly based on the conclusion to the parable, the man has used, accumulated, and made plans about his possessions in a way that does not consider *God* to be the ultimate reference point: "he stores up treasures for himself and is not rich toward God" (v. 21).[32] This is why he is the paradigmatic "fool," so reminiscent of the fool in the Psalms, who plans and acts as if God is not present and does not care or provide judgment upon wickedness (for example, Ps 14:1).

---

29. Malherbe, "The Christianization of a *Topos* (Luke 12:13–34)," in *Light from the Gentiles*, 339–51, here, 348.

30. On this parable and the broader theme of the right use of possessions in the face of death, see Matthew S. Rindge, *Jesus' Parable of the Rich Fool: Luke 12:13–34 among Ancient Conversation on Death and Possessions*, Early Christianity and Its Literature, vol. 6 (Atlanta: Society of Biblical Literature, 2011).

31. Halvor Moxnes, *The Economy of the Kingdom: Social Conflict and Economic Relations in Luke's Gospel* (Philadelphia: Fortress Press, 1988), 88–89.

32. See here one of the primary theses of Luke Timothy Johnson, *Sharing Possessions: What Faith Demands*, 2nd ed. (Grand Rapids: Eerdmans, 2011), namely, the way we respond to others with our possessions is the way we respond to God.

Jesus's criticism of the economic practices of his day suggests what some of the alternatives might be, but fortunately Jesus moves from his criticisms of his world's economy to setting forth God's economy in Luke 12:22–34. Jesus suggests that God's economy 1) rejects the belief that resources are ultimately *scarce* and must be secured and hoarded for us to have life, and instead trusts God as the God of abundance who provides and gives for his people and all creation (12:24–31); 2) is oriented toward God and his kingdom entirely and will then find, as a result, that life's necessities are provided (12:31–32); 3) advances the practice of giving and generosity as a means of freeing oneself from anxiety and enslavement to wealth and possessions (12:31); and 4) articulates a radical giving and sharing of one's possessions with those in need that results in being repaid eternally by God (12:33–34). In 12:33 Luke uses three imperatives to emphasize Jesus's advocacy of almsgiving as the solution to those who greedily accumulate possessions for themselves: "*sell* your belongings," "*give* alms," and "*make* purses for yourselves that will not grow old." The rich man's folly lay in storing up his incredible fortune for his own use (12:21) instead of sharing it with the poor and thereby securing for himself the heavenly treasure which does not depreciate in value.[33]

Jesus's command to give alms as the antidote to greed is found also in Jesus's response to the Pharisees who marvel that he doesn't wash before a meal (Luke 11:37–41). Jesus accuses the Pharisees of scrupulously cleansing the outside of the cup but being internally filled with "greed [*arpagēs*] and wickedness" (11:39b). Jesus's response: "give alms with respect to the things inside and see, all will be clean for you" (11:41).[34] Again, Jesus sets forth acts of mercy as the means of atonement for the greed of the Pharisees.[35] If they give alms and engage in acts of mercy, then they will not be susceptible to Jesus's charge that they have ignored "justice and love for God" (11:42). The obvious implication is that love for God is manifested in merciful acts for others—not unlike what Jesus taught in his parable of the so-called Good Samaritan (10:25–37).

---

33. Downs, *Alms*, 129: " . . . almsgiving is the antidote to the punishment experienced by those who store up treasures for themselves but are not rich toward God, as exemplified in the parable of the Rich Fool in 12:16–21." Throughout the NT (and the OT as well), acts of mercy to the poor have a vertical focus on God himself as the one who sees, receives, and recompenses for the gift. See throughout Gary A. Anderson, *Charity: The Place of the Poor in the Biblical Tradition* (New Haven: Yale University Press, 2013).

34. See here Christopher M. Hays, *Luke's Wealth Ethics: A Study in Their Coherence and Character*, WUNT 2.275 (Tübingen: Mohr-Siebeck, 2010), 120–23. My translation reflects his argument that *ta enonta* is an accusative of respect.

35. Downs, *Alms*, 127.

Our brief foray into Paul's, Luke's, and Jesus's teaching suggests that the first movement in the divine economy is moving from greed to acts of mercy. Recognizing the subtle and deceptive pull of greed is difficult, as the repeated biblical warnings make clear. Greed is a disordered love or desire that turns our hearts from God who alone is able to provide security, who alone grants gifts of food and clothing, and who gives us the resources to enjoy *by sharing with others*. Greed can prevent us from even *seeing and recognizing* the needs of our neighbors right before our own eyes. In place of greed, Jesus and Paul advocate almsgiving, acts of mercy, and sharing out of one's abundance with others. Mercy towards others imitates God, demonstrates lives ordered toward justice and love for God, and can even atone for or cleanse our propensity to accumulate wealth and possessions.

From Competitive Patronage to Economic Solidarity

Notably, the ancient Roman economy was embedded within important social institutions such as the family, guest-friends, political structures (such as the emperor), and a strict hierarchical social status.[36] Thus, money was not the only (or even perhaps primary) form of economic exchange, for social institutions exerted an enormous influence upon economic behavior and one's ability to acquire wealth. One very important ancient social institution embedded within the ancient economy was patronage, namely, the reciprocal exchange of favors and gifts.[37] Helen Rhee notes that "patron-client relations were grounded in and formed a part of the Greco-Roman ethic of reciprocity, which was basic, informal, and ubiquitous in various social relations."[38] Amidst the variety of patronage categories, the exchange of favors usually took place between "friends" of unequal status in terms of the social hierarchy.[39] The relationships are characterized by "a very

36. On the notion of an "embedded" economy, see Karl Polanyi, *The Great Transformation: The Political and Economic Origins of Our Time* (Boston: Beacon Press, 1957).

37. For what follows, see especially Peter Garnsey and Richard Saller, *The Roman Empire: Economy, Society and Culture*, 2nd ed. (Berkeley: University of California Press, 2015), 173–84; Richard P. Saller, *Personal Patronage under the Early Empire* (Cambridge: Cambridge University Press, 1982), 1, argues that patronage involved three elements: 1) reciprocal exchange of resources and services, 2) an element of solidarity or personal loyalty, and 3) asymmetrical social status.

38. Helen Rhee, *Loving the Poor, Saving the Rich: Wealth, Poverty, and Early Christian Formation* (Grand Rapids: Baker, 2012), 14.

39. Seneca's *On Benefits* is the most well-known ancient treatise devoted to the subject.

strong element of inequality and difference in power."[40] In exchange for
small portions of food, money, legal protection, loans, and meals the clients
were expected to engage in public acts that might contribute to the social
standing of their patron.[41] Patrons often held banquets for their clients
and often used the meal as an opportunity to distinguish their most valued
clients through offering better food and superior seating arrangements.
Failure to make a return on a received gift or to advertise the generosity of
one's benefactor was considered an act of ingratitude and could result in
enmity between the patron and the client. Given that social exchange was
at the heart of patronage, patrons did not initiate relationships with those
who might reflect poorly upon or fail to contribute to the social status of
the patron.[42] Giving was highly calculated.

Central to the institution of patronage are *reciprocity* and *competition*.
Given that resources—namely, honor, status, food, money, and power—are
scarce, patronage assumed a system of intense competition with one another
for these resources.[43] The patron is continually seeking to improve his status
through constant gift giving, while the client is simultaneously indebted to
the patron and caught in a suffocating web of obligations to him from which
he can hardly escape. For this reason, and especially in light of the fact that
patronage involved asymmetrical relationships, Downs is right that "there
is an inherent potential for patron-client relations to become exploitative."[44]

One significant practice related to patronage was the public acts of
benefaction or euergetism, namely, the bestowal of contributions for the
benefit of the city.[45] Public benefactions could take the form of building
projects, such as public baths, theaters, and synagogues; provision of games
and entertainment, money, meals; and provision of food. Benefactors were
often called upon to finance grain distributions for their citizens during food
shortages, but their favors were usually not granted to the lower strata of

---

On which see Miriam T. Griffin, *Seneca on Society: A Guide to* De Beneficiis (Oxford: Oxford
University Press, 2013).

40. Moxnes, *The Economy of the Kingdom*, 42.

41. Garnsey and Saller, *The Roman Empire*, 176.

42. Garnsey and Saller, *The Roman Empire*, 180–81.

43. Rhee, *Loving the Poor, Saving the Rich*, 15.

44. David J. Downs, "Is God Paul's Patron? The Economy of Patronage in Pauline Theology," in *Engaging Economics*, 129–56, here, 137.

45. See especially Paul Veyne, *Bread and Circuses: Historical Sociology and Political
Pluralism* (London: Allen Lane, 1990). On patronage and euergetism as *distinct but related*
conceptions of economic exchange, see Stephen Joubert, "One Form of Social Exchange or
Two? 'Euergetism,' Patronage, and Testament Studies," *BTB* 31 (2001): 17–25.

society. In return for their love of their cities, the benefactors received public displays of gratitude and honor.[46] Benefaction was not designed, however, to benefit the poor, slaves, or non-citizens (even if the poor did sometimes receive some indirect benefit), given that the poor were unable to make returns for favors and did not occupy a social class.[47] Participating in the patronage system, in other words, presumed that you had something to offer—which the poor did not.[48] Rather, patrons offered benefactions primarily as a means of accruing honor; the gifts thereby strongly reinforced the existing social hierarchy.[49] We have seen, for example, the way in which meals were used as opportunities to advertise one's social status.[50] No systematic attempt or structural approach to alleviate poverty among the poor existed in Greco-Roman society.[51]

Given that the Old Testament and ancient Judaism were remarkably ambivalent about the social institutions based on reciprocity because of its tendency to lead to exploitation and inequality,[52] it should not surprise us to find that Jesus and Paul directly oppose economic relationships of exchange characterized by reciprocity, competition, and a strong sense of social hierarchy. Instead, one finds both Jesus and Paul advocating for an alternative economy, one where the poor are seen and cared for, where wealth does not result in status hierarchy, and where gifts are given freely and acts of mercy

---

46. Cicero says that honor (not morals or pity for the poor) is the motivation for benefaction in *On Duties* 1.44.

47. See here Peter Brown, *Poverty and Leadership in the Later Roman Empire* (Hanover, NH: University Press of New England, 2002), 4–5. For my parenthetical qualification, see Anneliese Parkin, " 'You Do Him No Service': An Exploration of Pagan Almsgiving," in *Poverty in the Roman World*, ed. Margaret Atkins and Robin Osborne (Cambridge: Cambridge University Press, 2006), 60–82.

48. See Longenecker, *Remember the Poor*, 71–73.

49. Hays, *Luke's Wealth Ethics*, 61–63.

50. For example, see Peter Garnsey, *Food and Society in Classical Antiquity*, Key Themes in Ancient History (Cambridge: Cambridge University Press, 1999), 113–27.

51. Finley, *The Ancient Economy*, 39–40 See, however, the early rabbinic development of the *tamhui* (soup kitchen) and *quppa* (charity fund) as means of eliminating begging and poverty. See here Gregg E. Gardner, *The Origins of Organized Charity in Rabbinic Judaism* (Cambridge: Cambridge University Press, 2015).

52. See here the important study of Seth Schwartz, *Were the Jews a Mediterranean Society? Reciprocity and Solidarity in Ancient Judaism* (Princeton, NJ: Princeton University Press, 2010), 168: "I have not found any passage in either Ben Sira, the Josephan corpus, or the Talmud that . . . celebrates reciprocity . . . as the glue that holds society together, and which idealizes it to the extent of ignoring the oppression, exploitation, and injustice into which reciprocity-based relationships inexorably lapse."

are performed in compassionate solidarity in the expectation of reciprocity and reward *from God*.[53]

In his Sermon on the Plain (Luke 6:17–49), Jesus inverts the social order by pronouncing blessings on those who would not have played a significant role in the ancient economy, namely, the poor and the hungry (6:20–22), and pronounces woes on the rich and satiated (6:24–25). Jesus's antipathy to reciprocity ethics is seen clearly in his command: "love your enemies and do good to those who hate you" (6:27).[54] This is almost the exact opposite of one prevalent notion of justice in the ancient world, namely, benefiting one's friends and harming one's enemies.[55] Jesus even calls his disciples to respond to "negative reciprocity"—being cursed, struck on the face, and having one's garment stolen—with gift.[56] Jesus's command to "give to everyone who asks from you" (6:30a) is a repudiation of the received wisdom that one should be calculating and discriminating toward whom one grants gifts and favors.[57] Jesus's rejection of any form of reciprocity ethics is most evident in his commands in 6:32–35a:

> If you love those who love you, what credit [*charis*] is that to you? For even sinners love those who love them. And if you do good deeds to those who do good things for you, what credit [*charis*] is that to you? Even sinners do the same thing. And if you lend to those from whom you expect to receive a return, what credit [*charis*] is that to you? Even sinners lend to sinners so that they will receive back the same amount. But love your enemies and do good deeds and lend expecting nothing.

Jesus's repeated refrain "even sinners act this way" indicates that his economy and the world's economy are incommensurable ways of exchanging resources. The human economy suggests that good deeds have as their mo-

---

53. On which, see John M. G. Barclay, *Paul and the Gift* (Grand Rapids: Eerdmans, 2015), 39–45.

54. See here especially the helpful treatment of Jesus's love command by Alan Kirk, "'Love Your Enemies,' the Golden Rule, and Ancient Reciprocity (Luke 6:27–35)," *JBL* 122 (2003): 667–86.

55. For example, Hesiod, *Works and Days* (lines 342, 354): "Call your friend to feast but leave your enemy out. . . . Give to him who is giving to you but not to him not giving."

56. On negative reciprocity, see Marshall Sahlins, *Stone Age Economics* (London: Tavistock, 1974), 195–56.

57. Joel B. Green, *The Theology of the Gospel of Luke* (Cambridge: University of Cambridge Press, 1995), 114–15.

tivational basis the calculated expectation for a good return. The ground for Jesus's rejection of reciprocity ethics and his command to love, give, and do good to all is explicitly indicated to be the character of the merciful God and an expectation for a return from God. Jesus's disciples will be "sons of the Most High" if they, like God, are merciful and gracious to those who are unmerciful and ungracious (6:35b). "Be compassionate just as your Father is compassionate" (6:36).[58] This is a non-reciprocal, non-contractual, non-calculating form of exchanging goods and resources. One is motivated to reject an economy that receives "credit" from fellow humans for favors and gifts, since what really matters is "credit" before God. Instead of giving with an expectation of return, Luke endorses giving in order to gain "credit" from God.[59] Furthermore, God's mercy, and our call to imitate it, is not only why we show mercy and compassion but also why we refrain from judging others (vv. 37–38). The divine economy set forth by Jesus rejects the competitive, status-oriented, and domineering tendencies of patronage and benefaction and instead calls people to imitate God the Father, who gives mercifully and compassionately to all. Let's look at three of Jesus's parables that provide windows into this divine economy.

In the so-called parable of the Good Samaritan we find one of Jesus's clearest teachings on the nature of the hospitality and acts of mercy required of those who would be his disciples (10:25–37). In response to the lawyer's question, "What must I do to inherit eternal life?" (10:25), Jesus engages in a scriptural argument by asking how he interprets Torah (10:26). The lawyer responds with a summary of Torah: love God and love neighbor as yourself (10:26–27; see Deut 6:5; Lev 19:18). Jesus affirms the answer: "Do this and you will live" (10:28b). But the lawyer's follow-up question, "Who is my neighbor?" reveals his desire "to justify himself"—Lukan language that shows he is concerned with status (see 7:29–30; 16:14–15; 18:9). Likely, he expects Jesus will vindicate him by establishing a definition of "neighbor" that fits his categories. His question, further, exploits the ambiguity of "the neighbor" in Leviticus 19:18. Jesus's response uses the parable to interpret Leviticus 19:18 as encompassing love of strangers. Thus, Jesus expands Torah's command to love neighbor (Lev 19:18) to include the command to love strangers (Lev 19:33–34), for the latter text commands Israel to "love [the

---

58. Kirk, "'Love Your Enemies,' the Golden Rule, and Ancient Reciprocity (Luke 6:27–35)," 683.

59. Jonathan Marshall, *Jesus, Patrons, and Benefactors: Roman Palestine and the Gospel of Luke*, WUNT 2.259 (Tübingen: Mohr-Siebeck, 2009), 216: "Generosity toward others who cannot reciprocate is repaid from God's abundance."

stranger] as yourself." So, strangers belong to the referent of "neighbor," and hospitality is the doing of Torah.[60]

Jesus sets hospitality *above* (not against) the purity regulations that drew boundaries to exclude sinners and outcasts.[61] The priest and the Levite who see the half-dead man (10:30) of unknown ethnicity are in a hermeneutical quandary.[62] The question is whether they should risk defilement by extending hospitality to the man (Lev 21:1–3, 10–11; Num 19:11–19) or show no mercy to neighbor but maintain ritual purity (Lev 19:18, 33–34; Hos 6:6; Mic 6:6–8).[63] The story maintains a priority for the love commandment embodied in acts of mercy to the needy stranger (Lev 19:33–34) over ritual purity. Hospitality to the stranger is an expression of "compassion" (10:33) and "mercy" (10:37). Conversely, a strict enforcement of the purity regulations creates a hierarchy whereby the priest and Levite have privileged status and the outcasts remain excluded.

Jesus transforms the lawyer's question from "who is my neighbor?" (10:29) to "who do you suppose *became* a neighbor?" (10:36). Jesus's question is rhetorical genius for it elicits the response "the one who showed mercy" (10:37a)—an answer that gives priority to hospitality to a stranger *over* purity, exalts the hospitable Samaritan as heir of life *over* priest and Levite, and demonstrates that the extension of hospitality between Samaritan and stranger creates a family or friendship relationship between outsiders.[64] The man's forced response, "the one who showed mercy," requires that he put together two notions he supposed to be incompatible—"Samaritan" and "neighbor." Jesus's answer is framed in terms of obedience to Torah as he uses the call to love strangers in Leviticus 19:34 to interpret the love command in Leviticus 19:18b. The Samaritan's hospitality is non-reciprocal, as the half-dead man robbed of his goods has nothing to exchange or give to the Samaritan, and in this way the Samaritan functions as an example ("go and do likewise," 10:37) of Jesus's call to do what is good and merciful without an expectation for a return (see 6:27–36; 14:12–24).

---

60. Green, *The Gospel of Luke*, 425, rightly notes that the story "serves a hermeneutical function. It interprets the summation of the law provided by the legal expert."

61. See Lev 21:17–23; 1QM 7.4–6; see Luke 11:37–44.

62. See Richard Bauckham, "The Scrupulous Priest and the Good Samaritan: Jesus' Parabolic Interpretation of the Law of Moses," *NTS* 44, no. 4 (1985): 475–89.

63. Kenneth E. Bailey, *Through Peasant Eyes* (Grand Rapids: Eerdmans, 1980), 44–46.

64. On the relationship between Jews and Samaritans during the time of Jesus, see J. Massyngbaerde Ford, *My Enemy Is My Guest: Jesus and Violence in Luke* (Maryknoll, NY: Orbis, 1984), 79–83.

In another meal scene (Luke 14:1–14), when one of the guests interrupts Jesus's teaching and interjects "blessed is the one who eats bread in the kingdom of God" (14:15b), Jesus tells a parable to clarify who will enjoy divine hospitality at "the resurrection of the righteous."[65] Given that Jesus has come proclaiming "the kingdom of God" and has enacted it through eating and drinking, the reader should view the parable as an explication of Jesus's own ministry and as an example of his teaching on extending hospitality to those who cannot reciprocate (14:12–14; see 15:1–2).[66] In the parable, the host has "invited many" to "a great feast" (14:16). When the host sends his servant to tell the guests "come for everything is now ready" (14:17b), the reader sees in this statement Jesus's extension of divine hospitality to all the people. The time of *divine welcome* and the messianic banquet is *now*, but the tragedy is that the guests refuse the Lord's hospitality. Acquisition of possessions and status (fields, oxen, marriage) prevent them from receiving the Lord's hospitality (14:18–20).

The first set of guests rejects the invitation, and so the host bestows his hospitality on those who cannot reciprocate (14:12–14), that is those without status or possessions, and *"he brings in* the poor, the crippled, the blind, and the lame" (14:21b).[67] This list of guests evokes Luke 4:18–19 (see Isa 61:1; 35:5–6) *and is a call to join Jesus's ministry in extending "the year of the Lord's welcome" to the poor.*[68] Jesus's call to the Pharisees to bestow hospitality on the poor and outcasts demands that they recognize and treat them as family and friends, namely, as part of their social group. Jesus's demand that they not invite "your friends, your brothers, your kinsmen, or your rich neighbors" (14:12) highlights the role of hospitality in extending kinship alliances. To invite the poor and the outcast is to treat them as family and to bring them inside one's social network.[69] Only those who can see that they are all recipients of divine welcome and beneficence will feast at the final messianic

---

65. Both the parables in Luke 13:23–30 and 14:16–24 evoke the eschatological banquet feast (see Isa 2:2–4; 25:6–9; 65:13–14; Zech 8:7–8, 19–23). Further, see Dennis E. Smith, *From Symposium to Eucharist: The Banquet in the Early Christian World* (Minneapolis: Fortress, 2003), 166–71.

66. So David P. Moessner, *Lord of the Banquet: The Literary and Theological Significance of the Lukan Travel Narrative* (Minneapolis: Fortress, 1989), 158, states: "The great reversal of 14:15–24 is already coming true as the outcasts invited in 14:21–22 are the ones coming to the 'banquet' with Jesus in 15:1–2." Similarly, see Robert C. Tannehill, *The Narrative Unity of Luke-Acts*, vol. 1 (Minneapolis: Fortress Press, 1986), 184; Smith, *From Symposium to Eucharist*, 270–71.

67. On which, see Moxnes, *The Economy of the Kingdom*, 129–34.

68. Hays, *Luke's Wealth Ethics*, 130: "This allusion is significant because the out-group members mentioned are the types of people Luke's Jesus comes to save, and he calls the rich to display similar benevolence towards them." See also Smith, *From Symposium to Eucharist*, 269.

69. Relevant again is Moxnes, *The Economy of the Kingdom*, 130–34

banquet (14:14). A second time the host demands that his servant "go into the streets and the lanes" to find more guests and "to compel them to come in so that my house will be filled" (14:23b). Jesus's audience must *both* accept his invitation *and* imitate his hospitality ethics as host to the poor and the outcast if they would taste of the Lord's banquet (14:24).[70]

We have seen in an earlier chapter that Jesus's meal practices embody the divine economy of hospitality by creating a hospitable place of welcome for those on the margins of society to experience the life-giving presence of Jesus and the kingdom of God. In Jesus's farewell testament to his disciples (Luke 22:14-38), he commissions his disciples to continue his table-practices and instructs them in how to conduct themselves as hosts in a manner that embodies Jesus's sacrificial death on their behalf (22:15-20). Proper stewardship of the Lord's Table requires that they reject the reciprocity and pursuit of status that pervade the practice of benefaction (22:25). Presiding as leaders over the table is not an opportunity for "greatness" (22:24) or acting with the exploitative authority of kings, lords, the powerful, or benefactors.[71] Standard hospitality and meal practices were often used as opportunities for increased status and power, but Jesus declares "Not so for you!" (22:26). Instead, meals must be a place where rule is manifested by conducting oneself as "the youngest" and "one who serves [food]" (22:26b). Thus, when Jesus asks, "Who is greater, the one reclining or the one serving?" (22:27a), he alludes to their competitive dispute over who was the greatest (22:24) and reminds them: "I have been in your midst as one who serves" (22:27b). The statement recalls the meal he has served where he has given his sacrificial body and blood for their food and drink (22:14-20). Jesus has shown his "greatness" through table service. Given that the meal is to be repeated "in remembrance" of Jesus (22:19b), one can be certain that the apostles' stewardship over the food discloses the Lord to those who participate in this table.

The witness of the rest of the New Testament writings further suggests that the early church sought to resist the competitive and often exploitative economic practices of patronage and benefaction by practicing forms of "economic mutualism" and the sharing of resources with all the members of the church.[72] We have already seen Paul's criticism of the Corinthian

---

70. Marshall, *Jesus, Patrons, and Benefactors*, 272, 279.

71. See the pithy comment of Garnsey, *Food and Society in Classical Antiquity*, 33: "In antiquity, food was power."

72. On "economic mutualism," see Justin J. Meggitt, *Paul, Poverty and Survival*, Studies of the New Testament and Its World (Edinburgh: T&T Clark, 1998), 157-59.

church for practicing the Lord's Supper in a way that was consistent with the practices of patronage, which thereby highlighted the poverty and low social status of the poor (1 Cor 11:17–34). Paul, instead, demands that the church celebrate the Lord's Supper in a manner that is consistent with the loving, other-regarding, sacrificial death of the Lord who is the true host of the meal. This will happen only when the meal is used as an opportunity for the have-nots *to eat and drink together with those who are wealthier*. In Galatians, Paul affirms that he is eager to teach his Gentile churches "to remember the poor" (Gal 2:10).[73] Likewise, we have seen that Acts narrates how the Jerusalem church sold their possessions and distributed them "to everyone who had need" (2:45) with the result that none were in want in their community (4:34). Barnabas functions as a representative model for these early Christians who, in spite of some landed wealth, reject systems of reciprocity and benefaction by selling their land and using their resources for the mutual economic benefit of the church.

While Paul has often *wrongly* been viewed as having had little regard for those in poverty, many of his exhortations presume that local churches share their resources with each other so that there is no poverty or lack.[74] This notion of economic mutualism, or the corporate solidarity that results in the sharing of resources with everyone, even seems to be evident in Paul's warning to the Thessalonians that "if anyone is not willing to work, let that one not eat" (2 Thess 3:10b) and the command that each one should "eat their own bread by working quietly" (3:12b). Paul's exhortations suggest that some within the church who were able to work and provide for themselves were taking advantage of the church's (too!) indiscriminate sharing of resources.[75] Paul expects his churches to

- "bear one another's burdens" (Gal 6:2), to "not grow weary in doing good," and "to work for the good of all" (Gal 6:9–10);
- provide financial support for the needs of believing widows (1 Tim 5:3–16);
- "help the weak" and "pursue what is good for each other and for everyone" (1 Thess 5:14, 15b);

73. On this as a reference to Paul's general missionary practice more broadly and not the Jerusalem collection, see Longenecker, *Remember the Poor*, 157–219; David G. Horrell, *Solidarity and Difference: A Contemporary Reading of Paul's Ethics*, 2nd ed. (London: Bloomsbury T&T Clark, 2016), 256.

74. See here especially Longenecker, *Remember the Poor*, 135–56.

75. Meggitt, *Paul, Poverty and Survival*, 162.

- "share with the saints in their needs [and] pursue hospitality" (Rom 12:13); and
- "devote themselves to good deeds where there are great needs, so they will not be unfruitful" (Titus 3:14; see 3:8).

More statements from Paul could be added, but these exhortations suggest that Paul expected his churches to do good deeds to one another by sharing their resources with all those who had need. Paul's concern for the economic well-being of the churches he established is most clearly seen, however, in the monetary collection he undertook from his churches in Macedonia, Galatia, and Achaia "for the poor among the saints in Jerusalem" (Rom 15:26). Paul's collection is an enormously important (and controversial) subject in Pauline theology, but here I simply want to show, primarily from 2 Corinthians 8–9, how Paul's monetary collection resisted the patterns of reciprocity at the heart of patronage and benefaction and contributed to the mutual solidarity of Paul's churches through the sharing of resources with those in need.

First, while the collection does function as a sign of unity between Jewish and Gentile Christians, the primary purpose of the collection is clearly to provide economic relief and assistance to those suffering in Jerusalem (2 Cor 8:13–15).[76] The economic challenges in Judea due to frequent famines "confirms that life-threatening poverty very likely affected many of the lower classes in Jerusalem as well as elsewhere."[77]

Second, Paul expects that all of his churches will contribute to the collection, and he even upholds the Macedonians for their voluntary generous giving even in the midst of their own impoverishment (2 Cor 8:1–4). The concepts of *sharing, partnership,* and *fellowship* permeate Paul's language when he describes his churches' contributions to the collection (for example, Phil 4:14–19; Rom 15:26; 2 Cor 8:4; 9:13).[78]

Third, Paul argues that the goal of the collection is "equality" (*isotēs,* 8:14). In other words, the Jerusalem church is currently experiencing great economic hardship, and Paul's churches are currently able to use what they have to provide for their needs (2 Cor 8:13–15). This equality is the result of the Gentile churches' redistribution of the "surplus/abundance" of their wealth in order to remedy the "lack" in Judea (2 Cor 8:14). Paul's attempt to

---

76. On the purpose of the collection, see Horrell, *Solidarity and Difference,* 257–60.

77. Horrell, *Solidarity and Difference,* 259.

78. See Julien M. Ogereau, "Paul's κοινωνία with the Philippians: *Societas* as a Missionary Funding Strategy," *NTS* 60 (2014): 360–78.

instill a sense of solidarity and mutuality in his churches is further seen in his note that a time may come when the Jerusalem church's "abundance may also become available for our need" (8:14b). Paul supports his argument for mutuality and equality with Exodus 16:18: "The one who gathered much did not have too much, and the one who gathered a little did not have too little" (2 Cor 8:15). In other words, the Corinthians' sharing of resources is the way in which God provides so that no one has too great of a surplus and no one goes without. This is a form of economic mutualism "that entails a more or less horizontal exchange of resources among those of lesser means."[79]

Fourth, the Corinthians' giving of their resources to the collection is a participation in God's economy and it is not, therefore, an opportunity for them to receive honor, thanksgiving, and increased social standing or status.[80] This point is brought home through Paul's repeated claim that the Corinthians' monetary giving is a participation in *the gift/grace of God* (for example, 8:1, 4, 6, 7, 9). When Paul's churches give to the collection, their act is rooted in the very self-giving act of "the one who, even though he was rich, became poor for your sakes so that you might become rich by his poverty" (2 Cor 8:9). Presumably this is why the Macedonians can provide an abundance of wealth out of "their deep poverty" (2 Cor 8:2). Human giving is rooted in the divine economy of Christ's gift, which is "God's indescribable gift" (2 Cor 9:15). Likewise, God *is the one who gives* the abundance of the seed to the Corinthians in order that they might participate in the collection (2 Cor 9:6–10).[81] For this reason, Paul does not give any indication that the gift of the Corinthians *will be reciprocated through the form of thanksgiving, increased social status, or honor*. Paul does promise that God will continue to provide for their needs and that God will "increase the harvest of your righteousness" (9:10b), which likely refers to their reward of a right relationship with God.[82] But Paul provides no hint that they will receive a return of thanksgiving or honor for their gift.[83] Rather, their generosity and sharing of their resources is an act of worship that brings glory *to God* (2 Cor 9:13; see 1 Cor 16:1–2). God "enriches" the Corinthians with the opportunity to give

---

79. Downs, *Alms*, 169.

80. On the collection as a cultic act of worship, see David J. Downs, *The Offering of the Gentiles: Paul's Collection for Jerusalem in Its Chronological, Cultural, and Cultic Contexts*, WUNT 2.248 (Tübingen: Mohr-Siebeck, 2008), 120–60.

81. For more on this point, see Nathan Eubank, "Justice Endures Forever: Paul's Grammar of Generosity," *JSPL* 5, no. 2 (2015): 169–87, here, 179–80.

82. Downs, *Alms*, 172.

83. So Eubank, "Justice Endures Forever," 181–82.

generously and this results not in thanksgiving to the church in Corinth, as we might expect but, rather, in "thanksgiving to God through us" (9:11). In this way, when the Corinthian church engages in the horizontal "supplying the needs of the saints," this act results in the "overflowing of many acts of thanksgiving to God" (9:12).

Both Paul and Jesus (in Luke) show that participating in God's economy requires disentangling oneself from competitively using resources as a means of acquiring status, honor, and privilege. Given that we as God's people belong to Christ's body (Rom 12; 1 Cor 12), share together the same Spirit (1 Cor 12:13; Eph 4:4-6), and have experienced divine hospitality (Luke 14:16-24; 22:15-20), we are called to a form of mutual solidarity that uses our resources for free and generous gift-giving. We do this in imitation of our merciful God, who gives good gifts to all people, who generously provides us with abundance to share, and who ultimately brings into existence an economy whereby divine gifts arise out of human poverty.

From Structural Complicity to Prophetic Critique

Finally, let's very briefly look at three texts that present prophetic warnings to the wealthy who uncritically participate in the baser aspects of the ancient economy and legally but unjustly profit through exploiting and oppressing others. The first text, Jesus's parable of the rich man and Lazarus in 16:19-31, functions as a scathing critique of the luxurious greed of the wealthy, who not only fail to show hospitality and perform charitable acts of mercy to the poor but who do not even notice their existence. The parable is told within the literary context of Jesus's warning against the love of money: "No servant can serve two masters, for either he will hate the one and love the other, or he will be devoted to one and despise the other. You cannot serve God and Mammon" (16:13). Jesus personifies money as if it were a "Master" or "Lord" since greed can exert a powerful force upon people to orient their lives toward it. The Pharisees, who, we are told by Luke, "were lovers of money" (16:14), laughed at and mocked Jesus's radical criticism of material gains. Jesus's economic beliefs were too extreme for the Pharisees who, in Luke's view, probably see wealth toward God as easily compatible with material wealth and the latter as often confirming one's righteousness before God. Their economy is not so stark and requires no great dualistic opposition between wealth and God. Jesus's position is so disjunctive, in fact, that he characterizes the Pharisees as "money-lovers" who point to their wealth as a sign of favor with God, presumably, and thereby "justify themselves before humans" (v. 15).

The rich man "clothed in purple and fine linen joyously feasts in luxury every day" (16:19b) while Lazarus suffers "having been tossed outside his [that is, the rich man's] gate" (16:20).[84] The rich man functions as a symbol of the wealthy landowners who profited off the peasants' labor.[85] At the very least, the rich man was obligated to show hospitality to the stranger "lying at his gate"—an obligation that is obvious to those familiar with Torah.[86] Lazarus, however, represents the lowest stratum of poverty in ancient Palestine. The "absolutely poor" are those who are "hungry and thirsty, have only rags for clothes, and are without lodging or hope. For the necessities of life they are dependent on the help of others, for example, through begging."[87] Further, malnourishment was (and is) invariably connected with physical diseases and deficiencies.[88] Lazarus, covered in sores, is one of these poor who is longing "to be filled with some food falling from the table of the rich man" (16:21; see 15:16), but even table-scraps are denied him. In fact, we are not even told that Lazarus was seen or recognized by the rich man.[89] When the two men die, Lazarus is accompanied "by the angels" (16:22; see 15:10) into "Abraham's bosom," while the rich man descends to Hades (16:22b–23) where "he sees Abraham at a distance and Lazarus in his bosom" (16:23b).

The reason for the rich man's punishment is obvious: it is not the result of his wealth but of his luxurious consumption and refusal to share with the poor stranger at his gate![90] Jesus's use of "Abraham" as a character and "Abraham's bosom" as an image of the messianic feast is not accidental, given Abraham's reputation as a paragon of hospitality. Had the rich man been a son of Abraham, he would have bestowed hospitality upon the stranger at

---

84. On the meaning of Luke's characterization of the rich man in 16:19, see Dennis E. Smith, "Table-Fellowship as a Literary Motif in the Gospel of Luke," *JBL* 106 (1987): 613–38, here 623–26.

85. Moxnes, *The Economy of the* Kingdom, 89–90.

86. See especially Deut 14:28–29; 15:1–8.

87. Ekkehard W. Stegemann and Wolfgang Stegemann, *The Jesus Movement: A Social History of Its First Century* (Minneapolis: Fortress Press, 1999), 92.

88. On malnutrition and attendant diseases, see Garnsey, *Food and Society in Classical Antiquity*, 43–61.

89. Longenecker, *Remember the Poor: Paul, Poverty, and the Greco-Roman World*, 81: "Jesus' parable sets out a scenario in which the realities of 'conjunctural poverty' were of no impact upon the cocooned world of the rich man."

90. Many interpreters wrongly assume the rich man is punished simply because he is rich. See, for example, James A. Metzger, *Consumption and Wealth in Luke's Travel Narrative*, BIS 88 (Leiden: Brill, 2007), 146–55. Better here is Hays, *Luke's Wealth Ethics*, 153–59.

his gate.[91] It is fitting, then, that the inhospitable rich man is denied access to the feast with the hospitable Abraham, for the rich man is not of the same lineage or heritage (see Luke 3:8; 13:26–29). Those who do not extend hospitality to those to whom the Messiah bestows welcome will not share in the Messiah's feast. Further, in response to the rich man's request to send Lazarus back to warn his household, Abraham twice tells him "they have Moses and the prophets, let them listen to them" (16:29; see 16:31). According to Jesus, the rich man is a Torah-breaker and prophet-rejecter, for these Scriptures teach hospitality to the poor, love of neighbor, and the extension of one's possessions to those in need (see 11:37–54).[92]

The second text that prophetically warns the wealthy, the epistle of James, criticizes the economic oppression of the poor by those with land and wealth. Two sections of the letter are particularly relevant. In James 2:1–7 the writer imagines a scenario in which two men enter into the assembly: one is dressed in fine clothes with a gold ring and the other is a poor person dressed in dirty rags (2:2). If the assembly shows partiality to the rich man and disdains the poor man, that is to say, if they operate according to the normal societal conventions by conferring honor upon the wealthy, then they are guilty of "partiality" (2:1) and through their improper discrimination "have become judges with evil thoughts" (2:4).[93] James chastises this behavior, given that the wealthy are those who use the judicial courts to oppress and exploit (2:6) those whom God has chosen "to be rich in faith and heirs of the kingdom that he has promised to those who love him" (2:5). God's election of the poor might seem arbitrary, but James is consistent in his depiction of God as the one who exalts the humble and humiliates the proud (1:9–10; 4:6).[94] James states why bluntly: "the rich man will wither away with his pursuits" (1:11; see 4:13–17). In God's economy, it is the poor man who is honored (2:5), and by "dishonoring the poor man," the assembly has shown itself to be friends with the world and not God (see 4:4–6).

---

91. Thus, the rich man's threefold reference to Abraham as his "father" (16:24, 27, 30) demonstrates that biological kinship is of no significance. See John O. York, *The Last Shall Be First: The Rhetoric of Reversal in Luke*, JSNTSup 46 (Sheffield: JSOT Press, 1991), 68–69.

92. See the OT texts quoted by Jesus (for example, Isa 61:1 and 58:6 in Luke 4:18–19; Lev 19:16, 18, and 33 in Luke 10:26–29). See Christopher J. H. Wright, *Old Testament Ethics for the People of God* (Downers Grove, IL: InterVarsity Press, 2004), 146–81, 253–80.

93. See Roy Bowen Ward, "Partiality in the Assembly: James 2:2–4," *HTR* 62, no. 1 (January 1969): 87–97.

94. Mariam Kamell, "The Economics of Humility: The Rich and the Humble in James," in *Engaging Economics*, 157–75.

Steven Friesen rightly notes that "this section asserts there are two alternatives: the system of the world and the system of God's kingdom."[95] James does not engage in much nuance here, but he squarely blames an uncritical participation in the normal workings of the ancient economy and court system as leading to inequality and exploitation of the poor. Rather than exalt the virtues of the wealthy landowners, James sees the pursuit of luxury, wealth, and status as the greed, envy, and thirsty desire for acquisition that results in violence and oppression (4:1–2).[96] The wealthy landowners are responsible for living in luxury (5:2–3, 5), storing up treasures and wealth for their own consumption (5:3), exploiting and withholding just payment from those laboring in their fields (5:4), and oppressing the righteous (5:6). We have already seen that land ownership was one of the primary ways of making wealth, that the owners (and cities) were primarily consumers, and that the peasants and agricultural laborers lived at a subsistence level. Thus, James condemns one of the primary features of the ancient economy for the way in which it enables the rich to accumulate wealth and capital at the expense of the poor. In addition, he criticizes the wealthy for using the surplus for a wasteful and luxurious lifestyle. James argues that "resources are distributed unequally in society because landowners exploit workers, because the rich manipulate the justice system, and because the rich squander their immoral gains on self-indulgence."[97]

In the third and final text we examine, Revelation 17–18, the seer celebrates the destruction of "the whore of Babylon" (Rev 18:2), namely, the Roman imperial economic system that is controlled by Satan himself. Rome's economic system is castigated for a) extravagant luxury and consumptive greed (18:3, 7, 9, 11–14)[98]; b) benefiting the local and imperial elites at the

---

95. Steven J. Friesen, "Injustice or God's Will? Early Christian Explanations of Poverty," in *Wealth and Poverty in Early Church and Society*, ed. Susan R. Holman, Holy Cross Studies in Patristic Theology and History (Grand Rapids: Baker, 2008), 17–36, here, 25.

96. On the theme of greed and envy, see Luke Timothy Johnson, "James 3:13–4:10 and the Τόπος περὶ φθόνου," *NovT* 25 (1983): 327–47.

97. Friesen, "Injustice or God's Will?," 26. Kamell, "The Economics of Humility," frequently makes assertions that the rich are not faulted for being rich per se, but rather critiques "the common people who respond to him [that is, the rich man in 2:2–3] with notable groveling" (173). But this ignores what James says about the rich in 2:6–7 and 5:1–6 and underestimates the extent to which the rich, as portrayed by James, unjustly profit from the arrangement of the current economic system.

98. On this, see especially Richard Bauckham, "The Economic Critique of Rome in Revelation 18," in *Images of Empire*, ed. Loveday Alexander, JSOTSup 12 (Sheffield: Sheffield Academic Press, 1991), 47–90. On Rome's attempt to regulate luxury and excessive consumption

expense of the majority (18:15–19); c) the exploitation involved in human slavery as it trades and imports "bodies, that is human lives" (18:13); d) the idolatry of worshipping wealth (18:7); and e) violently killing the righteous and those who criticized Rome's economic, political, and military idolatry (18:20–24). The harlot's boast, "I sit as a queen; I am not a widow, and I will never see grief" (18:7b), gives voice to the economy's idolatrous self-divinization and belief that luxury, consumption, and acquisition—even at the expense of the good of others—will fulfill one's deepest desires.[99] The author's exhortation is radical—withdraw completely from the economic injustices of the entire economy: "Come out of her, my people, so that you will not share in her sins or receive any of her plagues" (18:4). Even if it should mean martyrdom or financial deprivation, the seer calls for a total withdrawal from the idolatry and evil of the Roman economic system, since God will destroy the whore of Babylon *and* vindicate the righteous.[100]

Participating in the Divine Economy

As we have seen, and we've only scratched the surface, the New Testament has much to say about wealth and the human economy. Following are three brief suggestions—all in need of further nuance and practical/pastoral wisdom for local contexts—for how Christians who long to extend hospitality can respond and participate in God's economy.

The first necessary response is one of *seeing the needs of others and an attendant disposition of compassion*. The rich man in Luke 16 never even *saw* Lazarus, whereas the Samaritan not only saw the beaten and half-dead man but also "felt compassion when he saw him" (10:33). This is an empathic response that enters into the suffering and needs of others, and this compassion might be tied to grief, sadness, or anger at experiencing the needs of another fellow human being. Susan Holman refers to this as "sensing need" and as the "process by which we are aware of persons outside of ourselves who are effectively 'touching' our nerves in response to particular

---

through sumptuary laws, see Andrew Wallace-Hadrill, *Rome's Cultural Revolution* (Cambridge: Cambridge University Press, 2008), 315–55.

99. Similarly, see Richard Bauckham, *The Bible in the Contemporary World*, 60; Rosner, *Greed as Idolatry*, 92–94; J. S. Perry, "Critiquing the Excess of Empire: A Synkrisis of John of Patmos and Dio of Prusa," *JSNT* 29 (2007): 437–96.

100. Friesen, "Injustice or God's Will?," 23.

concerns."[101] Before we can use our possessions in any meaningful way for others, the Scriptures suggest that we feel James's outrage against those who would oppress their employees (James 5:1–6), the helplessness and *hunger* of Lazarus (Luke 16:19–31), and the compassion and mercy of the Samaritan (Luke 10:29–37).

As a second response, Christians of *any age* need to be aware of the ways in which our human economies may produce desires and patterns of behavior antithetical to the divine economy. No human economic arrangements are value-free, but rather each economic system offers visions of ultimate reality, an account for what is wrong with the world, the necessary human virtues to rightly participate in the economy, and visions of the good life.[102] I am not suggesting that Christians should withdraw completely from human economic arrangements, as if that were even a possibility. The Bible is certainly not opposed to labor, production, the circulation of goods and resources, or money. I am arguing, however, that Christians should not sacralize any human economy but must pay attention to ways in which an uncritical acceptance of its order of things may shape us in ways that make it virtually impossible to participate in the divine economy.[103] *And* we should reflect upon how our economic arrangements may be redeemed and ordered toward love and desire for God and love for others.[104] Whatever arguments one might want to make in favor of *the autonomous individual's economic self-interest* as a necessary component of a market-economy, the divine economy consistently advocates the collective community (instead of the individual), solidarity (not self-sufficiency or autonomy), abundance (not scarcity), and uncalculated generosity (not competition or calculated investment).[105] Luke's Gospel in particular has provided us with memorable examples of the mismatch between the virtues and ordering in God's economy and those in human economic patterns (Luke 12:13–21; 14:7–14; 16:15–31).

I have already mentioned that an uncritical participation in our consumerist, capitalist ideology can involve us in an endless cycle of con-

---

101. Susan R. Holman, *God Knows There's Need: Christian Responses to Poverty* (Oxford: Oxford University Press, 2009), 16.

102. Nelson, *Economics as Religion*; Cavanaugh, *Field Hospital*, 56–73.

103. On the theological necessity of reading and discerning the workings of our economy as it pertains to new forms of greed, see Wannenwetsch, "The Desire of Desire: Commandment and Idolatry in Late Capitalist Societies," 316–17.

104. Bell, *The Economy of Desire*, 191; Long, *Divine Economy*, 235.

105. Again, see Bell, *The Economy of Desire*; Long; *Divine Economy*; Tanner, *Economy of Grace*.

sumption that makes us oblivious to the real needs of others.[106] Today, the idolatry of greed tends to consist in an endless desire to consume and obtain luxury goods and services. We have seen that greed is so dangerous, even being condemned as idolatry, precisely because a love of wealth can shape us to be people who desire, worship, and long for financial prosperity rather than God. If we are unable to discern the forms that the vice of greed takes in our age and the ways in which it deceives us into trusting and worshipping that which is not God, then we are in danger of idolatry and apostasy (1 Tim 6:9–10). I suggest that the Bible's deep understanding of human desire explains why the biblical writings do *not reject self-interest* as a motivating factor in participating in God's economy and specifically as a motivation for sharing one's wealth. Rather, the biblical authors appeal to human self-interest (for example, "store up treasures for yourself in heaven"; 1 Tim 6:18–19; Matt 6:19–21; Luke 12:31–34; 14:12–14; 2 Cor 9:8–15; Phil 4:14–19), but they make it clear that by generously sharing one's resources with others one can expect a return *from God*. Thus, when we share our wealth and possessions *with others in need* we are worshipping and thereby *rightly desiring God.*

The biblical witness suggests that we pay attention to the ways in which human economies exploit, dominate, and oppress the vulnerable. We saw this in the third text discussed above, where the seer calls us to hear the exhortation "Come out of her my people, so that you will not share in her sins" (Rev 18:4). Structural economic injustice can take on many forms in our culture, including the commodification of sex and the exploitation of young women (often children), *legal and institutionalized* real estate practices that have kept many African Americans and their neighborhoods and schools in poverty,[107] local economic profiteering from the mass incarceration of minorities,[108] and low wages, accompanied by

---

106. Cavanaugh, *Being Consumed*, 91: "For a number of reasons, desire in consumer society keeps us distracted from the desires of the truly hungry, those who experience hunger as life-threatening deprivation."

107. Beryl Satter, *Family Properties: How the Struggle over Race and Real Estate Transformed Chicago and Urban America* (New York: Picador, 2010); Robert J. Sampson, *Great American City: Chicago and the Enduring Neighborhood Effect* (Chicago: University of Chicago Press, 2013).

108. Elizabeth Hinton, *From the War on Poverty to the War on Crime: The Making of Mass Incarceration in America* (Cambridge, MA: Harvard University Press, 2016); Michelle Alexander, *The New Jim Crow: Mass Incarceration in the Age of Colorblindness* (New York: The New Press, 2012); Nicole Gonzalez Van Cleve, *Crook County: Racism and Injustice in America's Largest Criminal Court* (Stanford, CA: Stanford University Press, 2016).

unsafe working conditions, paid to undocumented immigrant workers.[109] I have no profound pieces of advice or simple solutions for any of these deeply troubling realities, but I do believe that Christians are called to a) *see and to recognize* the systemic, structural ways in which our economic systems exploit the vulnerable, b) speak against structural economic injustice and work to rescue those who are enslaved, and c) look for ways to ensure that the economy benefits all people, especially the poor and marginalized.

A third response, arising in many sectors of the church, is a resurgence of commitment to corporate generosity, acts of mercy, and economic mutual solidarity. And this is a good thing. I have argued throughout this book that hospitality to strangers, and here, acts of mercy, are not simply add-ons or even entailments of the Christian faith. Rather, through acts of mercy we imitate God and ensure that God will repay us at the resurrection of the dead. Those who respond to confiscation of their property with generous gift-giving imitate the God who is kind and merciful to everyone (Luke 6:35–36). Our communion with Christ's embrace of poverty necessitates sharing one's resources, even out of our own poverty, in order to enrich us (2 Cor 8:9; 9:11–13). Feeding the hungry, giving drink to the thirsty, clothing the naked, providing homes for the homeless, caring for the sick, and visiting prisoners arise out of the deep belief in Christ's love for the poor (Matt 25:31–46). The early church's commitment to the divine economy created institutions where bishops were charged with caring for the poor, hospitals to serve the sick, homes devoted to caring for orphans, and ways to rescue abandoned infants from infanticide.[110] When the church orders its life in such a way that acts of mercy toward the vulnerable, generous gift giving and circulation of resources for those in need, and communion and solidarity with the marginalized are the norm, the church embodies God's economy and witnesses to God's ordering of material resources for his ends.

---

109. See ch. 5 on hospitality and the immigrant.

110. See throughout Rhee, *Loving the Poor, Saving the Rich.* The sermons of John Chrysostom are an excellent resource here as well. See, for example, Rudolf Brändle, "The Sweetest Passage: Matthew 25:31–46 and Assistance to the Poor in the Homilies of John Chrysostom," in *Wealth and Poverty in Early Church and Society,* ed. Susan R. Holman (Grand Rapids: Baker Academic), 127–39.

Study Questions

1. Are you content with your possessions and resources? Why or why not? If you're not content, what would you need to be content?

2. Brian Rosner and others have argued that there are profound similarities between the economy in Western societies and God. To what extent do you agree or disagree?

3. In what ways does the Bible's teaching on wealth, possessions, and economic practices conflict (or not) with the consumerist, capitalist economy of the United States of America?

4. Describe any instances when you have witnessed structural economic injustice. How can followers of Jesus respond prophetically to instances when human lives are destroyed and abused through economic exploitation?

5. In what ways are you combatting greed with generosity and acts of mercy? If you are not, why not?

Epilogue

A simple but no less profound theme has emerged in my examination of the scriptural teachings on hospitality to strangers: God's hospitality to us necessarily results in and creates hospitality to others. Divine hospitality elicits human hospitality. The singular foundation for our identity is God's act in Christ of extending welcome, hospitality, and friendship to us. This divine welcome, a welcome to us without consideration of individual or collective social worth or merit, draws us into the life of God and makes us God's family and friends. This divine welcome transcends the boundaries and limitations of both our societal and ecclesial expectations in such a way that God's people bear an identity that is, by the world's standards, stigmatized, since it includes people who would ordinarily be outcasts, marginalized, or considered less valuable or worthless. In other words, God's hospitality creates a community that embodies this hospitality both in its social composition *and* in its practices of continuously seeking opportunities to extend God's welcome to whoever are the strangers, the outcasts, the vulnerable, and the stereotyped in our context.

Because I believe that the Scriptures are God's Word that addresses us when we read, listen, and submit ourselves to it, I have tried to move beyond simply describing the biblical texts to showing how the texts address us, our problems, our questions, and our needs as embodied people in our context. My attempt to integrate text and life may be convincing to some and not to others. But my hope and prayer for the church today in North America is that congregations and individuals would discover or rediscover the Scriptural teaching that hospitality to strangers—both divine hospitality and human hospitality—is at the core of our faith and a *necessary* practice for all those who claim to follow Jesus.

Bibliography

Aasgaard, Reidar. *"My Beloved Brothers and Sisters!": Christian Siblingship in Paul.* ECCon 265. New York: T&T Clark, 2004.

Alexander, Michelle. *The New Jim Crow: Mass Incarceration in the Age of Colorblindness.* New York: The New Press, 2012.

Alexander, T. Desmond. "Lot's Hospitality: A Clue to His Righteousness." *JBL* 104, no. 2 (June 1985): 289–91.

Allison, Dale C., Jr. *The Jesus Tradition in Q.* Harrisburg, PA: Trinity Press International, 1997.

Allison, Dick. "Spiritual Friendship: Portrait of a Prison Ministry." In *Prison: Christian Reflection,* edited by Robert B. Kruschwitz, 62–66. Waco, TX: Baylor University Press, 2012.

Anderson, Gary A. *Charity: The Place of the Poor in the Biblical Tradition.* New Haven, CT: Yale University Press, 2013.

Arterbury, Andrew E. "Breaking the Betrothal Bonds: Hospitality in John 4." *CBQ* 72, no. 1 (January 2010): 63–83.

———. *Entertaining Angels: Early Christian Hospitality in Its Mediterranean Setting.* NTMon 8. Sheffield: Sheffield Phoenix Press, 2005.

Ashton, John. *Understanding the Fourth Gospel.* 2nd ed. Oxford: Oxford University Press, 2007.

Avalos, Hector. *Health Care and the Rise of Christianity.* Peabody, MA: Hendrickson, 1999.

Bailey, Kenneth E. *Through Peasant Eyes.* Grand Rapids: Eerdmans, 1980.

Barclay, John M. G. "'Do We Undermine the Law?': A Study of Romans 14:1–15:6." In *Paul and the Mosaic Law,* edited by James D. G. Dunn, 287–308. Tübingen: Mohr-Siebeck, 1996.

———. *Paul and the Gift.* Grand Rapids: Eerdmans, 2015.

Barth, Markus. *Rediscovering the Lord's Supper: Communion with Israel, with Christ, and among the Guests.* Atlanta: John Knox Press, 1988.

Barton, Stephen C. "Money Matters: Economic Relations and the Transformation of

Value in Early Christianity." In *Engaging Economics: New Testament Scenarios and Early Christian Reception*, edited by Bruce W. Longenecker and Kelly D. Liebengood, 37–59. Grand Rapids: Eerdmans, 2009.

Bates, Matthew W. *The Hermeneutics of the Apostolic Proclamation: The Center of Paul's Method of Scriptural Interpretation*. Waco, TX: Baylor University Press, 2012.

Bauckham, Richard. *The Bible in the Contemporary World: Hermeneutical Ventures*. Grand Rapids: Eerdmans, 2015.

———. "The Economic Critique of Rome in Revelation 18." In *Images of Empire*, edited by Loveday Alexander, 47–90. JSOTSup 12. Sheffield: Sheffield Academic Press, 1991.

———. "The Scrupulous Priest and the Good Samaritan: Jesus' Parabolic Interpretation of the Law of Moses." *NTS* 44, no. 4 (1985): 475–89.

———. *The Testimony of the Beloved Disciple: Narrative, History, and Theology in the Gospel of John*. Grand Rapids: Baker, 2007.

Beck, Richard. *Unclean: Meditations on Purity, Hospitality, and Mortality*. Eugene, OR: Cascade, 2011.

Bell, Daniel M., Jr. *The Economy of Desire: Christianity and Capitalism in a Postmodern World*. Grand Rapids: Baker, 2012.

Bellah, Robert N., Richard Madsen, William M. Sullivan, Ann Swidler, and Steven M. Tipton. *Habits of the Heart: Individualism and Commitment in American Life*. Rev. ed. Berkeley: University of California Press, 2008.

Block, Daniel I. "Echo Narrative Technique in Hebrew Literature: A Study in Judges 19." *WTJ* 52, no. 2 (Fall 1990): 325–41.

Blomberg, Craig L. *Contagious Holiness: Jesus' Meal with Sinners*. Vol. 19, *New Studies in Biblical Theology*. Downers Grove, IL: InterVarsity Press, 2005.

Bouma-Prediger, Steven, and Brian J. Walsh. *Beyond Homelessness: Christian Faith in a Culture of Displacement*. Grand Rapids: Eerdmans, 2008.

Boyle, Gregory. *Tattoos on the Heart: The Power of Boundless Compassion*. New York: Free Press, 2010.

Brändle, Rudolf. "The Sweetest Passage: Matthew 25:31–46 and Assistance to the Poor in the Homilies of John Chrysostom." In *Wealth and Poverty in Early Church and Society*, edited by Susan R. Holman, 127–39. Grand Rapids: Baker Academic, 2008.

Brink, Laurie. *Soldiers in Luke-Acts: Engaging, Contradicting, and Transcending the Stereotypes*. WUNT 2.362. Tübingen: Mohr-Siebeck, 2014.

Brown, Peter. *The Body and Society: Men, Women, and Sexual Renunciation in Early Christianity*. New York: Columbia University Press, 1988.

———. *Poverty and Leadership in the Later Roman Empire*. The Menahem Stern Jerusalem Lectures. Hanover, NH: University Press of New England, 2002.

Bryon, Gay L. *Symbolic Blackness and Ethnic Difference in Early Christian Literature*. London: Routledge, 2002.

Burridge, Richard A. *Imitating Jesus: An Inclusive Approach to New Testament Ethics*. Grand Rapids: Eerdmans, 2007.

Bushway, Shawn, and Raymond Paternoster. "The Impact of Prison on Crime." In *Do

Prisons Make Us Safer? The Benefits and Cost of the Prison Boom, edited by Steven Raphael and Michael Stoll, 119–50. New York: Russell Sage Foundation, 2009.

Byars, Ronald P. *The Sacraments in Biblical Perspective*. Interpretation. Louisville: Westminster John Knox Press, 2011.

Byrne, Brendan. *The Hospitality of God: A Reading of Luke's Gospel*. Collegeville, MN: The Liturgical Press, 2000.

Cacioppo, John T., and William Patrick. *Loneliness: Human Nature and the Need for Social Connection*. New York: W. W. Norton & Company, 2008.

Campbell, Douglas A. "Participation and Faith in Paul." Pages 37–60 in *"In Christ" in Paul: Explorations in Paul's Theology of Union and Participation*, edited by Michael J. Thate, Kevin J. Vanhoozer, and Constantine R. Campbell. WUNT 2.384. Tübingen: Mohr-Siebeck, 2014.

Campese, Gioacchinno. "'But I See That Somebody Is Missing.'" In *Ecclesiology and Exclusion: Boundaries of Being and Belonging in Postmodern Times*, edited by Dennis Doyle, Pascal D. Bazzell, and Timothy J. Furry, 71–91. Maryknoll, NY: Orbis, 2012.

Carey, Greg. *Sinners: Jesus and His Earliest Followers*. Waco, TX: Baylor University Press, 2009.

Carroll R., M. Daniel. *Christians at the Border: Immigration, the Church, and the Bible*. Grand Rapids: Baker Academic, 2008.

Castles, Stephen, and Mark J. Miller. *The Age of Migration: International Population Movements in the Modern World*. 4th ed. New York: Palgrave Macmillan, 2009.

Cavanaugh, William T. *Being Consumed: Economics and Christian Desire*. Grand Rapids: Eerdmans, 2008.

———. *Field Hospital: The Church's Engagement with a Wounded World*. Grand Rapids: Eerdmans, 2016.

———. *The Myth of Religious Violence*. New York: Oxford University Press, 2009.

Chadwick, Henry. *The Early Church*. Harmondsworth, UK: Penguin, 1967.

———. "Justification by Faith and Hospitality." StPatr 4 (1961): 281–5.

Cleveland, Christina. *Disunity in Christ: Uncovering the Hidden Forces That Keep Us Apart*. Downers Grove, IL: InterVarsity Press, 2013.

———. "A Liberation Theology for Single People." April 11, 2016. Accessed September 1, 2016. http://www.christenacleveland.com/blog/2016/4/a-liberation-theology-for-single-people.

Coloe, Mary L. "Welcome into the Household of God: The Foot Washing in John 13." *CBQ* 66:3 (July 2004): 400–15.

Crossan, John Dominic. *In Parables: The Challenge of the Historical Jesus*. New York: Harper and Row, 1975.

Culy, Martin M. *Echoes of Friendship in the Gospel of John*. NTMon 30. Sheffield: Sheffield Phoenix Press, 2010.

Danker, Frederick W. *Jesus and the New Age according to St. Luke: A Commentary on the Third Gospel*. St. Louis: Clayton Publishing House, 1972.

DeFranza, Megan K. *Sex Difference in Christian Theology: Male, Female, and Intersex in the Image of God*. Grand Rapids: Eerdmans, 2015.

Bibliography

de Jonge, Marius. *Jesus, Stranger from Heaven and Son of God: Jesus Christ and the Christians in Johannine Perspective*. Missoula, MT: Scholars Press, 1977.

de la Torre, Miguel. *Trails of Terror and Hope: Testimonies on Immigration*. Maryknoll, NY: Orbis, 2009.

DeYoung, Curtiss Paul, Michael O. Emerson, George Yancey, and Karen Chai Kim. *United by Faith: The Multiracial Congregation as an Answer to the Problem of Race*. New York: Oxford University Press, 2003.

Dorrien, Gary. *Social Ethics in the Making: Interpreting an American Tradition*. Malden, MA: Wiley-Blackwell, 2011.

Downs, David J. *Alms: Charity, Reward, and Atonement in Early Christianity*. Waco, TX: Baylor University Press, 2016.

———. "Is God Paul's Patron? The Economy of Patronage in Pauline Theology." In *Engaging Economics: New Testament Scenarios and Early Christian Reception*, edited by Bruce W. Longenecker and Kelly D. Liebengood, 129–56. Grand Rapids: Eerdmans, 2009.

———. *The Offering of the Gentiles: Paul's Collection for Jerusalem in Its Chronological, Cultural, and Cultic Contexts*. WUNT 2:248. Tübingen: Mohr-Siebeck, 2008.

Duin, Julia. *Quitting Church: Why the Faithful Are Fleeing and What to Do about It*. Grand Rapids: Baker, 2009.

Dying to Get In: Undocumented Immigration at the US-Mexican Border. Directed by Brett Tolley. Mooncusser Films, 2007.

Dying to Live: A Migrant's Journey. Directed by Bill Groody. Groody River Films, 2005.

Edwards, James R., Jr. "A Biblical Perspective on Immigration Policy." In *Debating Immigration*, edited by Carol M. Swain, 46–62. Cambridge; Cambridge University Press, 2007.

Edwards, Korie L. *The Elusive Dream: The Power of Race in Interracial Churches*. Oxford: Oxford University Press, 2008.

Edwards, Ruth B. "The Christological Basis of the Johannine Footwashing." In *Jesus of Nazareth: Lord and Christ: Essays on the Historical Jesus and New Testament Christology*, edited by Joel B. Green and Max Turner, 367–83. Grand Rapids: Eerdmans, 1994.

Emerson, Michael O., and Christian Smith. *Divided by Faith: Evangelical Religion and the Problem of Race in America*. New York: Oxford University Press, 2000.

Eubank, Nathan. "Justice Endures Forever: Paul's Grammar of Generosity." *JSPL* 5, no. 2 (Fall 2015): 169–87.

Ferngren, Gary B. *Medicine and Health Care in Early Christianity*. Baltimore: The Johns Hopkins University Press, 2009.

Fields, Weston W. "The Motif 'Night as Danger' Associated with Three Biblical Destruction Narratives." In *'Sha'are Talmon': Studies in the Bible, Qumran, and the Ancient Near East Presented to Shemaryahu Talmon*, edited by Michael Fishbane and Emmanuel Tov, 17–32. Winona Lake, IN: Eisenbrauns, 1992.

———. *Sodom and Gomorrah: History and Motif in Biblical Narrative*. JSOTSup 231. Sheffield: Sheffield Academic Press, 1997.

Finger, Reta Halteman. *Of Widows and Meals: Communal Meals in the Book of Acts.* Grand Rapids: Eerdmans, 2007.

Finley, Moses I. *The Ancient Economy.* Berkeley: University of California Press, 1999.

Fitzgerald, John T. "Christian Friendship: John, Paul, and the Philippians." *Interpretation* 61, no. 3 (July 2007): 284–96.

———. "Paul and Friendship." In *Paul in the Greco-Roman World: A Handbook*, edited by J. Paul Sampley, 319–43. Harrisburg, PA: Trinity Press, International, 2003.

Flemming, Dean. *Why Mission? Reframing New Testament Theology.* Nashville: Abingdon, 2015.

Flett, John G. *Apostolicity: The Ecumenical Question in World Christian Perspective.* Downers Grove, IL: InterVarsity Press, 2016.

Ford, J. Massyngbaerde. *My Enemy Is My Guest: Jesus and Violence in Luke.* Maryknoll, NY: Orbis, 1984.

Fowl, Stephen E. *Philippians.* THC. Grand Rapids: Eerdmans, 2005.

Friedman, Milton, and Rose Friedman. *Free to Choose.* New York: Avon Books, 1980.

Friesen, Steven J. "Injustice or God's Will? Early Christian Explanations of Poverty." In *Wealth and Poverty in Early Church and Society*, edited by Susan R. Holman, 17–36. Holy Cross Studies in Patristic Theology and History. Grand Rapids: Baker, 2008.

Gardner, Gregg E. *The Origins of Organized Charity in Rabbinic Judaism.* Cambridge: Cambridge University Press, 2015.

Garnsey, Peter. *Food and Society in Classical Antiquity.* Key Themes in Ancient History. Cambridge: Cambridge University Press, 1999.

Garnsey, Peter, and Richard Saller. *The Roman Empire: Economy, Society and Culture.* 2nd ed. Berkeley: University of California Press, 2015.

Garrett, Susan. *The Demise of the Devil: Magic and the Demonic in Luke's Writings.* Minneapolis: Fortress Press, 1989.

Gaventa, Beverly Roberts. *From Darkness to Light: Aspects of Conversion in the New Testament.* OBT. Philadelphia: Fortress, 1986.

———. "'You Proclaim the Lord's Death': 1 Corinthians 11:26 and Paul's Understanding of Worship." *Review and Expositor* 80, no. 3 (Summer 1983): 377–87.

Gill, David. "*Trapezomata*: A Neglected Aspect of Greek Sacrifice." *HTR* 67, no. 2 (April 1974): 117–37.

Gittins, Anthony J. *Gifts and Strangers: Meeting the Challenge of Inculturation.* New York: Paulist Press, 1988.

Goffman, Erving. *Stigma: Note on the Management of Spoiled Identity.* London: Simon and Schuster, 1963.

Gooch, Peter D. *Dangerous Food: 1 Corinthians 8–10 in Its Context.* Waterloo, Ontario: Wilfrid Laurier University Press, 1993.

Gorman, Michael J. *Becoming the Gospel: Paul, Participation, and Mission.* Grand Rapids: Eerdmans, 2015.

Gowan, Donald E. "Wealth and Poverty in the Old Testament: The Case of the Widow, the Orphan, and the Sojourner." *Interpretation* 41, no. 4 (October 1987): 341–53.

Green, Joel B. *Conversion in Luke-Acts: Divine Action, Human Cognition, and the People of God.* Grand Rapids: Baker, 2015.

———. *The Theology of the Gospel of Luke*. Cambridge: University of Cambridge Press, 1995.

Greene-McCreight, Kathryn. *Darkness Is My Only Companion: A Christian Response to Mental Illness*. Rev. ed. Grand Rapids: Brazos Press, 2015.

Greer, Rowan A. *Broken Lights and Mended Lives: Theology and Common Life in the Early Church*. University Park: The Pennsylvania State University Press, 1986.

Griffin, Miriam T. *Seneca on Society: A Guide to* De Beneficiis. Oxford: Oxford University Press, 2013.

Groody, Daniel G. "Jesus and the Undocumented Immigrant: A Spiritual Geography of a Crucified People." *Theological Studies* 70, no. 2 (July 2009): 298–316.

Hahn, Scott W. *Kinship by Covenant: A Canonical Approach to the Fulfillment of God's Saving Promises*. ABRL. New Haven, CT: Yale University Press, 2009.

Hartch, Todd. *The Rebirth of Latin American Christianity*. Oxford: Oxford University Press, 2014.

Harvey, Jennifer. *Dear White Christians: For Those Still Longing for Racial Reconciliation*. Grand Rapids: Eerdmans, 2015.

Hays, Christopher M. *Luke's Wealth Ethics: A Study in Their Coherence and Character*. WUNT 2.275. Tübingen: Mohr-Siebeck, 2010.

Hays, Richard B. *1 Corinthians*. Interpretation. Louisville: Westminster John Knox Press, 1997.

———. *Echoes of Scripture in the Gospels*. Waco, TX: Baylor University Press, 2016.

———. *The Moral Vision of the New Testament: A Contemporary Introduction to New Testament Ethics*. San Francisco: HarperCollins, 1997.

Heaton, E. W. "Sojourners in Egypt." *Expository Times* 58 (1946): 80–82.

Heil, J. P. *The Meal Scenes in Luke Acts: An Audience-Oriented Approach*. Atlanta: SBL Publications, 1999.

Hellerman, Joseph H. *When the Church Was a Family: Recapturing Jesus' Vision for Authentic Christian Community*. Nashville: B&H Publishing, 2009.

Henderson, Suzanne Watts. "'If Anyone Hungers . . .': An Integrated Reading of 1 Cor 11.17–34." *NTS* 48, no. 2 (April 2002): 195–208.

Heuertz, Christopher L., and Christine D. Pohl. *Friendship at the Margins: Discovering Mutuality in Service and Mission*. Downers Grove, IL: InterVarsity Press, 2010.

Heyer, Kristin E. *Kinship across Borders: A Christian Ethic of Immigration*. Washington, DC: Georgetown University Press, 2012.

Hill, Wesley. *Spiritual Friendship: Finding Love in the Church as a Celibate Gay Christian*. Grand Rapids: Brazos Press, 2015.

Hinton, Elizabeth. *From the War on Poverty to the War on Crime: The Making of Mass Incarceration in America*. Cambridge, MA: Harvard University Press, 2016.

Hock, Ronald F. *The Social Context of Paul's Ministry: Testimony and Apostleship*. Philadelphia: Fortress Press, 1980.

Holman, Susan R. *God Knows There's Need: Christian Responses to Poverty*. Oxford: Oxford University Press, 2009.

Hooker, Morna. "Interchange in Christ." In *From Adam to Christ: Essays on Paul*, 13–25. Cambridge: Cambridge University Press, 1990.

Horrell, David G. *Solidarity and Difference: A Contemporary Reading of Paul's Ethics.* 2nd ed. London: Bloomsbury T&T Clark, 2015.

―――. "Theological Principle or Christological Praxis? Pauline Ethics in 1 Corinthians 8.1–11.1." *JSNT* 67 (September 1997): 83–114.

Hultgren, Arland J. "The Johannine Footwashing (13.1–11) as Symbol of Eschatological Hospitality." *NTS* 28, no. 4 (October 1982): 539–46.

Hume, Douglas A. *The Early Christian Community: A Narrative Analysis of Acts 2:41–47 and 4:32–35.* WUNT 2.298. Tübingen: Mohr-Siebeck, 2011.

Huntington, Samuel. *Who Are We? The Challenges to America's National Identity.* New York: Simon and Schuster, 2004.

Hurtado, Larry W. *Lord Jesus Christ: Devotion to Jesus in Earliest Christianity.* Grand Rapids: Eerdmans, 2003.

Hütter, Reinhard. "Hospitality and Truth: The Disclosure of Practices in Worship and Doctrine." In *Practicing Theology: Beliefs and Practices in Christian Life*, edited by Miroslav Volf and Dorothy C. Bass, 206–27. Grand Rapids: Eerdmans, 2002.

Jefford, Clayton N. *Reading the Apostolic Fathers: An Introduction.* Peabody, MA: Hendrickson, 1996.

Jenkins, Philip. *The Next Christendom: The Coming of Global Christianity.* Oxford: Oxford University Press, 2002.

Jipp, Joshua W. "The Beginnings of a Theology of Luke-Acts: Divine Activity and Human Response." *JTI* 8, no. 1 (Spring 2014): 23–44.

―――. *Christ Is King: Paul's Royal Ideology.* Minneapolis: Fortress, 2015.

―――. *Divine Visitations and Hospitality to Strangers in Luke-Acts: An Interpretation of the Malta Episode in Acts 28:1–10.* NovTSup 153. Leiden: Brill, 2013.

―――. "Hospitable Barbarians: Luke's Ethnic Reasoning in Acts 28:1–10." *JTS* (2017): forthcoming.

―――. "Paul's Areopagus Speech of Acts 17:16–34 as *Both* Critique *and* Propaganda." *JBL* 131, no. 3 (2012): 567–88.

―――. "Philanthropy, Hospitality, and Friendship." *Christian Reflection* (2015): 65–72.

Johnson, Luke Timothy. *Among the Gentiles: Greco-Roman Religion and Christianity.* AYBRL. New Haven, CT: Yale University Press, 2009.

―――. "The Body in Question: The Social Complexities of Resurrection in 1 Corinthians." In *Contested Issues in Christian Origins and the New Testament*, 295–315. NovTSup 146. Leiden: Brill, 2013.

―――. *Brother of Jesus, Friend of God: Studies in the Letter of James.* Grand Rapids: Eerdmans, 2004.

―――. "Imagining the World Scripture Imagines." *Modern Theology* 14, no. 2 (April 1998): 165–80.

―――. "James 3:13–4:10 and the Topos περὶ φθόνου." *NovT* 25, no. 4 (October 1983): 327–47.

―――. *The Literary Function of Possessions in Luke-Acts.* SBLDS 39. Missoula, MT: Scholars Press, 1977.

―――. *Religious Experience in Earliest Christianity.* Minneapolis: Fortress Press, 1998.

———. *Sharing Possessions: What Faith Demands.* 2nd ed. Grand Rapids: Eerdmans, 2011.

Jones, Robert P. *The End of White Christian America.* New York: Simon and Schuster, 2016.

Joubert, Stephen. "One Form of Social Exchange or Two? 'Euergetism,' Patronage, and Testament Studies." *BTB* 31, no. 1 (2001): 17–25.

Just, Arthur A. *The Ongoing Feast: Table Fellowship and Eschatology at Emmaus.* Collegeville, MN: The Liturgical Press, 1993.

Kamell, Mariam. "The Economics of Humility: The Rich and the Humble in James." In *Engaging Economics: New Testament Scenarios and Early Christian Reception,* edited by Bruce W. Longenecker and Kelly D. Liebengood, 157–75. Grand Rapids: Eerdmans, 2009.

Karris, Robert J. *Eating Your Way through Luke's Gospel.* Collegeville, MN: Liturgical Press, 2006.

Keifert, Patrick R. *Welcoming the Stranger: A Public Theology of Worship and Evangelism.* Minneapolis: Fortress, 1992.

Kennedy, Rebecca F., C. Sydnor Roy, and Max L. Goldman, eds. and trans. *Race and Ethnicity in the Classical World: An Anthology of Primary Sources in Translation.* Indianapolis: Hackett Publishing, 2013.

Kim, Seyoon. "*Imitatio Christi* (1 Corinthians 11:1): How Paul Imitates Jesus Christ in Dealing with Idol Food." *BBR* 13, no. 2 (2003): 193–226.

Kirk, Alan. "'Love Your Enemies,' the Golden Rule, and Ancient Reciprocity (Luke 6:27–35)." *JBL* 122, no. 4 (Winter 2003): 667–86.

Knauth, R. J. D. "Alien, Foreign Resident." In *Dictionary of the Old Testament: Pentateuch,* edited by T. Desmond Alexander and David W. Baker, 27–33. Downers Grove, IL: InterVarsity Press, 2003.

Koenig, John. *New Testament Hospitality: Partnership with Strangers as Promise and Mission.* Eugene, OR: Wipf and Stock, 2001.

Koester, Craig R. *Symbolism in the Fourth Gospel: Meaning, Mystery, Community.* 2nd ed. Minneapolis: Fortress Press, 2003.

———. *The Word of Life: A Theology of John's Gospel.* Grand Rapids: Eerdmans, 2008.

Konstan, David. *Friendship in the Classical World.* Cambridge: Cambridge University Press, 1997.

Koser, Khalid. *International Migration: A Very Short Introduction.* Oxford: Oxford University Press, 2007.

Köstenberger, Andreas J. *The Missions of Jesus and the Disciples according to the Fourth Gospel: With Implications for the Fourth Gospel's Purpose and the Mission of the Contemporary Church.* Grand Rapids: Eerdmans, 1998.

Labberton, Mark. *The Dangerous Act of Worship: Living God's Call to Justice.* Downers Grove, IL: InterVarsity Press, 2012.

Lampe, Peter. "The Eucharist: Identifying with Christ on the Cross," *Interpretation* 48, no. 1 (January 1994): 36–49.

Lane, William L. "Unexpected Light on Hebrews 13:1–6 from a Second Century Source." *Perspectives in Religious Studies* 9, no. 3 (Fall 1982): 267–74.

Lasine, Stuart. "Guest and Host in Judges 19: Lot's Hospitality in an Inverted World." *JSOT* 29 (June 1984): 37–59.

LaVerdiere, Eugene. *Dining the Kingdom of God: The Origins of the Eucharist according to Luke.* Chicago: Liturgy Training Publications, 1994.

Lee, Dorothy. "The Gospel of John and the Five Senses." *JBL* 129, no. 1 (Spring 2010): 115–27.

Leithart, Peter J. *Delivered from the Elements of the World: Atonement, Justification, Mission.* Downers Grove, IL: InterVarsity Press, 2016.

Leshem, Dotan. *The Origins of Neoliberalism: Modeling the Economy from Jesus to Foucault.* New York: Columbia University Press, 2016.

Levitt, Peggy. *God Needs No Passport: Immigrants and the Changing American Religious Landscape.* New York: The New Press, 2007.

Logan, James Samuel. *Good Punishment? Christian Moral Practice and US Imprisonment.* Grand Rapids: Eerdmans, 2008.

Long, D. Stephen. *Divine Economy: Theology and the Market.* London: Routledge, 2000.

Lyons, William John. *Canon and Exegesis: Canonical Praxis and the Sodom Narrative.* JSOTSup 352. Sheffield: Sheffield Academic Press, 2002.

Macaskill, Grant. *Union with Christ in the New Testament.* Oxford: Oxford University Press, 2013.

Malherbe, Abraham J. "The Christianization of a *Topos* (Luke 12:13–34)." In *Light from the Gentiles: Hellenistic Philosophy and Early Christianity: Collected Essays, 1959–2012,* by Abraham J. Malherbe, 339–51. NovTSup 150. Leiden: Brill, 2013.

———. "Godliness, Self-Sufficiency, Greed, and the Enjoyment of Wealth: 1 Timothy 6:3–19." In *Light from the Gentiles: Hellenistic Philosophy and Early Christianity: Collected Essays, 1959–2012,* by Abraham J. Malherbe, 507–57. NovTSup 150. Leiden: Brill, 2013.

Marshall, Christopher D. *Beyond Retribution: A New Testament Vision for Justice, Crime, and Punishment.* Grand Rapids: Eerdmans, 2001.

Marshall, Jonathan. *Jesus, Patrons, and Benefactors: Roman Palestine and the Gospel of Luke.* WUNT 2.259. Tübingen: Mohr-Siebeck, 2009.

Marshall, Peter. *Enmity in Corinth: Social Conventions in Paul's Relations with the Corinthians.* WUNT 2.23. Tübingen: Mohr-Siebeck, 1987.

Martin, Clarice J. "A Chamberlain's Journey and the Challenge of Interpretation for Liberation." *Semeia* 47 (1989): 105–35.

Martin, Dale B. *Slavery as Salvation: The Metaphor of Slavery in Pauline Christianity.* New Haven, CT: Yale University Press, 1990.

Marty, Martin E. *The Public Church: Mainline-Evangelical-Catholic.* New York: Crossroad, 1981.

———. *When Faiths Collide.* Blackwell Manifestos. Malden, MA: Blackwell, 2005.

Matson, David Lertis. *Household Conversion Narratives in Acts: Pattern and Interpretation.* JSNTSup 123. Sheffield: Sheffield Academic Press, 1996.

Matthews, Victor. "Hospitality and Hostility in Genesis 19 and Judges 19." *BTB* 22, no. 1 (Spring 1992): 3–11.

Bibliography

Matthews, Victor H., and Don C. Benjamin. *Social World of Ancient Israel: 1250–587 BCE.* Peabody, MA: Hendrickson, 1993.

McDermott, Gerald, and Harold A. Netland. *A Trinitarian Theology of Religions.* New York: Oxford University Press, 2014.

McGowan, Andrew B. *Ancient Christian Worship: Early Church Practices in Social, Historical, and Theological Perspective.* Grand Rapids: Baker, 2014.

Meeks, Wayne A. *The First Urban Christians: The Social World of the Apostle Paul.* New Haven, CT: Yale University Press, 1983.

———. "The Man from Heaven in Johannine Sectarianism." In *The Interpretation of John,* edited by John Ashton, 169–206. Philadelphia: Fortress Press, 1986.

———. "The Man from Heaven in Paul's Letter to the Philippians." In *The Future of Early Christianity: Essays in Honor of Helmut Koester,* edited by Birger Pearson, 329–36. Minneapolis: Fortress, 1991.

Meggitt, Justin J. *Paul, Poverty and Survival.* Studies of the New Testament and Its World. Edinburgh: T&T Clark, 1998.

Meilaender, Gilbert C. *Friendship: A Study in Theological Ethics.* Notre Dame, IN: University of Notre Dame Press, 1981.

Metzger, James A. *Consumption and Wealth in Luke's Travel Narrative.* BIS 88. Leiden: Brill, 2007.

Michaels, J. Ramsey. *The Gospel of John.* NICNT. Grand Rapids: Eerdmans, 2010.

Miller, Patrick D., Jr. "The Gift of God: The Deuteronomic Theology of the Land." *Interpretation* 23, no. 4 (October 1969): 454–65.

———. "Israel as Host to Strangers." In *Israelite Religion and Biblical Theology: Collected Essays,* 559–62. JSOTSup 267. Sheffield: Sheffield Academic Press, 2000.

Mitchell, Alan C. "The Social Function of Friendship in Acts 2:44–47 and 4:32–37." *JBL* 111, no. 2 (Summer 1992): 255–72.

Mitchell, Margaret M. *Paul and the Rhetoric of Reconciliation: An Exegetical Investigation of the Language and Composition of 1 Corinthians.* Louisville: Westminster John Knox Press, 1992.

———. "Pauline Accommodation and 'Condescension' (συγκατάβασις): 1 Cor 9:19–23 and the History of Influence." In *Paul beyond the Judaism/Hellenism Divide,* edited by Troels Engberg-Pedersen, pp. 197–214. Louisville: Westminster John Knox Press, 2001.

Moessner, David P. *Lord of the Banquet: The Literary and Theological Significance of the Lukan Travel Narrative.* Minneapolis: Fortress Press, 1989.

Moloney, Francis J. *A Body Broken for a Broken People.* San Francisco: HarperCollins, 1997.

———. *Love in the Gospel of John: An Exegetical, Theological, and Literary Study.* Grand Rapids: Baker, 2013.

Moltmann, Jürgen. "Open Friendship: Aristotelian and Christian Concepts of Friendship." In *The Changing Face of Friendship,* edited by Leroy S. Rouner, 29–42. Notre Dame, IN: University of Notre Dame Press, 1994.

More, Michael S. "Ruth: Resident Alien with a Face." *Christian Reflection* (2008): 20–25.

Moxnes, Halvor. *The Economy of the Kingdom: Social Conflict and Economic Relations in Luke's Gospel*. Philadelphia: Fortress Press, 1988.

Murphy-O'Connor, Jerome. *1 Corinthians*. NTM. Wilmington, DE: Michael Glazier, 1979.

Nelson, Peter K. "Luke 22:29–30 and the Time Frame for Ruling and Dining," *Tyndale Bulletin* 44, no. 2 (November 1993): 355–57.

Nelson, Robert H. *Economics as Religion: From Samuelson to Chicago and Beyond*. University Park: Pennsylvania State University Press, 2001.

———. *The New Holy Wars: Economic Religion vs. Environmental Religion in Contemporary America*. University Park: Pennsylvania State University Press, 2010.

Netland, Harold A. *Christianity and Religious Diversity: Clarifying Christian Commitments in a Globalizing Age*. Grand Rapids: Baker Academic, 2015.

Newbigin, Leslie. *The Gospel in a Pluralist Society*. Grand Rapids: Eerdmans, 1989.

Nicholson, G. C. *Death as Departure: The Johannine Descent-Ascent Schema*. Chico, CA: Scholars Press, 1983.

Nouwen, Henri J. M. *Reaching Out: The Three Movements of the Spiritual Life*. New York: Doubleday, 1975.

O'Day, Gail R. "I Have Called You Friends." *Christian Reflection* (2008): 20–27.

Oden, Amy G. *And You Welcomed Me: A Sourcebook on Hospitality in Early Christianity*. Nashville: Abingdon, 2001.

———. *God's Welcome: Hospitality for a Gospel-Hungry World*. Cleveland: The Pilgrim Press, 2008.

Ogereau, Julien M. "Paul's κοινωνία with the Philippians: *Societas* as a Missionary Funding Strategy." *NTS* 60, no. 3 (July 2014): 360–78.

Pao, David W. *Acts and the Isaianic New Exodus*. Grand Rapids: Baker Academic Press, 2000.

———. "Waiters or Preachers: Acts 6:1–7 and the Lukan Table Fellowship Motif," *JBL* 130, no. 1 (Spring 2011): 127–44.

Parkin, Anneliese. " 'You Do Him No Service': An Exploration of Pagan Almsgiving." In *Poverty in the Roman World*, edited by Margaret Atkins and Robin Osborne, 60–82. Cambridge: Cambridge University Press, 2006.

Parsons, Mikeal C. *Acts*. PCNT. Grand Rapids: Baker Academic Press, 2008.

Pearce, J. K. *The Land of the Body: Studies in Philo's Representation of Egypt*. WUNT 1.208. Tübingen: Mohr-Siebeck, 2007.

Penner, Todd. *In Praise of Christian Origins: Stephen and the Hellenists in Lukan Apologetic Historiography*. ESEC. New York: T&T Clark, 2004.

Perry, J. S. "Critiquing the Excess of Empire: A Synkrisis of John of Patmos and Dio of Prusa." *JSNT* 29, no. 4 (June 2007): 437–96.

Pervo, Richard I. *Acts*. Hermeneia. Minneapolis: Fortress Press, 2009.

Pitre, Brant. *Jesus and the Jewish Roots of the Eucharist: Unlocking the Secrets of the Last Supper*. New York: Doubleday, 2011.

———. *Jesus and the Last Supper*. Grand Rapids: Eerdmans, 2015.

Placher, William. "Visiting Prisoners." In *The Blackwell Companion to Postmodern Theology*, edited by Graham Ward, 177–91. Oxford: Blackwell Publishing, 2007.

Pohl, Christine D. *Making Room: Recovering Hospitality as a Christian Tradition*. Grand Rapids: Eerdmans, 1999.

Polanyi, Karl. *The Great Transformation: The Political and Economic Origins of Our Time*. Boston: Beacon Press, 1957.

Porter, Michael. *On Competition*. Cambridge, MA: Harvard University Press, 1998.

Porterfield, Amanda. *Healing in the History of Christianity*. Oxford: Oxford University Press, 2005.

Praeder, Susan M. "Acts 27:1–28:16: Sea Voyages in Ancient Literature and the Theology of Luke-Acts." *CBQ* 46, no. 4 (October 1984): 683–706.

Radner, Ephraim. *A Time to Keep: Theology, Mortality, and the Shape of a Human Life*. Waco, TX: Baylor University Press, 2016.

Rah, Soong-Chan. *Many Colors: Cultural Intelligence for a Changing Church*. Chicago: Moody Publishers, 2010.

———. *The Next Evangelicalism: Freeing the Church from Western Cultural Captivity*. Downers Grove, IL: InterVarsity Press, 2009.

Raphael, Steven, and Michael Stoll. "Introduction." *Do Prisons Make Us Safer? The Benefits and Cost of the Prison Boom*, edited by Steven Raphael and Michael Stoll, 1–24. New York: Russell Sage Foundation, 2009.

Reasoner, Mark. *The Strong and the Weak: Romans 14:1 – 15:13 in Context*. SNTSMS 103. Cambridge: Cambridge University Press, 1999.

Reinders, Hans S. *Receiving the Gift of Friendship: Profound Disability, Theological Anthropology, and Ethics*. Grand Rapids: Eerdmans, 2008.

Rhee, Helen. *Loving the Poor, Saving the Rich: Wealth, Poverty, and Early Christian Formation*. Grand Rapids: Baker Academic Press, 2012.

Rice, Joshua. *Paul and Patronage: The Dynamics of Power in 1 Corinthians*. Eugene, OR: Pickwick Publications, 2013.

Ricoeur, Paul. *Oneself as Another*. Chicago: The University of Chicago Press, 1992.

Rindge, Matthew S. *Jesus' Parable of the Rich Fool: Luke 12:13–34 among Ancient Conversation on Death and Possessions*. Early Christianity and Its Literature. Vol. 6. Atlanta: Society of Biblical Literature, 2011.

Robinson, B. P. "The Place of the Emmaus Story in Luke-Acts." *NTS* 30, no. 4 (October 1984): 481–97.

Rosner, Brian S. *Greed as Idolatry: The Origin and Meaning of a Pauline Metaphor*. Grand Rapids: Eerdmans, 2007.

———. "Soul Idolatry: Greed as Idolatry in the Bible." *Ex Auditu* 15 (1999): 73–86.

Rowe, C. Kavin. *Early Narrative Christology: The Lord in the Gospel of Luke*. Berlin: Walter de Gruyter GmbH & Co. KG, 2006.

———. "The Grammar of Life: The Areopagus Speech and Pagan Tradition." *NTS* 57, no. 1 (January 2011): 31–50.

Rudolph, David J. *A Jew to the Jews: Jewish Contours of Pauline Flexibility in 1 Corinthians 9:19–23*. WUNT 2.304. Tübingen: Mohr-Siebeck, 2011.

Ruiz, Jean-Pierre. *Readings from the Edges: The Bible and People on the Move*. Studies in Latino/a Catholicism. Maryknoll, NY: Orbis, 2011.

Safe Families for Children, "Safe Families for children—the beginning" (flash video).

Posted December 9, 2015. Accessed September 4, 2016. https://vimeo.com /148396998.

Sahlins, Marshall. *Stone Age Economics*. London: Tavistock, 1974.

Saller, Richard P. *Personal Patronage under the Early Empire*. Cambridge: Cambridge University Press, 1982.

Sampson, Robert J. *Great American City: Chicago and the Enduring Neighborhood Effect*. Chicago: The University of Chicago Press, 2013.

Sanneh, Lamin. *Disciples of All Nations*. Pillars of World Christianity. Oxford: Oxford University Press, 2008.

———. *Translating the Message: The Missionary Impact on Culture*. 2nd ed. Maryknoll, NY: Orbis, 2009.

Satter, Beryl. *Family Properties: How the Struggle over Race and Real Estate Transformed Chicago and Urban America*. New York: Picador, 2010.

Schlosser, Eric. "The Prison Industrial Complex." *Atlantic Monthly*, December 1998.

Schnabel, Eckhard J. *Early Christian Mission*. 2 vols. Downers Grove, IL: InterVarsity Press, 2004.

Schottroff, Luise. "Holiness and Justice: Exegetical Comments on 1 Corinthians 11.17–34." *JSNT* 23, no. 79 (January 2001): 51–60.

Schreck, Christopher J. "The Nazareth Pericope: Luke 4:16–30 in Recent Study." In *L'évangile de Luc—The Gospel of Luke*, 2nd ed. Edited by Frans Neirynck. Leuven: Leuven University Press, 1989.

Schwartz, Seth. *Were the Jews a Mediterranean Society? Reciprocity and Solidarity in Ancient Judaism*. Princeton, NJ: Princeton University Press, 2010.

Skinner, Christopher W. *Reading John*. Cascade Companions. Eugene, OR: Cascade Books, 2015.

Skinner, Matthew L. *Intrusive God, Disruptive Gospel: Encountering the Divine in the Book of Acts*. Grand Rapids: Brazos, 2015.

Slade, Peter. *Open Friendship in a Closed Society: Mission Mississippi and a Theology of Friendship*. New York: Oxford University Press, 2009.

Smith, Christian. *Lost in Transition: The Dark Side of Emerging Adulthood*. Oxford: Oxford University Press, 2011.

Smith, Dennis E. *From Symposium to Eucharist: The Banquet in the Early Christian World*. Minneapolis: Fortress Press, 2003.

———. "Table-Fellowship as a Literary Motif in the Gospel of Luke." *JBL* 106, no. 4 (December 1987): 613–38.

Smith, James K. A. *Desiring the Kingdom: Worship, Worldview, and Cultural Formation*. Vol. 1, Cultural Liturgies. Grand Rapids: Baker, 2009.

———. *You Are What You Love: The Spiritual Power of Habit*. Grand Rapids: Brazos, 2016.

Smith-Christopher, Daniel L. "Between Ezra and Isaiah: Exclusion, Transformation, and Inclusion of the 'Foreigner' in Post-Exilic Biblical Theology." In *Ethnicity and the Bible*, edited by Mark Brett, 117–42. Leiden: Brill, 2002.

Snyder, Susannah. "Fright: The Dynamics of Fear within Established Populations." In

Bibliography

Asylum-Seeking: Migration and Church, 85–126. Explorations in Practical, Pastoral and Empirical Theology. London: Ashgate, 2012.

Soerens, Matthew, and Jenny Hwang. *Welcoming the Stranger: Justice, Compassion & Truth in the Immigration Debate*. Downers Grove, IL: InterVarsity Press, 2009.

Spencer, F. Scott. "Neglected Widows in Acts 6:1–7." *CBQ* 56, no. 4 (October 1994): 715–33.

Stapleford, John E. *Bulls, Bears and Golden Calves*. 2nd ed. Downers Grove, IL: InterVarsity Press, 2009.

Stark, Rodney. "Epidemics, Networks, and the Rise of Christianity." *Semeia* 56 (1992): 159–75.

Stegemann, Ekkehard W., and Wolfgang Stegemann. *The Jesus Movement: A Social History of Its First Century*. Minneapolis: Fortress Press, 1999.

Stowers, Stanley K. *A Rereading of Romans: Justice, Jews, and Gentiles*. New Haven, CT: Yale University Press, 1994.

Strawn, Brent, ed. *The Bible and the Pursuit of Happiness: What the Old and New Testaments Teach Us about the Good Life*. Oxford: Oxford University Press, 2012.

Sturdevant, Jason S. "The Centrality of Discipleship in the Johannine Portrayal of Peter." In *Peter in Early Christianity*, edited by Helen K. Bond and Larry W. Hurtado, 109–20. Grand Rapids: Eerdmans, 2015.

Swartley, Willard M. *Health, Healing and the Church's Mission: Biblical and Moral Priorities*. Downers Grove, IL: InterVarsity Press, 2012.

Tannehill, Robert C. *The Narrative Unity of Luke-Acts*. Vol. 1. Minneapolis: Fortress Press, 1986.

Tanner, Kathryn. *Economy of Grace*. Minneapolis: Fortress Press, 2005.

Taylor, Charles. *A Secular Age*. Cambridge, MA: Harvard University Press, 2007.

Taylor, Mark Lewis. *The Executed God: The Way of the Cross in Lockdown America*. 2nd ed. Minneapolis: Fortress Press, 2015.

Thiessen, Gerd. *The Social Setting of Pauline Christianity*. Edinburgh: T&T Clark, 1982.

Thomas, John Christopher. *Footwashing in John 13 and the Johannine Community*. JSNTSup 61. Sheffield: JSOT Press, 1991.

Thompson, Alan J. *One Lord, One People: The Unity of the Church in Acts in Its Literary Setting*. LNTS 359. London: T&T Clark, 2008.

Thompson, James W. *Moral Formation according to Paul: The Context and Coherence of Pauline Ethics*. Grand Rapids: Baker, 2011.

Thompson, Michael. *Clothed with Christ: The Example and Teaching of Jesus in Romans 12.1–15.13*. JSNTSup 59. Sheffield: JSOT, 1991.

Tilling, Chris. *Paul's Divine Christology*. WUNT 2.323. Tübingen: Mohr-Siebeck, 2012.

Tran, Jonathan, and Myles Werntz, eds. *Corners in the City of God: Theology, Philosophy, and the Wire*. Eugene, OR: Cascade, 2013.

Trible, Phyllis. *Texts of Terror: Literary-Feminist Readings of Biblical Narratives*. OBT 13. Philadelphia: Fortress Press, 1984.

Tucker, J. Brian. *"Remain in Your Calling": Paul and the Continuation of Social Identities in 1 Corinthians*. Eugene, OR: Pickwick Publications, 2011.

Vacek, Heather H. *Madness: American Protestant Responses to Mental Illness*. Waco, TX: Baylor University Press, 2015.

Van Cleve, Nicole Gonzalez. *Crook County: Racism and Injustice in America's Largest Criminal Court*. Stanford, CA: Stanford University Press, 2016.

van Houten, Christian. *The Alien in Israelite Law*. JSOTSup 107. Sheffield: Sheffield Academic Press, 1991.

Vanier, Jean. *An Ark for the Poor: The Story of L'Arche*. Toronto: Novalis, 1995.

————. *Community and Growth*. 2nd ed. New York: Paulist Press, 1989.

————. *The Scandal of Service: Jesus Washes Our Feet*. L'Arche Collections. Toronto: Novalis, 1998.

Van Opstal, Sandra. *The Next Worship: Glorifying God in a Diverse World*. Downers Grove, IL: InterVarsity Press, 2015.

Van Seters, John. *Abraham in History and Tradition*. New Haven, CT: Yale University Press, 1975.

Veyne, Paul. *Bread and Circuses: Historical Sociology and Political Pluralism*. London: Allen Lane, 1990.

The Visitor. Directed by Tom McCarthy. Overture Films, 2008.

Volf, Miroslav. *Exclusion and Embrace: A Theological Exploration of Identity, Otherness, and Reconciliation*. Nashville: Abingdon, 1996.

Wacquant, Löic. *Prisons of Poverty*. Minneapolis: University of Minnesota Press, 2009.

Wadell, Paul J. *Becoming Friends: Worship, Justice, and the Practice of Christian Friendship*. Grand Rapids: Brazos, 2002.

Wagner, J. Ross. "The Christ, Servant of Jew and Gentile: A Fresh Approach to Romans 15:8–9." *JBL* 116, no. 3 (Fall 1997): 473–85.

Wainwright, Geoffrey. *Eucharist and Eschatology*. Oxford: Oxford University Press, 1981.

Wallace-Hadrill, Andrew. *Rome's Cultural Revolution*. Cambridge: Cambridge University Press, 2008.

Walls, Andrew F. *The Missionary Movement in Christian History: Studies in the Transmission of Faith*. Maryknoll, NY: Orbis, 1996.

Walters, James C. "Paul and the Politics of Meals in Roman Corinth." In *Corinth in Context: Comparative Studies on Religion and Society*, edited by Steven J. Friesen, Daniel N. Schowalter, and James C. Walters, 343–64. NovTSup 134. Leiden: Brill, 2010.

Wannenwetsch, Bernd. "The Desire of Desire: Commandment and Idolatry in Late Capitalist Societies." In *Idolatry*, edited by Stephen C. Barton, 315–30. New York: T&T Clark, 2007.

Ward, Roy Bowen. "Partiality in the Assembly: James 2:2–4." *HTR* 62, no. 1 (January 1969): 87–97.

————. "The Works of Abraham: James 2:14–26." *HTR* 61, no. 2 (April 1968): 283–90.

Watson, Francis. *Paul and the Hermeneutics of Faith*. London: T&T Clark, 2004.

Webber, Robert E. *Celebrating Our Faith: Evangelism through Worship*. San Francisco: Harper and Row, 1986.

Webster, Jane S. *Ingesting Jesus: Eating and Drinking in the Gospel of John*. SBLAB 6. Atlanta: Society of Biblical Literature, 2003.

Weiman, David, and Christopher Weiss. "The Origins of Mass Incarceration in New York State: The Rockefeller Drug Laws and the Local War on Drugs." In *Do Prisons*

Bibliography

Make Us Safer? The Benefits and Cost of the Prison Boom, edited by Steven Raphael and Michael Stoll, 73–116. New York: Russell Sage Foundation, 2009.

Wells, Samuel. *A Nazareth Manifesto: Being with God*. Malden, MA: Wiley Blackwell, 2015.

White, L. Michael. "Morality between Two Worlds: A Paradigm of Friendship in Philippians." In *Greeks, Romans, and Christians*, edited by David L. Balch, Everett Fergusson, and Wayne A. Meeks, 201–15. Minneapolis: Fortress, 1990.

Wilson, Brittany E. *Unmanly Men: Refigurations of Masculinity in Luke-Acts*. Oxford: Oxford University Press, 2015.

Wilson, Walter T. "Urban Legends: Acts 10:1–11:18 and the Strategies of Greco-Roman Foundation Narratives." *JBL* 120, no. 1 (Spring 2001): 77–99.

Winter, Bruce W. *After Paul Left Corinth: The Influence of Secular Ethics and Social Change*. Grand Rapids: Eerdmans, 2001.

Wise, Mary Alice. "The Hospitality House: Portrait of a Prison Ministry." In *Prison*, edited by Robert B. Kruschwitz, 79–83. Christian Reflection. Waco, TX: Baylor University Press, 2012.

Wright, Christopher J. H. *Old Testament Ethics for the People of God*. Downers Grove, IL: InterVarsity Press, 2004.

Yarhouse, Mark A. *Understanding Gender Dysphoria: Navigating Transgender Issues in a Changing Culture*. Downers Grove, IL: InterVarsity Press, 2015.

Yong, Amos. *Hospitality and the Other: Pentecost, Christian Practices, and the Neighbor*. Maryknoll, NY: Orbis, 2008.

York, John O. *The Last Shall Be First: The Rhetoric of Reversal in Luke*. JSNTSup 46. Sheffield: JSOT Press, 1991.

Index of Names and Subjects

Dead Sea Scrolls, 162
DeYoung, Curtiss Paul, 51
Didache, 40
Diversity, 50–52, 54, 70–75
Downs, David, 153–54, 156, 158

Edwards, James R., Jr., 145
Eusebius, 118–20

Fitzgerald, John T., 67
Flett, John, 116
Food. *See* Table-fellowship
Fowl, Stephen, 53–54, 71
Friesen, Steven, 171

Gittins, Anthony, 117
God, economy of, 151, 153, 155–56, 159–61,
 164, 167–68, 170–71, 175
Greed, 12, 148, 150, 152–53, 155–57, 163,
 168–72, 174; antidote to, 153–54; as disordered desire, 152–57; and patronage
 system, 157–68; prophetic warnings
 against, 168–72

Hays, Christopher M., 163
Hays, Richard, 61
Henderson, Suzanne Watts, 61–62
Hesiod, 160
Heuertz, Christopher, 94
Heyer, Kristin, 124
Hill, Wesley, 67, 72–73
Hinton, Elizabeth, 46
Holman, Susan, 172
Homer, 89, 105
Horrell, David, 54, 56, 68
Hospitality, divine, 10, 12, 17–18, 35,
 57–58; crosses social barriers, 40,
 53, 61, 63, 70–72, 127, 136, 142, 177; as
 foundation for human hospitality, 2,
 7, 17–18, 26, 28, 31, 34, 37, 53–54, 59–62,
 64–66, 70–71, 73–75, 102, 127, 139–43,
 161, 163–64, 168, 175, 177; as friendship
 to humanity, 3, 66–67, 70–75, 80, 82,
 89–94, 96, 143, 177; and the Great
 Banquet, 19–20, 22, 163–64; mediated
 through Christ, 17, 25–27, 35, 55, 70–72,

80, 82, 86–89, 92–94, 102, 177; mediated through the church, 37, 67, 93,
 104–5, 111–12, 117–18, 164; reveals God
 to humanity, 81–88, 90–92, 95, 105,
 164; to "the others," 22, 34, 38–39, 41,
 136, 139–43, 177; transforms to show
 hospitality, 38, 41, 92–94, 102, 139–43,
 163–64, 168, 177. *See also* Christ: as
 divine host; God, economy of
Hospitality, of humans, 3–6, 8, 12, 17,
 20, 69–70, 128–32, 136–44; challenges
 to, 12, 30, 35, 39, 74–75, 100, 147–57,
 163, 173–74; to Christ, 27, 82, 85, 121;
 creates friendship, 17, 29–31, 34, 37–38,
 43, 50, 53, 59, 61–63, 66–67, 71–74,
 91–92, 94–95, 104, 106, 113–14, 117, 162;
 extends salvation, 105, 108–12; fulfills
 Torah, 66, 121–22, 137–43, 162, 170; to
 immigrants, 8, 126–27, 133, 136–46;
 as indiscriminate, 18, 104, 110, 120;
 parameters of, 22, 40, 100–101, 114–15;
 of Paul, 103, 107–14, 121; to the poor,
 29, 69, 159, 163–66, 175; receiving
 hospitality, 103, 108–10, 112–15; to religious others, 102–4, 114–18; rewards
 of, 129–30, 132–33, 139, 169–70, 172; to
 strangers, 21, 82, 104, 127–33, 136–43,
 161–62, 164, 175, 177; to "the other," 2,
 8, 10, 18, 32, 37, 42–44, 47, 50–52, 53,
 61, 65–66, 75, 82, 100, 102, 104, 115–16,
 162–64, 177; as welcome, 20–21, 42,
 44, 53, 63–64, 66, 70, 82, 104, 128–30,
 142–43, 146, 163–64; with giving,
 152–54, 156–57, 159–62, 165–68, 173–75;
 with hosts and guests, 99–104, 107–10,
 112–18. *See also* Inhospitality
Hultgren, Arland, 89

Ignatius, 44
Immigrants, 8, 124–27, 133, 136–46
Inhospitality, 8–9, 23, 30, 39, 43, 52,
 72, 105, 128, 136, 143; consequences
 of, 132–33, 139, 169–72; as corrupted
 hospitality, 133–36; greed, 12, 148, 150,
 152–53, 155–57, 163, 168–72, 174; of
 Israel, 133–35; with the Lord's Supper,

Index of Scripture and Other Ancient Writings